Rental Property Investing

The Ultimate Real Estate Investing Guide

Vick Jelser

contained within this document, including, but not limited to, errors, omissions, or inaccuracies.

Table of Contents

Introduction

Investment is no longer a word that's reserved for the corridors of Wall Street and high finance. It's become a topic that's shared at the dinner table and discussed during dates. Both the young and the old can chew the fat off the nuances of investment. And one of the most common markets that people invest in is real estate.

It's no surprise that real estate remains a favorite among investors—it's not just a viable way to build lasting wealth, but also a relatively safe bet. Land, which is a defining part of real estate, is always in high demand. This makes this market especially profitable and attractive. Add to this the various niches in real estate, and you have a market that welcomes investors to find their own uniquely comfortable and exciting space.

As mentioned before, land is an integral part of real estate. In fact, properties may not be termed real estate if they aren't situated on some portion of earth. As the wheels of population increase and migration continues to churn with ever-increasing velocity, the demand for land has also risen up. People need homes, schools, offices, bunkers, religious places of worship, and the like. Those who are able to attend to this need, either by providing land or guiding people through the process of acquiring it, are almost certain to become rich. This is a fact that, in all likelihood, may exist until the end of time.

As such, people are encouraged to look into the real estate industry as a viable source of wealth creation and an honest way to add value to the general society. And like every human endeavor, the amount of knowledge gained will determine one's chances of success. It's presumed that you're aware of this fact and, as such, have chosen this book to provide you with the basic, prerequisite information for your future exploits in real estate. You've, indeed, chosen quite well!

This book is a well researched compendium of only the facts regarding real estate investing. After completing this book, you're certain to become versed in everything from the definition of real estate to the interest-free ways to generate funds to invest in properties. This book demystifies many complex subjects and uses easy-to-grasp language to carry you, the reader, along from one mind-broadening chapter to the next. While other books that have tackled the same problem of teaching real estate tend to leave their readers mostly confused, bored, and stultified—*Rental Property Investing* takes an interesting, casual, and informative approach to keep the reader hooked.

As its title foretells, many of the chapters in this book are focused on how to succeed as a landlord. But there's more. You'll also learn things like how to become a consistently successful investor, and both the common and not quite common pitfalls in this market.

One major problem faced by new investors in real estate is finding the money needed to purchase good properties. Typically, real estate properties are usually as expensive as the speed with which they could appreciate in value. The level of profitability that a property can attain would also affect its pricing. Say you have two properties that cost the same amount of money to build—but as a result of location, one will be 20% more expensive in 4 years, while the other will hit that number in 8 years. The current purchase cost for the former will justifiably be higher. And if an investor wants their returns quickly, it would be smarter for them to buy the more expensive property.

So how would you secure the capital to invest in profitable real estate, if your savings do not suffice? You may not want to rely on bank loans and similar interest-based financing, as these could eat into your profits in the long run. Also, depending on where you live, the interest rates may not be feasible or quite simply backbreaking.

Another major problem for real estate investors is that many still find themselves outside, peering into this fast-paced world. Even after investing their time and money into securing good deals, they might still feel like strangers in the market. This is a bad place to be, as it prevents you from getting real time and accurate information about the many twists in real estate. One of the first things a new investor must do is find their place in successful networks. You want to have access to not just the giants in the industry, but also those like you who are learning and maturing.

Other common issues in real estate include finding a viable career in real estate, finding a mentor, how to work as a real estate wholesaler, and how to market your properties. The solutions to these, and many others, are discussed at length in this book.

If you're short on funds, one way to invest in real estate is to become a part of a real estate investment trust (REIT). In this book, you'll gain in-depth knowledge about REITs and how to find them. You'll also discover the art of networking, and learn how to find and interact with your peers in the industry.

In addition, you'll discover the secrets to success as a landlord. Rental property, which is the focus of this book, is a common niche in real estate. However, very few people know how to truly exploit the vast opportunities in this sector of the market. For instance, owning an attractive building isn't all it takes to become rich as a landlord. In fact, every tenant you accept must first be scrutinized. Should you allow a bad tenant into your house, they can delay your chances of breaking even and progressing to the profit-making stage of your investment. This book will teach you how to spot a bad tenant, and how you can enjoy passive income from rental properties.

Regardless of the work that has gone into making *Rental Property Investing* valuable, you, the reader, still have a vital part to play in making sure this book actually brings about positive changes in your life. For instance, you should be committed to diligently applying the solutions shared within. It's not enough to just read a book like this one. You must practice the tips and ideas that it proffers.

The treasures in real estate are bountiful for those who know where to look and how to excavate them. This book is your guide to becoming a successful treasure hunting real estate investor!

Chapter 1:

The Mindset of an Investor

Many self-help books preach a "winning mindset" that can effectively be applied by anyone to any situation. The reliability of self-help books aside, there is some truth to a general winning mindset. For instance— whether you're an athlete, student, or bank manager—things like hard work, commitment, and routine would be necessary for your success.

However, different fields require that one possesses a particular and unique way of perceiving and analyzing problems if they will rise to the top. For example, extroversion is a determining factor of the level of a musician's success. Even if they're uncomfortable in crowds, they should be able to convincingly pretend to have fun on stage in front of hundreds or thousands of people. This same skill may not be required of an author, though. Certainly, not to the same degree.

This applies in the business world as well. Many types of investments demand long-term planning and expectations. Some may take a week for you to reap the rewards. For others, you may be required to have a decade's worth of patience. Investors understand this fact and, depending on where they've put their money, can wait as long as they need.

The successful investor also understands that risk is an immutable rule of the game. Despite your best efforts, a number of things could still go wrong. In view of this fact, investors employ various money management strategies to make sure they don't lose more money than they can afford to part with. Another way that investors prepare for the risks to come is by gaining as much knowledge as they can before jumping into any investment. Regardless of the experience gained by an investor and the level of success they've attained, they must begin each new investment by learning.

Networking may not necessarily be at the forefront of every investor's mind. But the thought process of the average *real estate* investor is oriented toward making new and lasting connections in the trade. This is how, in some cases, they access interest-free financing. It's also how they predict the market and avoid the errors that come with having blindspots—and no business person is so proficient that they're without blindspots.

The goal of most investments, if not all of them, is to make sufficient returns so that it justifies the time, money, and effort that you sacrificed. As such, you may correctly conclude that the mindset of investors is geared toward getting wealthy off their investments.

To summarize, the mindset of an investor (and real estate investors, in particular) is a combination of these things: long-term thinking, acceptance of and preparation toward risk, networking, and profit-making.

Tips to Being a Skilled Real Estate Investor

Although this chapter describes the similarities between thriving real estate investors, you should know that you're not expected to mimic any investor exactly. Individual investors are as unique as one person is from another. Also, you may face challenges which would require you to be creative. As such, you're expected to grasp these examples of foundational knowledge and, upon them, build *your* style of business.

Below is a blueprint for real estate investment that has been tested and proven true:

- **Have a plan**: If there's one thing you must remember as an investor, it's that the real estate market responds negatively to the "winging it" strategy. Unless you're endlessly wealthy, chances are that you'll encounter a continuous series of losses if you invest ignorantly and haphazardly.

   Before you put a dime into any deal, you should devise a careful plan that acknowledges all the risks involved in that particular investment.

- **Develop a niche**: There is more than one way to invest in real estate. The same is true for the exit strategies in this business. You may choose REITs over partnerships, and you may choose to lease your property as opposed to flipping it. All of it rests on your goals and plan.

   However, it's advisable to devote your focus to becoming an expert within a chosen subset of the real estate market. This way, your decisions will be better-informed and more accurate, and buyers will find it easy to trust you.

- **Know the market**: In general, you should study the real estate market to determine things like the best entry period and the most profitable properties to invest in. But it's also important that you analyze the niche in which you'll be focused. For instance, there are certain choices that you might have to make as a fix-and-flip investor which would be imprudent for people who are focused on rentals.

   Developing a network and paying for courses in real estate are some great ways to improve your knowledge of real estate.

- **Be honest**: In the high stakes world of real estate, news spreads quite fast. Should you give in to dishonest methods for the sake of hitting it big and fast, you may find that the possible consequences of such actions aren't worth it. One of the worst things that could happen to you as a real estate investor is to have a poor reputation in the market.

A bad name would discourage potential tenants, buyers, developers, contractors, financial institutions, and other investors from doing business with you. It's also hard to recover from the ostracism after it happens. In the long run, as such, it's more profitable to maintain honest and fair relationships.

- **Encourage referrals**: You can spread the word about your business by using marketing strategies like social media ads, YouTube ads, billboard ads, and cold calling. However, the most effective way to draw the right kind of attention to your business remains word-of-mouth.

Make sure your deals are fair and ask your tenants, for instance, to tell the people they know about available apartments in your building. Business cards can also be helpful in encouraging people to refer your business to anyone they know.

- **Stay educated**: Since the world is constantly changing and processes evolve, it's imperative that you stay abreast of the latest developments in your field. If there are new and more effective methods utilized by investors, you want to not only be in the know, but also have a solid grasp of them.

As such, it's essential to your continued success in real estate that you never stop learning. You should be as informed of the traditional styles of investing as you are of the new and avant-garde methods.

- **Understand the risks**: First, you must accept that there are no risk-free investments. Whether it's advertised as 100% safe or you think you've covered all the bases, it's imprudent to be convinced that nothing can go wrong. A better strategy is to try to learn as much as you can about the possible risks. You should identify and find ways to mitigate them.

One way to secure your finances in the event of a negative outcome is to employ money management techniques. This will ensure that, come what may, you'll be unlikely to lose all your savings to any investment. We'll discuss tips for money management later on in this book.

- **Invest in an accountant**: More precisely, you should get an accountant who specializes in real estate and understands the nuances of your niche. While you busy yourself with the day-to-day tasks, you need a professional to protect your financial interests. For instance, you may not have to pay as many taxes as you had thought. Accountants who have in-depth knowledge of taxes related to real estate will help you save a fortune. Although hiring a certified public accountant may be relatively expensive, they are usually worth every penny.

Chapter 2:

Raising Capital to Invest

This is a crucial part of your investment in real estate. Indeed, the type of financing you're able to get may determine how much profit you can make. For this section, we'll steer clear of loans. One reason for this is that interest-based financing often negatively impacts ROIs. To then make up for what you lose to a loan, you may choose to rent out or sell your property at a higher markup that's unattractive and discouraging to potential tenants and buyers.

Although the more common types of funding are loans like mortgages and seller financing, this chapter will show you five equally viable and loan-free options that exist. They are crowdfunding, angel investing, wholesaling, partnerships, and savings. These aren't methods by any means. But since they aren't talked about as much in real estate, chances are that you've never heard of them or just don't know how to make them work. You'll find the help you need below and finally understand how to get interest-free funding.

Crowdfunding

We may never know if startups like Oculus and MVMT watches would still exist without crowdfunding campaigns. We do know, however, that the dreams of many investors have been realized thanks to this method. But the efficacy of crowdfunding doesn't just work for startups alone. You can also rely on the support of this method to fund your real estate investment.

Like the startups mentioned above, you can pitch your real estate investment ideas to individuals who may, in turn, chip in what they can to finance your business. For real estate crowdfunding in particular, there is usually a minimum investment that excludes low-income earners from participating.

There are online websites dedicated to crowdfunding. However, some investors also rely on social media platforms like Facebook and Instagram to attract a much larger audience of potential investors.

Benefits of Real Estate Crowdfunding

- **Relatively stress-free funding**: With a mortgage, for instance, you may find the paperwork involved to be nerve-racking. Even if you're eventually approved for a loan, you would be required to pay a downpayment that may be unaffordable for you.

  Crowdfunding demands considerably low (or no) legwork. If you've got the necessary details to convince potential investors, you may not have to meet them in person. You can also secure this funding with zero down payment. This makes it a cheaper and all-round easier way to finance real estate projects.

- **Market your brand**: The beauty of this method of financing is that you gain much more than the capital you need at that moment. If successful, you'll also gain a network of investors that you can always cash in on. It's a great way to promote— not just individual projects, but your brand as a whole.

Prospective investors should be able to visit your website and see past projects and their respective ROIs.

You also want them to know the vision and mission of your company—then they can decide if your business is in alignment with their goals. By doing so, you would encourage them to choose you for the long haul.

- **Crowdfunding platforms are user-friendly**: If you're trying to convince people to buy into your idea, you want your platform of choice to be easily navigable. Thankfully, most crowdfunding sites are designed such that anyone can find their way around them without getting confused. In addition, these websites present texts and pictures in formats that are aesthetically appealing.

  Also, there are numerous available crowdfunding websites. You should select one depending on its reach and how well it fits your goals.

- **Constructive criticism**: Every business person and investor is an open channel for useful feedback. There is an advantage that crowdfunding sites have over social media platforms. The comments on Facebook, for instance, are often populated by trolls, bots, and outright negativity. Yet, you want to connect with prospective investors and learn their pain points.

  On platforms that are dedicated to crowdfunding, you will find serious and well-meaning investors who, with their feedback, will help you shape your idea to be more effective.

Angel Investing

Angel investors are typically high-net worth individuals who provide much-needed seed funding for startups. In many cases, they can be friends, family members, or colleagues. Other times, they can be total strangers who, upon hearing your pitch and understanding your business model, buy into your dream. Depending on your agreement with an angel investor, they might give you a one-time financial backing to help your idea get off the ground, or regular support to keep your business flying.

If you have a real estate company, an angel investor may want equity for their funding. Otherwise, you could find friends and family members who are willing to settle for a percentage of the ROI from a single deal.

Benefits of Angel Investing

- **It validates your business**: All it takes is for one investor to believe in your idea and trust you with their money. Other investors, upon hearing that you've secured an angel investor, will be many times more likely to also invest in your real estate project or company. In essence, a single angel investor can open the floodgates of capital to make your dream real.

- **You don't need a collateral**: To get most loans, a down payment or collateral may be required of you. Many times, both of those requirements may be a necessary prerequisite for a loan. Angel investors, however, will not ask you for either of those things. All they want is to share in the profits of your business.

- **Flexible business agreements**: To secure a loan from traditional sources or to get a deal from a venture capitalist, you'll be made to follow a rigid, non-negotiable process that may be unfavorable to your project in the long run. Angel investors are usually open to negotiating, and are more flexible with regards to the terms of agreement.

  In fact, an angel investor could give you capital for reasons beyond profit-making. For example, they could be sentimentally invested in the success of your business (in the case of friends and family members), or they might see your business or project as being necessary for the development of the community.

- **It's a cheap source of funding**: When you factor in the cost of down payments, interest rates, and other charges associated with many types of financing, you'll find that it adds up in the end. As much as a loan can help you realize your dream, chances are that you might feel a bit shortchanged. After all, you're losing money even before you start winning.

  With an angel investor, however, you're allowed an abundance of funds to invest into your project or business. You needn't "make do with," or cut corners to achieve your goals.

Wholesaling

Wholesaling in commerce generally refers to individuals or businesses that act as middle agents between the manufacturers of certain products and retailers. While there are similarities between the definition of wholesaling above and its meaning in the context or real estate, they cannot be transposed without confusion.

Although wholesalers in real estate connect buyers to sellers, one cannot draw parallels to its more general definition beyond this point. In the high stakes world of real estate, wholesalers play a more active role by being intermediaries for buyers and sellers. They approach and strike deals with property sellers, then present the contract (with a substantial markup) to buyers. Should they succeed in closing a deal, their profit is the difference between the actual selling price and the markup.

Benefits of Wholesaling

- **You don't need money to start**: If you don't have enough of your own capital to invest in real estate, this is an almost free way to make money in the real estate market. Besides the relatively small expense of things like transportation, you needn't spend a dime to close a deal as a real estate wholesaler. If you are skilled at negotiating and know where and how to find buyers and sellers of real estate, then you're home free.

- **Easy entry for beginners in real estate**: With many other methods of property investment, you may be required to have a degree or certain licenses. With fixing and flipping, for example, you at least need to know how to renovate buildings or be good at managing contractors. A formal or informal training isn't necessarily required for wholesalers.

  While it would help to have a mentor and build a network of property owners and potential buyers before starting out in this business, a large number of wholesalers have done just fine without such prerequisites. With the Internet and social media, you can learn as much as you need to know about wholesaling, and find clients easily.

- **Fast turnovers**: Usually, investors in real estate understand that they must wait for months or years before making returns on their investment. The real estate game, as you may know, is won by great patience. However, wholesaling can return profits at a much faster rate than other real estate investment methods. While it doesn't yield much in lump sum profits when compared to, say, property rehab investment—you can successfully close a wholesaling deal in a week or less.

- **High demand**: Everyone—from buyers and sellers to corporate financial and government institutions—needs wholesalers to help them find and close real estate deals. By choosing to be a real estate wholesaler, you'd be putting yourself in the coveted position of always being in business. Your only off-seasons (if you can quickly hone your client-finding and negotiating skills) would be when you choose to take a break.

- **No need for listings**: This business involves searching for motivated property owners who've probably already listed their homes. You just need to convince them to sell at a certain price and help them find a committed buyer. You may even recruit the services of deal scouts (for an agreed finder's fee, they'll search out distressed prospects for you) to find ready sellers.

- **Relatively low-risk**: Since you won't be spending money to purchase real estate or investing in anything besides the transportation of yourself or similar expenses, your failed deals won't exactly be financially crippling. The risks, really, are borne by the buyers and sellers. In fact, if you're able to quickly build a network that helps you easily locate investors and property owners who want to sell, you'll soon enjoy consistent earnings.

Partnerships

You could have an in-depth know-how of the real estate market, but not have the capital to bank on your skills and knowledge. Conversely, you may have an abundance of cash to rely on, but also be clueless about how to profitably invest in properties. These two kinds of people not only need each other, but their partnership is also typically more effective than the single investor who is both financier and active player.

Now, the above passive model of knowledge and funds teaming up to invest isn't the only way partnerships in real estate are done. In many cases, the partnership may involve more than two active partners. This means that everyone involved both finances and manages agreed-to real estate projects. Partnerships of these kinds aren't taxed as an entity in the U.S. Instead, they do pass-through, where the various partners pay income tax in relation to their share of the ROI.

Benefits of Partnerships

- **Opportunity for bigger ROI**: Whether you find yourself in a passive or active partnership, either one allows you to purchase properties that may be well above the limits of your personal funds. Investors can pool funds together to purchase particularly expensive and equally profitable real estate assets.

- **Division of labor**: If yours is a partnership where all involved are given equal responsibilities, tasks will be completed at a much faster rate and with little or no errors. This is as opposed to being a sole investor and having the responsibility of managing every aspect of a project.

- **Multiple perspectives**: While it's said that too many cooks spoil the broth, this adage may not always apply to real estate partnerships. If you're able to form a group of informed investors, what you'll have is individual partners looking out for the blind spots of others. This is beneficial to the accuracy of your investments, and it improves your chances of getting consistently high ROIs.

- **Shared risks**: Some people only think about the fact that, if all goes well, they'll be required to share a percentage of their profits with their partners—and so, they feel discouraged from choosing this method of investment. But it's also important to know that should anything go wrong, a partnership would prevent them from bearing the loss and setback alone. This also means that you stand a better chance of bouncing back quickly when you have partners.

Savings

This is the oldest and most self-reliant method of financing there is. Saving bits of your personal income to invest in real estate someday isn't something that's commonly talked about as a viable means of funding your real estate project. One reason for this is that many people don't have the earning power to hit their financing target quickly enough. As a result of inflation, you want to be able to grow your savings before the market becomes even more expensive. As such, this option best serves middle- or high-income individuals. If you find yourself in this category, make sure you keep your money in high-yield savings accounts.

Benefits of Savings

- **All the profits are yours**: Since this method doesn't involve partners, angel investors, or venture capitalists, you can be sure that 100% of your ROI belongs to you. This large bounty will make it easier for you to finance your next project. You'll find that with the successful completion of each real estate deal, the next one will require considerably less effort and time.

- **The cheapest kind of financing**: Whether you just want to own a property (or properties), or you intend to use exit strategies like fixing and flipping, the cheapest path to these points is by using your own money. You needn't be held back by down payments and recurring interests when you can personally finance your dreams.

Chapter 3:

The Importance of Goal Setting

A well laid out plan is more easily achievable than cliched methods like going with your gut, or "winging it." In this chapter, we'll see why goal setting is crucial to success in any venture, and how to correctly plan your long-term and short-term goals.

But first, what does it mean to set goals? To engage in goal setting, you'll need to have precise intended results for certain changes made and problem-solved. Goals shouldn't just be vague ideas of what an individual wants (even though that's how they're commonly defined). Instead, they should be clear charts that guide people from where they are to where they hope to be. By setting goals, you become an active agent in your story and exercise some control over the so-called "wheels of fate."

Goal setting is also a credible way to measure success. Otherwise, you might adopt the insatiable pop culture idea of success, which is simply measured by how many new and expensive things one owns. Blind materialistic pursuit is a vice, while goal setting is a virtue.

You might wonder if there's a difference between having a goal and setting one. The former is more akin to wishful thinking. But by writing down specific goals and mapping a plan to reach them, you'd be more likely to actualize them.

If your job, for example, involves a long and expensive commute, your goal could be to find remote jobs. This is arguably a step up from complaining or wishing things were better. You should immediately follow this goal by writing a plan for finding those telecommuting jobs. This example can be classified as a long-term goal, since it could take a long while to find a new and remote job. Medium and short-term goals include completing a weeklong course or scheduling a massage appointment.

The SMART Way to Plan Goals

Over time, various methods have been proffered to improve an individual's likelihood of reaching their goals. None have caught on like the SMART approach, though. It's a five-step checklist to verify the doability of any goal. Outlined below are some of the steps to use this method and what's required to complete them.

S - Specific

Vague goals like, *I want to be successful*, may never be realized, since success has a multiplicity of meaning. First, you need to determine the area(s) of life with which you desire success. Next, you should have a clear definition for success in those areas. For instance, publishing a book is enough success for some people, while others will only celebrate after selling 100 copies. You need to be clear and specific when writing your goals to avoid distraction and eventual disinterest.

M - Measurable

It's beneficial to your staying power that you keep track of the big and small steps that bring you closer to reaching your goals. This can be done daily, weekly, or monthly. The important thing is that you devise an objective method to remind yourself that you are, indeed, inching closer to success.

A - Achievable

While it's laudable to "dream big" and chase down particularly challenging goals, you also want to be realistic in your pursuit. You want to set your sights on a target that offers just the right amount of challenge without being impossible. To do this, you should consider your skills, access to funds, network, and time. The last (but not the least) one—time—is often forgotten or disregarded by many would-be investors. But it may be the most crucial factor in determining what your goals should be.

R - Relevant

Goals, by themselves, do not offer any intrinsic reward. They have to mean something to you for their completion to feel truly gratifying. This is why you shouldn't pursue a goal merely because it's popular, easy, or just because. You have to make sure that your goals are in line with your values and principles, and that they move you toward a state of relative contentment.

T - Timed

It's true that if one thinks they have forever to complete a task, they'll most likely take forever to get it done. This is why deadlines are important to the expedition of any project. If you don't want to be 80-years-old and still hoping to fulfill the dreams you had at age 20, you must compel yourself to act quickly by setting a deadline.

How to Set Long-Term Goals

Long-term goals are those ones that are expected to be fulfilled in the far future. They typically exceed a year and, as such, require a lot of patience to complete. They usually involve a number of complexities, like being able to foresee multiple eventualities and have a contingency plan for each one. An example of a long-term goal is growing a profitable startup. Knowing that the average startup needs at least two to three years before making profits (there is also a 25% chance of failing altogether), such a goal would require years of careful planning.

You should know, however, that the rewards of long-term plans (while not always the case), are usually more gratifying and lasting than those of short-term plans. This fact isn't exactly surprising, since goals that will only be realized far into the future are often more personal (or they become personal during the long process of reaching them). If you're excited about planning your long-term goals, use the list below as a guide:

- **Does it align with your personal or company values?**: One reason for many failed long-term objectives is burnout. It's difficult to stay motivated for particularly long stretches of time, especially when your chosen goals don't really matter to you.

  You can try this exercise to see if what you're about to adopt as a long-term goal is in-line not only with your best interest, but with your core values as well: try to imagine your ideal future. It's that simple. Think about the kind of relationships and career you hope to have in the length of time that it would take to accomplish your goals. Ask yourself questions like, *In what state would I like my emotional, physical, and mental health to be in 'x' years or months?* You should only pursue goals that have passed this assessment.

- **Prioritize certain goals**: Contrary to what you may believe, the human mind becomes less efficient and productive when under the strain of multiple, simultaneous problems. In reality, whatever is worth doing must be given great attention. As such, consider writing (in order of their importance), a list of all your goals. Start working on the first goal and only take on the second one on two conditions:

  - if you can do so without compromising the most important goal

  - if it's essential

  By taking this approach to long-term goals, you'll end up making the best use of your time and, in more general terms, life.

- **Mince your goals**: Long-term objectives are usually also highly challenging and expensive. By viewing and trying to claim the goal in its entirety, you may damage your courage. A better way to work on your long-term goals is to cut them into milestones.

This way, all you have to do is complete a small and simple task each month or week. It makes the long-term goal seem less intimidating, and may even help you achieve it at a faster pace.

- **Keep track of your progress**: Chances are that you'll forget you even had a goal if it takes a long time to accomplish it. As such, you should devise a way to monitor every positive move you make toward the full realization of your goal. This is where you start to enjoy the benefits to dividing your long-term objective into smaller, more easily achievable projects.

  There are various online and offline project management applications that you can utilize to stay on top of your goals. Tools like Trello, Basecamp, and Asana will help you manage not just your personal goals, but everyone involved in the project, too. You can create scheduled reminders and due dates for every short-term goal on those platforms.

- **Be willing to adapt**: By checking in on your progress, you have the opportunity to also assess your methods and make necessary changes to improve them. You should accept the fact that you will gain new information and encounter unforeseen challenges during the course of any project. Your ability to course-correct and adopt tried-and-true solutions will mean the difference between an accomplished goal and failure.

Below are some examples to help you identify long-term goals:

- scaling your startup

- founding a profitable startup

- rebranding your company

- climbing the ranks to become a manager

- getting a degree or certification

- writing a book

- becoming published

- learning a new language

- improving your credit score

- adopting a child

- owning your first home

The Importance of Long-Term Goals

Everyone, regardless of their socioeconomic status and beliefs, needs to cultivate the habit of setting and completing long-term goals. It's a nonnegotiable part of life and happiness. And if you succeed as a player in the world of real estate, there's no question that you must have long-term strategies for your investments. Outlined below are some of the ways that everyone benefits from long-term goals.

- **It helps you work with clarity of mind**: About 86% of business leaders attest to the fact that defining a shared goal is a necessary ingredient for company growth (Toussaint, 2020). However great your products, services, and business model might be, you have to set precise, clear, and well-defined goals. Doing so will help you carry out your tasks with purpose and intention. It'll also help you resist distractions as you chip away, relentless, toward success.

- **It helps you determine what success means to you**: You'll often find that when you look inwards for your personal meaning of success, it differs a fair bit from society's standards. Our desires lie not on a spectrum, but as unique points on an infinite spread. And one's personal path to success is often found in their pursuit of a long-term goal. A reason for this is that long-term goals typically require passion, patience, and assiduousness to be realized—and these are the same necessary factors for personal fulfillment.

How to Set Short-Term Goals

Short-term goals are quickly realizable and, typically, simple objectives. The length of a short-term goal is usually less than a year. As we saw earlier, even long-term goals are made more realizable by chopping them into small bits. Short-term goals make otherwise tedious daily tasks more purposeful. Whatever you hope to achieve, whether you want to get fit or finish reading a book, short-term goals are your best bet.

Use the list below to map out feasible and effective short-term goals:

- Determine the areas of your life in which you'd like to be successful. This shouldn't be as general or vague as long-term goals. Think about specific categories in your career, for example, and devise quantifiable ways to measure your progress. Keep in mind that you can select categories from both professional and personal areas. Excellence in your personal life may positively impact your career, and vice versa. Some categories to consider improving include punctuality and organizational skills.

- Prioritize goals that have clear and relatively quick gains. If your short-term goal is to learn a skill for financial reasons, determine how long it would take for you to start profiting off the skill and in which practical ways that skill can be used.

- Try to avoid goals that would drastically upend the structure of your life. While short-term goals may require you to change some of your routines and habits, it's important that this change isn't too shocking. Consider gradually modifying your days, weeks, and months in line with your goals.

The Importance of Short-Term Goals

- **They can help you envision your purpose with even more clarity and precision**: While it's important for long-term goals to be well-defined, they are often so far into the future that they tend to be somewhat abstract. As the name suggests, short-term goals are much closer in time and space to you. And this makes them more conceivable and comprehensive.

- **They encourage helpful routines**: Short-term goals can be daily or weekly repetitive tasks. By completing them, you may learn habits that would make you more productive and efficient. These useful habits may be specific, like writing at a particular time everyday. They could also be general virtues like diligence and consistency.

- **They are useful for positively reinforcing good behavior**: Your short-term goals may seem like small tasks, but completing each one will fill you with a sense of achievement that'll bolster you to continue progressing. You'll find that every completed goal validates your abilities and rewards you with confidence.

- **They keep you grounded in what's real and attainable**: When you set relatively short-time frames for your goals, you may inadvertently want to make them realistic. This means that such tasks would fit your skills and budget, and be neither too simple nor too complex.

Chapter 4:

How to Find Good Rental

Properties

After making the choice to get involved in rental real estate, it's important that you approach this decision with care and prudence. The fact that a property looks right to you isn't enough to justify an investment. This is especially true if you're still a beginner in this market. More experienced investors may find success by merely eyeballing properties. Those who are still green, however, are yet to develop the right instincts for such a move. Also, with respect to the preceding chapter, whichever property you choose must be in the same direction as your long- and short-term goals.

It's also crucial that you don't make investment decisions based on popular opinion. Real estate trends, in a general sense, are considered fairly unpredictable and unreliable. The market, however, has certain knowable characteristics. For these reasons, your investment choices in real estate should be founded upon tested and proven criteria. Below are tips for finding profitable and stress-free real estate properties:

- **You need the right tenants**: Possibly the most important aspect of rental investments are the tenants. You could do everything right and still lose money, simply because you let in the wrong crop of people. The area in which your property is located will determine your tenant-base.

  For instance, buying a house near a university means that your tenants are likely to be students. Should you rent to them, be prepared for when they're unavailable in the summer.

- **Determine the nature of the property tax**: High property taxes are usually a turnoff for many potential investors. However, this should not necessarily prevent you from making money in the real estate market. What should matter is whether or not the property tax matches the value of the property. Should your investment prove to be highly profitable, this would make up for having to pay even astronomically high taxes.

  Unfortunately, some real estate in run-down and troubled areas also have high property taxes. Others, while presently relatively low, may rise sometime in the future. To protect yourself from such unfavorable eventualities, you should perform adequate due diligence on your property(ies) of choice.

- **Consider your property's value of appreciation**: If you purchase a building for rental purposes, it's expected that your main focus will be on the monthly (or periodic, in any case) cash flow. However, there could come a day when you decide to sell the property. For this reason, it's important that your property is able to succeed whether you rent it out or sell it.

  Take, for instance, houses that are almost an hour away from schools, restaurants, and malls. While you might be able to get tenants for such properties, it's less likely that buyers will invest in them.

- **Is the neighborhood filled with crime?**: Before buying any property, you may want to be sure that the neighborhood doesn't have a high crime rate. In fact, you should ask some people in the area about things like police presence and break-ins. Meet with the local police to determine the crime statistics in the neighborhood. It's also important that you don't downplay even petty crimes. All the factors that could potentially be a security issue must be treated with equal seriousness.

- **Are new companies popping up in the area?**: One of the perks of investing in a fast-developing area is that it's attractive to entrepreneurs and job seekers. Most people want to live close to where they work, as this would eliminate the need to wake up too early and prevent them from arriving late to work. Try visiting the local library in your intended area of investment to find out the job availability in the neighborhood. You may also check various news media to learn the areas that new and established companies are moving to.

Developing areas are typically great for property appreciation. As such, you should be able to sell your house at an increased value in the future.

- **Consider your property's proximity to certain amenities**: Unless it's a vacation home, people generally want to live in areas with good public transportation and a decent variety of gymnasiums, restaurants, and cinemas. As such, you want to tour your selected locations and look for where you can get a good mix of residential properties and public amenities. You may be able to access informational literature on this subject in City Halls in your neighborhoods.

- **What new projects are happening in the area?**: Other informational literature you might need may be in the municipal planning development office in your area. You want to know about the ongoing constructions and projects that have been zoned into the neighborhood. While this tells you about businesses that are moving into the area, you can also learn about other residential real estate projects.

- **You should check for the number of vacancies in the area**: Usually, areas with low vacancy rates are the best bets for potential landlords. This means that such a place would have more potential tenants than available apartments. As a landlord in an area with low vacancy, you'd have more leeway to increase your rent. Should you choose an area with high vacancy, tenants would have more readily available choices and you, as a landlord, may be unable to set profitable rents.

- **Determine the average rent in your area**: Whether the neighborhood has a high or low vacancy rate, your ROI will still be badly affected if the average rent cannot cover things like taxes and mortgages. This is not to say that you should completely give up on such neighborhoods. You could carry out some research to find out if the average rent is likely to rise in the next few years. This will, at least, make the risks clearer— and you may decide that you can take them.

- **What are the insurance factors?**: Man-made damages like burglary aside, you should check your selected areas to know if they are prone to natural disasters. The cost of regular insurance coverage may eat into your bottom line, preventing you from making profits from your rental income. It's important that you check for the likelihood of "acts of God," like tsunamis and earthquakes, hitting your property.

Chapter 5:

Networking

You may have heard the term 'networking' and chalked it up to just another self-help and business buzzword. While it's admittedly a fairly common word, networking is a potent ingredient for success in real estate. It involves an exchange of ideas among people who are in the same line of work or share a common interest. People within a network may also aid each other financially and in various other ways.

Networking is a vital part of any business, as it brings you in contact with other professionals in the same field who could be your mentors or partners. It's, in fact, a defining factor that separates consistently successful people from those who fail more times than they win. Regardless of the level of your skill and education, it's still important that you build a strong network. In fact, real estate investors who are bereft of experience and adequate knowledge are still able to succeed with the right network alone. The same isn't always true for those who have all but the right connections.

Below are more impressive reasons why you should be a part of a strong network:

- **Help other businesses, entrepreneurs, and investors find success**: This fact is rarely talked about, but it's arguably the most important rule of networking: You should give more than you take. Your mindset as you connect with various professionals should be oriented toward helping them achieve their dreams, as opposed to always trying to get them to assist you.

  While it's virtuous to altruistically help the members of your network, this needn't be the case. The more you share and help others, the more likely they'll help you in return.

- **A great place to find ideas**: Thinking about how to make the most out of a seemingly ordinary property? You may find that some people in your network have faced the same challenge and overcame it. They could share their solutions with you, which would shield you from costly trials and errors.

  You also don't have to worry about being a bother to the people in your network. People are often too happy to help in this way. For one, it makes them feel needed (who doesn't appreciate this), and they know that their assistance will be reciprocated.

- **It could help you advance your career**: By attending social events and making your face known to entrepreneurs and executives, you'll have the opportunity to get the right attention and build a sterling reputation. When making first impressions, it's important that you're seen as dependable, knowledgeable, and helpful. This isn't to say that you should pretend to be someone you're not, only to change after gaining the friendship of your network. In fact, if you're ambitious, you should continue to be supportive and reliable if you want to grow as an investor.

- **Learn the latest information in your industry**: Even with the Internet, those who find out about new developments on social media are often too slow. Important and niche business news is often circulated with various networks before they become public and common knowledge. This is one reason why it's important to not only be connected, but for your network to be wide and informed.

  You should know that the people in your business circle may not reach out to you with new information. Depending on the level of your influence on and intimacy with your contacts, you may have to actively ask for information.

- **You may find enduring and personal relationships**: While it could start off as a formal and business relationship, chances are that it could mature into something less stiff. Indeed, many close and long-term friendships start off in this way. Since the people in your network will share many of your interests and goals, you'll find it quite easy to develop a close bond with them.

- **You'll always have an answer to your question:** This is only unlikely depending on the size of your network. If you are connected with a large population of professionals, at least one person in your circle will have an answer to your question. On the off chance that you don't get an immediate and definite answer to your question, you'll certainly be able to bounce ideas around until you arrive at an answer.

How to Build a Powerful Network

- **Create win-win situations**: No one wants to be the loser in a relationship. One mistake made by new businesspeople is that they inadvertently (or deliberately) try to take advantage of everyone in their network. The problem here isn't just that people are turned off by selfishness; but that word also gets around quickly. Should you continue that way, soon you'll be unable to make business relationships at all.

- **You don't need everyone**: It isn't enough that an individual is wealthy or works, generally, in your industry. One question you might want to ask is this: Do they share your values? Also, ask this: Does this person have the influence, knowledge, and experience to help me further my career? Although a large network is advised, you shouldn't try to connect with just anybody.

- **Deepen your bonds by being a connector**: You don't always have to be on the lookout for new people to make a part of your network. Instead, you can serve your network by introducing different members to each other. This way, other people can benefit from the richness of your network.

- **Reconnection is more important than connection**: Introducing yourself to people for the first time is great; but there are often those contacts that you haven't touched base with in years. Such contacts may be unwilling to help you, since it might feel too obvious that you only need them for self-seeking reasons. For this reason, it's important that you keep in touch with your contacts regularly. Ask after their well-being and seek out ways to be of value to them.

- **You can build a network on social media**: Today, most people would agree that the Internet is the best place to find and develop rewarding business relationships. Social media, in particular, allows you to access and reach out to individuals who may become your mentors, business partners, or close friends.

Chapter 6:

The Difference Between Real

Estate and Personal Property

All property you'll ever get falls into two basic categories: Real property or personal property. The determining factor of which property falls into what category depends on how possible it is to move it.

Real Estate (Real Property)

Real property is simply property, like land, that you cannot move. Real property is land or any other thing attached to it. This explains why land is called real estate. Things like wood, metal, and other building materials are not exactly real property—but they join the category when they become attached to land. Trees or plants growing on land can also be in the real property category, as long as they do not need routine cultivation or labor.

So when you think about buying a real property, you are considering a land, a home, or a building including mineral resources. The key thing to remember is that real property is land and other things attached to land.

Personal Property

Personal property is any property that can be moved. It is divided into two categories: chattels and intangibles. Chattels is a term used to describe all types of property. Most times, people refer to tangible property like purses or clothing as chattels. Chattels can sometimes be attached to land, and become a part of real property and then they are called fixtures. In other cases, fixtures do not become real property regardless of being attached to real property. For instance, when a lease term ends, a tenant could be allowed to remove the fixtures they installed even without having rights to the real property.

Intangibles are a category of personal property not regarded as tangible. Ideally, intangible properties cannot be seen or touched. This category of property only serves as a precise way of attaching legal rights to property, and not things. Intangible things could be bank accounts, intellectual property, franchises and licenses, insurance policies, and investments like bonds or stocks.

Why Do You Need to Classify Your Property?

Because of the distinction between real and personal property, different rules apply to them. Classifying your property is important, firstly because there may be concerns when a creditor wants to repossess equipment that is connected to a real property, or when someone decides to remove a fixture before moving out of a property. Property classification is also important for tax purposes.

Many U.S. states have been known to tax tangible property. However, the tax on personal property has almost been fully eliminated as states seek to lure new investments and retain manufacturing.

How Do You Know Which Category Your Property Falls Into?

It's simple to know a real property from a personal one. However, with certain fixtures, it becomes difficult to classify. Fixtures are usually personal properties that were attached to real properties at some point. When they are no longer attached, they become real property.

Before determining tax, a three-part test is carried out to classify a fixture connected with real property. The three part test involves:

- **Occupation or attachment**: The property evaluation is done by the jurisdiction to determine the way the property is attached, if it can be removed, and if the real property will be damaged during the removal.

- **Adaptation**: The way the property is used in relation to the real estate is determined.

- **Intent**: The jurisdiction determines if installing the property makes it a permanent feature of the real property, or if the real property changes the actual use of the fixture.

Besides tax, there are other differences between personal property and real property like:

- Personal properties are properties that can also be assets, while real property (real estate) is land and things that are connected to it on a permanent basis like walls, houses, etc.

- Personal properties are not usually durable, and often depreciate in value as time goes on—for instance, a car or furniture. Real properties last long and are very durable.

- The legal process for buying or selling personal property is relatively easier than real property, which is time-consuming and has many steps. Personal properties are not as complex and taxed as fixed properties. Understanding real properties is tedious, because you have to pay tax and handle other proceedings.

- It is easy to transfer personal properties from place to place, but real property being real estate can not be moved. It's not possible to move land or a house. Personal properties can be tangible,whereas real property is residential, industrial, agricultural, commercial, etc.

Why You Should Choose Real Estate

There are many reasons why you should invest in real estate. The benefits of buying real estate include having an excellent rate of returns, amazing tax advantages, wealth creation, etc. These are the most interesting reasons for investing in real estate:

- **The returns on real estate are higher than the stock market with even less volatility**: Ideally, the amount you lose in real estate reduces by the length of time you hold onto your property. The value of the home increases when the market improves. Real estate is different from the stock market because the high risk of the stock market never changes, and your investment can tilt negatively due to the many factors that are beyond your control. With real estate, you have better control over your property because it is a tangible asset that you can get capital appreciation from.

- **Real estate has a high tangible asset value**: Land and homes are always valuable. They are not like other assets, whose value may decrease over time. When you invest in real estate, you have homeowners insurance to protect your investment in the event of a worst-case scenario.

- **Real estate values are always on the rise**: Ideally, the longer you hold onto your real estate, the more money you make. Even in situations where the housing market slips, it always recovers—and people who retain their investments in times of uncertainty see their prices return to status quo, and they start appreciating again.

- **A real estate investment helps diversify your portfolio**: Portfolio diversification helps you to spread out the risk of investing. Real estate is always a safe tangible asset that reduces the risk in your investment portfolio. People have gotten wealthy mainly from real estate investments.

- **Many tax benefits are associated with real estate**: When you invest in real estate, you can get tax reductions on mortgage interest, cash flow from investment properties, property taxes, operating expenses and costs, insurance and depreciation, and other benefits.

Owning a home and renting it out makes you a business owner. The following expenses can be written off for you because of that:

- the mortgage interest paid on the loan

- maintenance expenses

- origination points paid on the loan

- real estate taxes, homeowners insurance, and HOA dues

- depreciation (spread out over 27.5 years)

While you need to confirm with your tax advisor before writing off any expenses, the possibility of even doing that is a benefit that you can't get with stocks and bonds investments. In stocks and bonds, the only way you can write off capital losses is when you sell the asset for a lower price than you bought it.

Forcing Appreciation

Real estate can be forced to appreciate. On its own, real estate appreciates around 3% to 5% every year, with no special effort besides home maintenance. However, you can force the appreciation rate to increase by renovating or repairing things in the home. While the return on your investments may not come back dollar for dollar, you might receive about 80%-90% of your renovation investment.

Again, you don't have to do major renovations. Completing the basement or adding a new room may boost the home value more than basic aesthetic renovations, but the value of your home will increase exponentially when you do even the littlest renovation to your bathroom and kitchen.

Passive Income

You can earn passive income from real estate investment. Renting out a single family or multifamily property provides you income that you do not have to work daily for. Every month, you receive passive income in the form of rent.

Leverage Your Funds

Usually, people who invest in real estate cannot afford to pay the full price for a property—especially first-time buyers. It may cost around $200,000 to buy a single-family home. The best thing about real estate is that it gives you the chance to leverage. Simply put, you buy the properties with other people's money. Financing the investment involves taking loans from banks, mortgage lenders, or credit unions to pay back over time. This makes you increase your real estate holdings without providing the entire monetary cost out-of-pocket.

Protection Against Inflation

Investing in real estate provides you with a buffer against inflation. Home values and rents also increase with the price of goods and services during an inflation. Buying real properties gives you rising monthly income and appreciation that make your finances stable, and reflect the increase in the cost of every other thing.

Opportunity to Build Capital

The main reason you invest in real estate is to get more money or boost capital. Selling a property whose value has risen automatically boosts your capital.

Chapter 7:

Flipping Houses

People who are new in the real estate industry often assume that they have to buy brand new properties to get into the industry or make profit. However, you can also make money in real estate by flipping houses.

House flipping is simply buying distressed properties, refurbishing them, and then reselling at a profit. Properties for flipping are usually bought through foreclosures, property auctions, or bank short sales.

To make money when house flipping, you have to purchase undervalued properties, renovate them to boost their resale value, and list the property on the market. Sometimes, you can purchase properties for flipping without doing extensive renovations—like in microflipping, which works better if you want to buy and sell properties faster without renovating them. In this case, you do careful research to find properties that you can buy below market value, and flip quickly to some other buyer. Usually, the homes do not need major repairs—and you make a lot of money if you can do many real estate transactions in a short period.

Generally, house flipping requires renovation and is a more popular form of flipping in real estate than microflipping.

How to Carry Out House Flipping

Before you flip a house, you need to know the important steps. Having adequate knowledge of the house flipping process helps to boost your chances of being successful and reduce the risk of the venture. These are some things to do before flipping houses:

- **Know your neighborhood**: Don't start house flipping until you have carried out significant research about the real estate market to determine the right location for your investment. If you don't feel equipped enough to do this on your own, then get a real estate agent to guide you. After you find a home you want to flip, you need to have a general contractor assess the property. Doing this helps you decide the estimation of the repairs to be carried out on the house, and if it fits your budget.

- **Plan your budget with the 70% rule**: Real estate investors often use the 70% rule for decision-making. According to this rule, an investor needs to pay only 70% of the after-repair-value (ARV) of a property after the cost of important repairs have been subtracted. The ARV is the home value after renovations are completed. As an example, the ARV of a home is $200,000 and it requires renovation of $25,000. This means 70% of the AVR is $140,000, and removing the cost of repairs leaves the sum at $115,000. By the calculation, you should not buy the home for more than $115,000.

- **Assess your skill set**: Your success as a house flipper largely depends on the kind of skills you have. Flipping a house requires skills like knowledge of design, construction, and real estate. You can still flip a house if you don't have the skills, but the implication is that you will need to hire professionals.

When you are ready to flip houses, gather a team of experts to help you like real estate agents, contractors, and insurance agents. Having a solid team makes it easy to find, fix, and sell the property.

- **Finance your project**: When you have figured out other important things in home flipping, you need to determine your finance plans. How do you intend to finance your project? Think about it and find out which of the many home financing options suits you the best.

- **Make your decision and buy your house**: When flipping a house, you'll encounter the most difficulty during the process of finding the right property. This is due to the fact that your priority is not about the current cost of the home, but the potential value when you resell it. You can consider distressed, foreclosed, and fixer-upper homes if you have a real estate agent and contractor who help you figure out how much work is needed.

After finding the right property, make an offer and close on the house. There might be competition from other buyers if the property is a good deal. All you need to do is figure out the maximum amount that you can spend on buying the house while still making profit.

- **Build sweat equity**: You don't have to quit on your goals of flipping a home if your budget is tight. You can build sweat equity to save some money. Sweat equity is the unpaid labor channeled into your project through mental effort or physical labor. Real estate entrepreneurs often realize that sweat equity is an important part of their success, as it provides the resources to continue pushing.

- **Flip the house**: After finishing repairs on your home, then you should resell it. Selling the property should be done as fast as possible, because the profit you'll make from the home reduces if it stays on the market longer. The main focus of house flipping should be making fast improvements and reselling the home fast. A real estate agent can help you with the house listing in the Multiple Listing Service database. Because real estate agents understand market fluctuation, you can figure out the right resale price with their help.

The Cost of Flipping a House

The overall cost of flipping a house depends on the buying cost, the renovations done, and the amount of time you need to sell it. The expectations you have should be based on:

The Financial Investment

You need to do a lot of calculations when buying and flipping a house to ensure that you make a profit from your venture that justifies the time and money spent on it. The initial cost of buying and refurbishing the home are not the only expenses to account for. Other important expenses include:

- down payment

- property taxes

- insurance payments

- closing costs

- utility costs

- marketing costs

- real estate agent fees

The Time Investment

Aside from the financial investment, house flipping also needs your time investment. The amount of time the project takes from you depends on the size and scope. All things being equal, the process of buying and flipping a home can take you over 6 to 12 weeks. If there are delays in certain processes like remodeling, or third-party approvals, you might spend several months before your house flipping project is completed.

Is House Flipping Right for You?

Considering the effort and dedication you need to do a house flip; you have to determine that you are capable of going through with it before you begin. So, how do you know that house flipping is right for you?

Knowing the advantages and disadvantages of flipping a house can help you decide if you want to do it or not.

Advantages of House Flipping

- there is a possibility of making a huge profit
- it suits individuals with a high skill level
- the risk is lower than with other real estate investments
- it provides relevant real estate experience
- it provides a better understanding of the local real estate market

Disadvantages of House Flipping

- there is a chance of investment loss
- the process requires external assistance and support
- it needs intense planning and budgeting
- the possibility of substantial unbudgeted costs arising
- it requires adequate knowledge of the real estate industry

House flipping is a great real estate business option if you figure out the finances and start with the right plan. But the success of this business is not instant, and you are prone to making mistakes and losing money. If you intend to flip a house, ease the process by having the right team of experts who can help you navigate your way around the real estate market and choose relevant homes.

House Flipping Mistakes

From the aesthetic point of view, house flipping looks easy. All you need to do is buy a house, do some cosmetic makeover, resell, and get your profit. People in the industry make the process look glamorous. To be fair, lots of properties are getting flipped—but the process is more tedious than it appears.

Many people who venture into flipping houses overlook the basic things, and end up without success. If you are considering house flipping, you need to understand the common mistakes that new real estate investors make so that you can avoid them.

Limited Finances

Real estate is expensive, and acquiring the property is the first expense you'll make. Although most deals claim to have low or zero money down options, it is hard to find the deals from a legit vendor. Before you buy a house to flip, it is important that you figure out your financing options and select the type that best suits your needs. When you buy properties with cash, you eliminate interest payments, but you have to consider the opportunity costs and property holding costs for tying up your cash. Factor in the cost of refurbishing the house to be sure that you're not spending more than is necessary on the buying cost. Ideally, you need to have enough money to be able to invest in house flipping.

Limited Time

House flipping is a time-intensive venture. You cannot find the right property for flipping instantly. Oftentimes, it takes several months. Besides the time spent finding the house, you also need to invest time in fixing it after you have bought it. If you handle the refurbishing task on your own, you will lose your free time doing major repairs. If you outsource the renovation task to someone else, supervising the work done will also make you spend more time.

After the renovation is complete, inspections have to be done to ensure the property is in line with the relevant building codes before listing it for sales. If the property does not meet up, you have to spend more time and money to bring it up to scale.

Selling the property is another aspect that requires time investment. If you have to show the property to prospective buyers on your own, you will invest a lot of time commuting to the property.

Limited Skills

People who majorly flip houses are professional builders and skilled professionals, like plumbers and carpenters who do it as a side income from their main jobs. These people usually have the necessary knowledge, skills, and experience needed to find and refurbish a house. In some cases, they have union jobs that give them unemployment checks while they focus on flipping the houses.

To get a better profit from house flipping, you need more sweat equity. Important skills like being able to lay a carpet, roof a house, hang drywall, and fix a kitchen sink are needed to flip a house. If you don't have these skills, then paying a professional to handle the repairs will lower your chance of making reasonable profit.

Limited Knowledge

Success in house flipping comes from knowing how to choose the right property, in the right place, and for the right reason. If the houses in a neighborhood sell for $100,000, you cannot possibly buy a property for $60,000 and sell at $200,000. It is possible to get good deals, like when you buy good houses for really low prices at foreclosures, but it is important to know which renovation to make and which to avoid. Another important thing to know is the tax laws and zoning laws that govern the property. This helps you figure out when to cut your losses and leave the project before it guzzles up all your money.

Limited Patience

People who have experience in the real estate industry often apply patience until they get the right property. But newcomers are quick to buy the first property they view, and they hire the first contractor that bids to handle the work they cannot do. Professionals are either handling their work on their own, or cashing in on their network of trustworthy contractors.

A real estate novice would always need a realtor to help in selling the property. But professionals sell their properties on their own in order to reduce expenses and boost profits. Most newbies expect that the process will be fast, and they'll earn good money in a short while. But professionals understand that flipping houses takes time and may have slim profit margins, so they apply patience when necessary.

Before you flip a house, ensure you have adequate knowledge regarding the risks involved so you do not overestimate your skills and knowledge, or underestimate the time and money needed.

Flipping Houses With No Money

You need money to flip a house—lots of it, and that's not overstating the fact. But what happens when you don't have enough money to venture into this line of real estate? There are other ways to access money for a house flipping investment.

Wholesaling

House flipping investors can make cool money in a short time from wholesaling houses. Wholesaling houses means finding properties for sale, creating a contract for them, and issuing the contract out to a new buyer. After completion of the sale, the percentage—which is usually around 5%-10%—is the profit of the wholesaler. Because the process of the wholesale does not exactly involve buying properties, it is a good point to start in real estate without money.

Remember that as an investor, however, you need to make active moves to achieve success. You will have to study the market, network with potential buyers, and learn how to negotiate contracts. These active efforts help you as an investor to succeed as a wholesaler, and the skills and connections you build are transferable when you eventually progress into flipping houses.

Partner With House Flipping Investors

One way to flip houses without money is by joining a partnership of house flipping investors. It is possible to merge with someone who is already flipping houses, and they could finance a few of your projects.

So if you find that you cannot take on an entire house flipping project alone, get a partner who has funds. With the right agreement, your partner can provide the funding as long as you add value to the table. Remember though, that since you are not bringing funds to the partnership, you need to make up for it by bringing lots of value in other aspects. You could know a deal, or supply the right contacts. It doesn't matter what you're bringing to the table, you just have to bring something. Becoming a partner to investors who can provide funding is a sure way to start flipping houses without money.

Option to Buy

Option to buy, also known as a lease option, is an opportunity for investors to buy a property after leasing. The process is straightforward: Renters get a property and agree to buy it when their lease contract ends. The cost of buying the property is determined during the original contract; but in many cases, rent payments can be credited to the final price. It is a good option if you are considering house flipping without money, because lease option properties do not need upfront payments.

If you decide to flip a property using this option, you have to negotiate potential renovations and repairs when you sign the contract. This is to make sure that the involved parties agree on any work done on the property. Always review the contract carefully, as the terms of an option to buy agreement are largely circumstantial. This is a good option for flipping houses without money; but if you are interested, you need to be adequately prepared and be very attentive to the details.

Seller Financing

Seller financing is another way to flip a house without money. If you want to invest in this way, find properties that advertise seller financing, or find a home to flip and share your idea with interested sellers. Instead of using a traditional lender, investors can work directly with former property owners. Most people who want to flip houses chose this method because of the flexibility of the loan terms. The investors may eventually pay a small down payment, have a favorable payment schedule, and better approval terms.

Crowdfunding

You can also get money for house flipping from crowdfunding—this involves getting multiple investors to sponsor a part of your funding. There are many sites online that link house flippers to crowdfunders to make the process easier.

Getting funds for your real estate projects as a beginner depends on how well you can access a network of experienced real estate investors. This means you have to actively advertise yourself, and insert yourself into local real estate spaces like clubs, meetups, and events. Putting yourself out there helps connect you with successful investors who can start you up, as well as other new investors.

Finding Houses to Flip

With the finance part of your house flipping investment taken care of, you should now be concerned with finding the right markets for flipping houses. The locations you should look out for are up-and-coming areas with low property prices which you can make good profit on after refurbishing. Consider getting properties in areas with increasing employment rates and more development projects. Choose markets with properties that sell quickly. While you search for an investor, also search for the right property, as these two elements are necessary for a successful flip.

Chapter 8:

Some Careers in Real Estate

The most popular career associated with real estate is "residential real estate agent," but it is not the only one. Even the most interesting and profitable career opportunities in real estate are connected to buying and selling residential properties. Still, a real estate license provides the opportunity to access other jobs. If you want a job that is more flexible, high-stakes, low-stakes, or provides more structure—you can always find a career that suits you in the real estate industry.

With a real estate license, you can venture into any one of these profitable and challenging new careers:

- **Real estate managing broker**: A real estate managing broker is way different from a real estate agent, although people use the two terms interchangeably. A broker is a real estate professional with the license and extensive education required to manage a real estate office with multiple agents. If you have already started the process of qualifying as an agent, you can set your sights on being a real estate broker if you want your career to grow.

- **Commercial real estate agent**: Residential real estate agents are known as the default agents in the real estate industry. But commercial real estate can be an even more prosperous niche, where your skills and strengths can be better utilized.

  Usually, a commercial real estate agent does more research than a residential agent. The job of the commercial agent is to help businesses get locations that will improve their inflow. Ideally, being a commercial real estate agent involves leasing a good office space—but most times, it involves things like determining the best location for a budding coffee business to build a store. As a result, commercial agents are particular about figuring out the statistics and data of a location before they close a deal.

- **Real estate investor**: There are two types of real estate investors that you can be: active and passive. An active investor is directly involved in the real estate process. For instance, a house flipper who directly buys and flips residential properties or supports the efforts of another investor or contractor who buys properties to flip. A passive investor does not have direct dealings with the process of acquiring properties.

- **Residential appraiser**: The job of a residential appraiser is to gather information on a residential property so it's possible to give recommendations based on the property's worth. Appraisers can do private work—like appraising individual homes before selling or mortgaging—or work for the government, like appraising a home to find out its worth for tax purposes.

- **Commercial appraiser**: The commercial appraiser has the same task as a residential appraiser—but in this case, they appraise commercial properties. They do not rely entirely on the knowledge from their licensing course, as they learn to determine the value of commercial properties from established appraisers.

- **Property manager**: A property manager oversees the maintenance of a residential or commercial property. They ensure that the property is smooth running and producing the necessary profit for the owner. For residential properties, a property manager may be tasked with many duties, like being a leasing agent and repairman.

The property size and skills of the property manager will determine which of the tasks will be outsourced. The property manager just coordinates the activities and ensures that the property is kept in good condition.

- **Leasing consultant**: The job of a leasing consultant is to ensure that a property is occupied by tenants. While it's important for the consultant to be available on evenings and weekends, there is still a level of flexibility that comes with the job. This is a suitable role for people who love marketing and negotiation. Leasing consultants have to promote specials or openings in their building through promotional events. Consultants have to have current knowledge of the latest digital marketing best practices.

- **Commercial leasing managers**: Commercial leasing managers are usually attached to office space or storefronts, and bargain deals and transactions with businesses. The commercial leasing manager may need to observe the changes in the marketplace, as these affect the budget which businesses will have when buying properties.

- **Foreclosure specialist**: Foreclosure specialists can be affiliated to banks or private lenders, and are tasked with the documentation and processes that are required during the foreclosure of a company. The foreclosure specialist analyzes the client's financial statements, and develops foreclosure cases to ensure that the property is sold off faster. You need good organizational and time management skills to succeed as a foreclosure specialist.

- **Real estate attorney**: A career as a real estate attorney is great if you want to explore education beyond real estate. A real estate attorney is relevant in many ways. Being an attorney means you can fight for tenant rights, or counsel investors before they make a major real estate investment.

- **Corporate real estate manager**: A corporate real estate manager works with a company to manage their real estate properties on their behalf. Big businesses often need to lease office space and commercial space. This job can provide the opportunity to work with companies that need an in-house person to oversee their real estate holdings.

Chapter 9:

Why Real Estate Is Get Rich Slow

Most of the people who invest in real estate quit after their first year. The major reason for this is because of the erroneous belief that you can build wealth very quickly from real estate. Regular real estate flipping industries portray the industry to be rosier than it actually is. People get into real estate thinking that all that is required of them is to find a cool property, fix it up, and wait a few days for buyers to come. Far from the picture-perfect idea people have, real estate is not a "get rich quick" scheme.

But What Does a "Get Rich Quick" Scheme Entail?

A get rich quick scheme is simplifying getting fast profit in a business or investment. It's a process where a person intends to make more than double their investment in rapid time. While it is great to want a substantial increase on your investment in a short while, it's important to remember that real estate cannot provide fast and easy money.

Ideally, real estate is a long-term investment. You need to work hard and have patience. There's no chance of making fast, quick money in real estate.

The major ways of making money from real estate are:

- **Appreciation**: having the value of an acquired property increase over time

- **Rental income**: receiving income from renting out properties to tenants

There are a lot of ways to make money in real estate, but none of them involves getting rich in the blink of an eye. Just like other businesses, real estate has its risks—so much that even when all the conditions are optimum, it takes months to make sales. New investors who have their sights set on big goals may be entirely underwhelmed by the profit they make after expenditure. Investing in real estate is not about making it huge on every deal, but about making the best that you can across several deals until a big opportunity comes into the scene.

Sometimes a real estate deal does not produce returns that are proportional to the amount of work put into it. The reality of an investing business is that there is no way you will close deals worth millions right after you join. While the real estate business has a reputation for making people millionaires, it needs time and work to grow. If you are hoping to be successful immediately, you might think that you are not in the right line of business when it doesn't happen.

Many times, the success in real estate that people describe as overnight happens over many years. Many real estate investors stay in the business for a long time before they find the niche or contact that makes their business grow. While you might be enticed by the idea of making more money from a single deal than your entire year's pay on your former job, you have to put in time and work to reach that level. Even when you reach the point where you earn a tremendous amount of money on one deal, you still have to consider other running costs before you close.

Being passionate about real estate can help you create wealth from it, but it's not going to happen within a month. If you are getting into real estate, consider it as much more than a hobby, and put in a huge amount of effort into it.

The Similarities Between Real Estate Investments and Other Wealth Building Strategies

The three main ingredients for a real estate investment are: patience, planning, and persistence. Leave all expectations of hitting it big in your first year.

Rather, your focus should be on creating a real estate based business with constant yearly growth, which provides you with the materials to meet your financial goals and eventually make your dreams come true.

Regardless of what you hear, achieving success in real estate requires hard work. Just like in other fields, you are responsible for the turnout of things. You must apply the fundamentals of the industry, as there are no shortcuts, tools, or products that will handle your work for you.

The Differences Between Real Estate Investments and Other Wealth Building Strategies

Real estate is among the fastest ways to build real wealth in the current economy. And no, this does not mean overnight wealth. The chief investment advice from most financial gurus is to save 10% of your paycheck in a 401(k) or IRA, and be patient for 40 years until you can retire with a fair amount of money in your savings.

But with a correct investment plan, real estate gives you the chance to boost your financial growth, because you get an opportunity to leverage (make profit from using other people's money) and hustle.

Think about a scenario where you earn $10,000 and save $200 monthly—after five years, your savings will have grown to about $22,000 based on the interest accumulated over time. But if you invest $10,000 into flipping a house successfully, your $10,000 can turn into $40,000 in six months time. Investing your returns into another house flip or maybe a rental property will give you a passive return, which is higher than you can get from other investments.

Real estate can make you wealthy, but it is not a "get rich quick" scheme like it has been portrayed as. Granted, you might get richer faster than in other kinds of investment, but only if you have the patience, persistence, and plan to achieve success.

Chapter 10:

How to Find the Right Mentor

Without Paying

The term 'mentor' is used in broad reference to anyone who's a boss, coach, successful person, or even a friend you typically go to for advice. It denotes a certain sense of superiority, in that you can learn from them, and they have something valuable to impart.

Mentoring is a process that should occur on its own and develop over time. You can't exactly (and shouldn't) force anyone into mentoring you. Instead, you should have something to offer in return for their guidance. Like in any relationship, having a real estate mentor is also a two-way street that requires giving and receiving from both parties. On your part, it could mean expressing gratitude and paying attention. On the other hand, it could also be a conscious effort to aid your mentor in achieving their goals and objectives.

In simpler terms, your real estate mentor should be one that can train and advise you on important matters and offer relevant feedback as you grow. Often, mentors are older. But age isn't a core feature for choosing a mentor, nor is it cast in stone; younger people can also be mentors to older mentees if they have the right values.

But even if your mentor has all the right qualities, you can't expect them to divulge all their knowledge on real estate to you. Of course, they will set you up to succeed and take after them, but it would be on your own terms and with the knowledge and expertise you've garnered from learning under them. Don't expect that having a mentor automatically sets you up to receive their big book of real estate success. Slow down.

In the same vein, a mentor is more than your go-to speed dial for all your problems, or only when you need something. You shouldn't bother them with small details that are irrelevant to real estate. No, they don't want to know about your favorite blend of coffee or why you only wear cuff links on Tuesdays. Your time with them should be spent in meaningful conversations that further your understanding of real estate, rather than on vague questions and existential crisis problems.

Qualities of a Good Mentor

Here are some reasonable qualities you can expect in a real estate mentorship:

- You and your mentor should have common passions in business and life, because real estate involves both aspects of investing.

- There should be mutual respect between you both.

- Convince your mentor of what they should invest their efforts and knowledge in with you. Mentors are often the busiest people in the business, so you don't want to cut into their precious time for nothing.

- Ensure that they can provide direct and honest feedback easily.

- You want to get a mentor that has similar tastes and strategy for navigating the market, otherwise their oversight would be pointless.

- Your mentor should show a willingness and eagerness to invest in your growth.

- Expect the relationship between your mentor to be valuable to all involved, with each party standing to gain in the process.

Types of Mentorship

As you begin the search for an ideal mentor, you have to be aware of the different cadres of mentorship and what you want to be seen as. Consider factors like preferred learning style, availability, and educational needs when determining who's right to mentor you.

That said, here are some forms of mentorship to consider:

- **Apprenticeships**: Sometimes, the best approach to learning about real estate is to be a tag along as your mentor navigates business as usual. This could mean putting in part-time hours at their business like an intern, or shadowing them when deals are made and closed. Apprenticeships offer you a taste of real estate life without the responsibilities of taking over yourself.

- **Mastermind Groups**: Depending on your area of residence, you will likely find some real estate investing groups in your locale. These groups are important learning structures that bring you in contact with your peers. They present a great means of networking and building relationships independent of your mentor. If you can't find one near you, consider searching online for virtual groups.

- **Personalized Coaching**: This form of mentorship relies on one-on-one coaching, intent on guiding you into the industry. Your mentor would have to be an experienced player in real estate, who can offer you personalized advice to navigate your way through deals and other hassles. This form of mentorship offers you the best chance of consistency in both learning and practice.

Myths Surrounding Real Estate Mentors

They'll teach you all you need to know, but even teachers don't teach students all they know. It's a given that your mentor may sometimes lead by the hand on what to do, but that's an exception. Good mentors help you to learn at your own pace, and from your mistakes. Now, with all these in place, they can now assist you in discovering yourself and what works best for you.

Standfast, someone will discover you soon. Sometimes, success doesn't come to those who wait; and the patient dog has to go dig up his bone at some point. Simply put, don't take a passive route to finding a mentor. Stay proactive.

Mentoring is all about the mentee. On the contrary, it's a two-way street of benefits. Both the mentor and mentee have a lot to benefit from each other. Think of it as a symbiotic relationship.

'Yesses,' so to speak, come to those who ask. Don't be surprised if many people turn down the opportunity to mentor you. It's all right, and they are not wrong. You have to let everything stew and keep your eyes peeled to ensure that your mentor is right for you.

Tips for Finding a Real Estate Mentor

There are people whose careers are to be mentors for a sale. They impart you with their knowledge and expertise for about an hour or two, and that's about it. But you don't have to go down that lane. There are other ways to get a mentor without having to spend a dime. Here are some tips:

- Look into learning programs. Programs like Roofstock Academy offer you all you need to know to kickstart your real estate business by taking advantage of the expertise and experiences of more successful people in real estate who have devised a system of obtaining, studying, and managing rental properties.

- Look into your network of real estate workers—from contractors to brokers to lenders to title companies—with a steady stream of real estate investors. These people will be more than willing to recommend you to someone. From there, you can arrange a meeting with your potential mentor to find out if the arrangement works for both parties.

- Attending networking events with other local investors can help bring you in contact with people who have achieved your goals and objectives repeatedly.

- Although it's possible to begin your real estate career without any form of mentorship, having a mentor will allow you to grow and learn the ropes faster. Mentorship is meant to improve your understanding of the industry, and save you from rookie mistakes you might not see coming.

- When choosing a mentor, it helps to consider your goals, both long-term and short-term, as well as your reason for choosing a career in real estate. This should help you choose a mentor who is both like-minded and experienced in the industry.

Why should they be like-minded? You will learn better and be less at odds with someone who has a similar value system to yours. Also, you will connect on more levels than just a mentor-mentee relationship, giving you enough room to improve.

And if you have already found a mentor, make sure you do your homework before diving in. Begin by building a network with experts in your preferred segment of the market, who share similar goals and strategies.

You also need to be sure that your network and whoever you choose as your mentor is capable at their job. Do background checks and check out their referrals to ensure that no one wastes your time. There are many things you must double-check in your real estate career. Your mentor should be one of those, including their experience levels and backgrounds.

Chapter 11:

What Is Analysis Paralysis?

Sometimes, you may get stuck on decision-making during crucial moments. Instead of making a choice outrightly, you find yourself making needless risk assessments, analyzing the market, and in an unending cycle of due diligence. This phenomenon is known as analysis paralysis, the inability to be decisive because of overthinking.

Analysis paralysis often happens when you are overly saturated with information, so much that you get too involved in weighing the pros and cons of every option and are unable to decide on one. In real estate, it's easy to get bogged down by analysis paralysis when making investment decisions. While it's not a bad idea to thoroughly consider your choices, the problem comes from having to choose between options. Thus, your inability to choose becomes an inhibition to productivity.

How It Works

Analysis paralysis doesn't happen with complex problems alone, it can also occur with routine issues. It often arises from trying to find an answer from too many variables. For instance, when trying to decide between having cereal or bacon and eggs for breakfast, your basic logic considers what you had the previous day and are currently craving. If you'd rather have something warm and cooked, you'd gravitate toward the latter; but if you don't mind some cold milk and crunchy flakes, you'd go for the former. That's simple.

However, analysis paralysis in this situation is different. Usually, it begins when the options you have to weigh have ambiguous parameters. It's why the question of what to have for breakfast takes a longer time to figure out than just choosing cereal or bacon and eggs. The former leaves you with a laundry list of foods, both ones you have and don't, easy and complex dishes, etc. The parameters to weigh are unending, and you may wind up missing breakfast. The latter, on the other hand, presents you with two options that are fairly easier to compute and weigh.

How to Beat Analysis Paralysis

Below are a few proven solutions for this stagnating issue:

- **Recognize it**: It's great advice to thoroughly cogitate before making decisions, including how they affect your life. So, you need to first understand the difference between analysis paralysis and a healthy decision-making process.

  Things start to feel overwhelming when you have to single out a correct choice from several other options, especially when you believe every option is useful. It's this pattern that leads to analysis paralysis and gets you nowhere close to decision-making.

- **Prioritize the decisions**: Don't treat all your decisions with the same level of interest and commitment. Analysis paralysis begins when you don't know how to share your attention between options. Find out decisions that are more pressing and important, and tackle them first. For instance, don't put work emails and clipping your nails on the same priority list.

  Here are some questions to ponder to help ease the process:

  - What are the repercussions of this decision if it goes awry?

  - Is your decision crucial to productivity?

  - What level of importance are you attaching to it?

  - Do you have to make the decision now?

- **Take a break**: Analysis paralysis traps you in a web of ruminating and going over the exact thoughts repeatedly. But you know better than to think that overthinking brings any solution whatsoever. In fact, it's by repeatedly going over possibilities even when you feel overwhelmed and fatigued that causes paralysis.

  Instead of getting trapped in this whirlwind, consider taking some time out to distract yourself with something relaxing and enjoyable. Prime yourself to avoid cogitating on the decision during that time.

- **Ask someone for advice**: Often, analysis paralysis is triggered by anxiety in the form of fear, worry, and thoughts that you may struggle to stray from. It can be challenging to get out of the loop, but not impossible. Consider seeing a therapist for help.

  Start by acknowledging the triggers of the condition, and find a way to avoid repeating the pattern. Steer clear of symptoms of depression or anxiety that may worsen the situation, and confide in a professional support system when it starts to get in the way of your quality of life, work, productivity, and relationships.

- **Make quick decisions**: If you struggle with timely decision-making, it might be time for you to start cutting down on your thinking time. Don't mistake longer thinking time for better decision-making, because that's how you begin to gloss over analysis paralysis. It won't feel good making decisions in a heartbeat, but it's something that you should practice. For instance:

  ○ Get snacks from the vending machine without having to think about what you're getting and why.

  ○ Go on a walk without assigning a route prior. Just follow your feet.

  ○ Watch something on Netflix that you find interesting without going through the synopsis and reviews.

71

- Grab some cereal from the store without comparing it to another one.

- Practice regularly until you're comfortable making decisions in a timely manner.

- **Set a deadline**: Some people feel better with pressure on their backs. They want to be able to feel the weight of overhanging deadlines to kick into gear. If this works for you, it might be time to put it to good use. Instead of taking the rest of your life to decide what you want for breakfast, try setting an alarm for decision-making an hour before then. You'll find how easily you choose a meal the closer the time comes.

- **Understand your goals**: Usually, it's not the fear of failing that stops you from making decisions, nor is it that there are too many options to choose from. Often, it's that you don't know why you can't make a choice. When this scenario occurs, recall why you need to make a choice: your goals. You'll find it easier to make decisions based on the outcomes of your goals.

- **Limit your information intake**: It can help to find out why you can't make choices easily. Often, the reason might come from lingering memories, prior decisions that didn't go so well, or trouble believing in your ability to choose. It could also be that choosing wrongly may impact your life and the lives of others around you. Such decisions are often more challenging to make than others.

So, while it helps to be aware of the pros and cons of decisions through studies and analysis, you may have to hold out on seeking too much information that leaves you spiraling.

It's totally normal to take your time in making decisions and consider other options and alternatives. In fact, what isn't normal is rushing through decision-making all the time. However, if you find yourself regularly weighed down with indecision and constantly stewing over some decisions, it might be time to take a closer look at the situation.

When you find yourself getting paralyzed by making decisions, try going with your impulse. Just pick a path that feels right and go through with it. Of course, things won't always work out this way. But it helps a lot that you make a decision rather than none at all.

As Jeff Boss put, in one of his writings for Forbes, "It doesn't matter in which direction you choose to move when under a mortar attack, just as long as you move."

To beat analysis paralysis, you don't have to make the right decision at once. In fact, it's trying to make the right call that got you there in the first place. All you have to do is make one call. Keep in mind that taking too long to make a decision is just as bad at making choices randomly or not making a choice at all.

When you start feeling paralyzed by too much analysis, take the time out to highlight your goals and needs and find the options that best match them. Do the pros and cons, and go with the best option.

Chapter 12:

The Problem With Real Estate

Gurus

Every industry has a set of people who pride themselves as 'experts' of the trade, trying to impart their knowledge onto others to accelerate their success. They are known as gurus, and aren't the best people to be around. While there are rare cases of legitimacy in this lot, the overwhelming majority are anything but legitimate. Many gurus just want to get you excited for their seminars and workshops and books so that they can make a quick buck.

So, How Does It Happen?

Gurus start to enter the picture when you realize that you may not know about real estate as much as you think. So, you want to brush up and stay up-to-date to effectively compete in the industry. Now, these self-acclaimed professionals pop into view with the promise of meeting your educational needs. Their promotions often include an exclusive workshop that runs for three hours. They love the weekends, so Saturdays are often their go-to dates for teaching people "insider secrets to success in real estate."

You'd get more out of your Saturday by staying at home to clean and declutter than going to one of these workshops or seminars. The reason is because it's impossible to squeeze wisdom gathered over several decades into a three-hour lesson. And the concepts of buying, flipping, renting, and renovating houses can't be reduced to bullet points and catchphrases. Otherwise, everyone could sell a house—even the rodent that ate your economics homework. Think of it like trying to learn all about ancient Egypt and its powerful pharaohs before lunchtime, when you can't even point out the country on the map.

How to Identify Fake Experts (Gurus)

It's the easiest thing to find real estate gurus, because they want to be seen and make no effort to market themselves any better than a one-stop destination to success. Here are things to look out for:

- **Seminars**: If an educational seminar is cheap or free, then it's not a one-off affair but a lure to entice you into their web, where you'll be convinced and serenaded with tall tales of how easy and successful their hidden secrets are.

- **Psychological trickery**: As the great seminar comes to an end after several hours of catchy words and marketing, you'll find a hard sell, which combines emotional appeal and fearmongering. They start going in for the kill by encouraging you to buy their advanced courses, because they couldn't impart all their hidden knowledge in one class. Who would have thought! They market the next step as the final destination to making it big in real estate... if only.

- **Down, down the rabbit hole**: Did you think the advanced course was the end of the line? Too bad. These gurus won't stop now that they've managed to get you into the second phase with them. Now, it's time for extra courses, bus tours, field trips, specialty classes, and personal mentorships for a premium.

- **Investments**: When you finally make it out of their web of courses and training, you'd think you can finally set out on your own to identify, analyze, and close deals. But you'd be wrong. Gurus won't fail to mention how difficult and cutthroat it is to break into the industry (forgetting that their classes were supposed to make it a walk in the park). Their solution is to provide you with ready deals to close quickly. They're the experts, after all—where's the harm in it? If it hasn't already occurred to you, these real estate gurus aren't successful because they understand the industry and invest wisely. No. Their success is tied to exploiting the gullibility and naivety of others.

- **Celebrity attachment**: You would think that celebrities would know better than to align themselves with real estate gurus. But you'd be wrong. Many HGTV celebrities, including public figures like Donald Trump, have given many real estate investment seminars the thumbs up many times. That hasn't stopped those programs from being cash cows for the gurus. So, don't let the buzz fool you.

  In fact, these celebrities are rarely present at the event, and they are no more than figureheads to attract people to the program. If you want to get firsthand insights on how any program works, then get in touch with one of the regular folks from the workshop. Find out if the gurus have helped them find their feet in the industry. If you can't find any, ask to be referred to some people in your locale who have benefited from the workshop. That way you can find out if and how it works.

  There's a chance that the guru has won these people over, so don't just take everything they tell you. Find out their investments and properties, and do some background checks to ensure how legit they are.

- **The upsell is everything**: There's also a chance that the guru might not wait till the end of the workshop to issue a call to action. Some may spend the entire time buttering you up with tall tales of their accomplishments and how their advanced course is the next best thing since Nutella. But they won't stop there. They will try to rope you in by getting you to make a down payment for their upcoming master class or sign up for their paid newsletter because, "it's a limited great deal that you won't find anywhere else." Well, if such a great deal is only available because they will do it in the moment, it's not the best option, don't you think? You'd be surprised to find that the deal is still on the table even two months after the supposed limited period.

- **Do your homework**: Before committing to any workshop, do your homework to ensure that the organizers are legit. It might be worse than a regular scam. But that's on the one hand. You need a workshop that teaches you practical skills and steps to help you become better at real estate. By building you up, there's nothing that you can't achieve.

Use sites like ConsumerAffairs and Scams Galore to check for reviews of workshops. It's normal to see a little negative feedback. But if many people are complaining about the same problem, that's your sign to look elsewhere.

- **No money-back guarantee**: One way to know if a guru is good is if their program offers a money-back guarantee. Gurus who want to teach you practical skills won't be afraid of customers wanting to take their business elsewhere, because they know the value they sell and its ability to keep people. But saying you can't get your money back can also be a guise to look legit. Visit the Better Business Bureau to find out if people really got their money back.

- **The promise of quick wealth**: Real estate isn't a get rich quick scheme like those gurus say it is on YouTube. As much as people buy properties every day, remember that you won't be dealing with a commodity that everyone can afford. So, there will be dry spells and productive streaks. The most successful real estate investors are those who put in the hours come rain or shine.

  You must also be patient, as it's the desire to hit it big quickly that drives people to the wrong gurus who promise instant wealth if you try their style. How effective has it got to be to work 100% of the time for everyone they ever taught?

Also, look out for those gurus who add mantras to their workshops and books. You might as well visit a hypnotist, because saying, "You can do it if you believe hard enough," to your neighbor isn't the most effective real estate strategy.

If a guru tells you that real estate is the quickest way to get rich, you should have a hand on your purse. The louder they say it, the tighter you should hold it close. What are the odds that you will find a stunning property in New York that has somehow missed the attention of every real estate broker, realtor, or investor in the area?

Many gurus usually preach the gospel of investing now to retire in five years. If only! They want to tell you just how easy real estate is, and that if you listen and follow them long enough, there are no odds too great that you cannot beat, no market too difficult that you cannot navigate. And work? Why work again when the market is your own game?

But anyone with two bits of sense knows that real estate is hard work. Properties are one of the most expensive commitments people have to make. So getting people to part with their assets or take a loan to invest in real estate won't happen with sweet words alone.

How, then, do you make any sense of the market without the gurus screaming in your ear?

Mentorship is the answer. As far as it goes, mentors are the better versions of gurus. They are more relatable and better understand your situation than any guru will be willing to. And their advice comes from experience, rather than the desire to sell books and masterclasses.

Chapter 13:

Investing in REITs

REIT is an acronym for real estate investment trust. It refers to a company that manages, owns, or funds real estate properties that generate income. REITs are designed to work like mutual funds, so it's similar to a capital pool made up of different investors. As a result, all of the parties involved get returns on their investment when the real estate generates revenue. This way, they can earn without owning, managing, or purchasing any property.

How They Work

REITs were established in 1969 by Congress as a constitutional amendment. The new provision allowed people to purchase shares in the portfolios of commercial real estate. Before then, this investment opportunity was only open to huge financial intermediaries and the wealthiest persons.

Some types of real estate properties you will find in an REIT portfolio are hotels, data centers, apartment complexes, healthcare facilities, warehouses, office buildings, self-storage, timberland, retail centers, and infrastructure (e.g., energy pipelines, cell towers, and fiber cables).

From a general point of view, REITs deal with one area of the real estate market. However, you may sometimes see specialty real estate investment trusts with diversified portfolios that may contain several types of properties at the same time. For example, an REIT with both apartment complexes and self-storage.

Many REITs are available on major stock exchange platforms for public trading. So, you can trade them like any other stock across a trading session. The real estate investment trusts found on these platforms have better liquidity and enough volume to be bought and sold repeatedly in the market.

How to Invest in REITs

Investing in real estate investment trusts can be a challenge, because there are many terms to learn and platforms to know. But it's not impossible for a beginner. All you need is to get in touch with a stock exchange. Then, you can start buying shares from a broker. Now, there are two ways to go about this: you can either get the shares of an REIT exchange-traded fund (ETF), a REIT mutual fund, or a non-traded REIT.

Real estate investment trusts found on the publicly traded stock market are available from brokers. Using this method, there are many options you can take, from getting a common stock to a debt security to a preferred stock of a publicly traded REIT.

IRS regulations and policies stipulate that all real estate investment trusts must pay shareholders 90% or more of total taxable profits as dividends. This is why REIT companies are tax-free for most corporate income taxes. Instead, shareholders are taxed upon receiving their dividends, like any other dividend.

Types of REITs

Outlined below are the various types of real estate investment trusts that you're likely to find:

- **Hybrid REITs**: This form of REIT is born from the combined strategies of mortgage and equity REITs.

- **Mortgage REITs**: In this REIT, money is lent to real estate operators or owners in the form of loans or mortgages. But sometimes, the transfer of funds is indirect and is via the acquisition of mortgage-backed securities. This form of REIT generates revenue through net interest margins—the spread between the cost of funding the loans and the interests generated by the loans.

- **Equity REITs**: Most REITs available on the market are equity REITs, which operate and own real estate properties that generate revenue. In this case, revenue generation comes from rent rather than the selling of properties.

The Risks Involved

When going into REITs, be careful of who you get your stocks from. If they aren't registered with the SEC, it's likely a bad idea. You should be able to confirm the validity of both non-traded and publicly traded REITs using the EDGAR system available on the SEC. You can also use this system as a yardstick for reviewing the quarterly and annual reports of REITs, including other offering prospectus.

You should also run background checks on the investment adviser or broker recommending an REIT to you. There's a free search tool on the SEC website that lets you look up the registration and license of any investment professional.

One downside to investing in REITs is that it doesn't encourage capital appreciation. The structure of the stock is such that investors get 90% of the REITs earnings all the time. As a result, there's only 10% left in taxable income to be poured back into the REIT to get new holdings. Another risk is that you will be charged regular income tax on your dividends, even though many REITs come with high transaction and management fees.

The United States government allowed investors to invest in large-scale commercial real estate from as early as 1960. However, it wasn't until the past decade that REITs have become a popular investment choice for many individual investors.

The appeal of REITs comes from the low interest rates—these allow investors to look beyond the mutual funds, exchange-traded funds (ETFs), and bonds on income-producing investments. Instead, they chose to invest in real estate—up until the meltdown in 2007 and 2008, which dissuaded most Americans from being part of real estate and owning tangible assets.

Like any other financial vehicle, REITs took a big hit in 2008. However, despite this setback, it continues to be a huge hit for many investors with diversified portfolios.

You can invest in REITs for passive income instead of buying and managing a property yourself. However, the downside is that you can't always expect huge profits—like with rent, which is steady and can be increased over time. This is because REITs sometimes perform poorly in the market, especially when interest rates increase.

So, instead of investing in any REITs that you find, look for ones that are publicly traded, have high-end properties that are in line with the present market trends, and are run by great management teams. It also helps to have an experienced tax accountant on your side to ensure that you get the best tax rates. For instance, you could use a Roth IRA (which is a tax-advantaged account), to invest in REITs.

Chapter 14:

Finding Your Niche in Real Estate

Marketing yourself as a real estate expert doesn't do much for your reputation recently. People are more enlightened and have unfettered access to the things that suit their preferences and needs, including real estate. Add to that the increasingly competitive industry, and you start to doubt your chances of success. But every successful real estate agent knows one truth, and that's to avoid the competition at all cost. Instead of trying to take on the entire industry, focus on a specific part of the market and carve a niche for yourself. This way, you will access a smaller but more lucrative market, where you can motivate customers, build trust, and build a more successful portfolio.

Real estate niche marketing involves finding and promoting your business in a specific area of interest. But you can't just choose any part of the market at random. You need one that complements your skills and expertise, because these factors are important to the success and productivity of your efforts. Think of finding your niche as identifying your passion. It shouldn't just be a job, but something you are passionate about.

Different Niches in Real Estate

The real estate market is flooded with niches for days. But not all of them will appeal to you or your skills. As such, I've curated a few niches from some of the most popular and frequent market used by most customers:

- **Location**: This real estate niche is the most common of the lot, and has to do with certain areas, counties, neighborhoods, zip codes, or cities. You've likely heard of real estate agents who sell themselves as the best in a particular area. Those are location-based realtors. Attaching their names to an area makes it easier for them to get customers without leaving their comfort zones, where they have worked for years. By showing how much they know the area and the market, clients trust them to provide good value for their money.

When choosing a location, make sure to go with one that allows you to make the most appointments and show the most houses without spending too much time on the road. Your location of choice should also be an area you're familiar with, or have extensively researched. It helps if you live close to this location.

- **Property-based**: Niches based on property types are broader because of the different sub-niches under them. To be in this niche, you have to choose a specific type of detail, process, or structure of the properties you want to sell. Here are some of the property types you will see on the market:

  o **Single-family homes**: These are usually free-standing residential buildings located on their own lands.

  o **Multifamily homes**: These often come as single buildings broken into several units to house more than one family living independently.

  o **Condo (condominium)**: Condos are residential units owned by individuals, but are located on shared land with other similar buildings.

  o **Co-ops**: These buildings are mostly found in New York. They are corporate-owned properties run by a co-op of the owners.

  o **Commercial property**: This is a building or sets of buildings used for commercial purposes—e.g., a retail building, office building, or warehouse.

  o **Historic properties**: Buildings in this category are usually more than 50-years-old, with a connection to history. It's often a building lived in by a famous person, created with a historical style, or linked to an event.

- **Flipping**: You can also get into flipping, which is like a second career of retouching up homes before selling them. Flipping can be done solo or through investors in the same niche. Whichever way you go, flipping is one of the most common niches. But it's also more demanding. A background in decor or construction would go a long way. But it's not compulsory, and your love for customizing properties will be enough.

To become a successful flipper, you need to build a network because you can't manage it on your own. Surround yourself with a team made up of electricians, contractors, and plumbers. This way, you can rehab houses quickly and get them back on the market.

- **Rental and vacation properties**: If you live in a popular vacation destination, why not take advantage of the niche there? This real estate niche is popular, thanks to TV channels like HGTV. But it's not all hype and no substance. Selling people a second home, which is also an investment, requires more skills than needed to sell a home once. One important part is knowing the tax burdens on second homes.

For the people that buy these properties, their focus is on resale value, taxes, and rent generation instead of luxury kitchens or school zones. So, if you want to go into this niche, go to the National Association of Realtors for a Resort and Second-Home Property Specialist Certification.

- **Buyer types**: We are often caught up in trying to sell properties, that we sometimes forget about the other half of the real estate market: buyers. These people are often in the market for a good deal or investment, and can be a reliable niche to target. If you want to go into the buyer-type market, come up with buyer personas for the different types of buyers you want to meet. This will help you look for properties that your target buyers will be interested in.

Here are some common buyer-type clients you will find in the market:

- ○ **Luxury buyers**: This class of buyers often includes individuals with a lot of money to throw around. Most of them are already property owners, too. By having several homes across the country, they can spend some time in different places throughout the year.

- ○ **Rent-to-own buyers**: This class of buyers isn't ready to purchase a property yet, because of the lack of finances to make a down payment. Some of them may be dealing with a bad credit score, which stops them from getting a mortgage. But with all these hindrances, they still want to invest in real estate with the goal of owning their own home without having to rent, which doesn't help build equity.

- ○ **Commercial property buyers**: Buyers in this category are usually business owners or representatives of businesses who need a space for work.

- ○ **First-time homebuyers**: These buyers are in the market for their first property, and are usually looking for affordable deals. In 2020, 33% of homebuyers fell into this category.

- **REO & Foreclosures**: This is one of the most technical niches in real estate, because it requires you to know and understand market trends. Why? So that you can effectively connect with lenders when discussing property value. To begin, it's best to not go solo. So, try applying through a brokerage or joining a team of realtors in this niche.

You will be getting in touch with asset managers and lenders, so you can nail down a great marketing strategy that gets you steady business. This niche can be challenging a lot of the time, but it is also one of the most lucrative sectors of the market.

There are many different opportunities in real estate, so it's hard to be a jack-of-all-trades even if you want to. As such, finding a niche is the best way to build a career in real estate. As a rule of thumb, ensure that your niche is in line with the things you like or are interested in. This will allow you to enjoy it and set you apart from the competition. Also, it will help you grow your personal brand, turn your marketing to bring in maximum returns, and take your customer experience to a whole new level.

In addition, having a niche helps you to understand and relate with your customers better. This helps to boost your brand image and set you apart as an authority figure. Clients prefer experts in a specific part of real estate to a jack-of-all-trades. So, you can expect a loyal and trusting customer base.

To show just how much you know your stuff, add it to your online platforms, like your social media accounts, website, and blog. First, make the post on your website before sharing the link to your social media to increase traffic to your website.

When potential clients see that you are good at a particular niche, lead conversion will be much easier, and you will have an edge in the market.

Chapter 15:

Real Estate Wholesaling

Real estate wholesaling is a method of real estate investing that deals with selling properties on the owner's behalf. Of course, you get a profit from the sale. It begins with entering an agreement with a seller, after which you sell the property to a buyer. Like regular wholesalers, you are a middleman who stands between the seller and the buyer. But unlike regular wholesalers, you don't need to buy the property to add it to your inventory.

Instead, the contract allows you to markup the price, sell on behalf of the owner, and keep the profit. Usually, the properties that make it to real estate wholesalers are distress sales or ones off the market. The owner is no longer interested in the property, but doesn't want to go through the process of listing it traditionally. So, the wholesaler steps in to take it off their hands.

The contract in real estate wholesaling doesn't last forever, though. It's only valid for a limited time. And if you can't sell off the property within the agreed time, it remains with the seller and you no longer have access to it. Also, you won't be compensated for your time. In fact, the only time money changes hands between the seller and wholesaler is when a sale is made. So, the only way real estate wholesalers make money is by selling properties for a higher price than the asking amount of the seller. The difference between the asking price and the selling price is the profit, which the wholesaler gets to keep.

You should only go into real estate wholesaling if you don't have enough funds to invest in properties. Because you don't need capital, and all that matters is your ability to sell. There's no exam to take, course to pass, or license to get into wholesaling. In fact, with some people and refined marketing skills, you will do just fine in wholesaling. Often, the buyers of wholesale real estate are flippers, rehabbers, and investors who don't want to negotiate with sellers or scout cheap properties on the market.

So, in simple terms, the job of a real estate wholesaler is to help sellers get rid of property and help real estate investors close deals.

What Percentage of Real Estate Wholesalers Fail?

As a real estate wholesaler, it's bad business to expect fair trades at all times. You should also consider the possibility of bad deals. There's no guarantee that you will sell every property you find, or make the profit margin you hoped for. This is truer for beginners to real estate wholesaling.

If you're a beginner wholesaler, there is a 50% chance that you will fail in this niche. As a result, you must be prepared both financially and mentally to deal with the situation. But don't feel bad—you won't always be the reason for a bad deal. Several factors can come into play, like a prospective buyer calling off a deal. It's not the best move, but there's nothing you can do about it. They reserve the right to not go through with the purchase. It's situations like this that need a backup plan, and you must be ready to act the part.

Is Real Estate Wholesaling Viable?

The answer to this question is the same as for any other investment or business: it's neither yes nor no, and depends on how you see it.

On one hand, real estate wholesaling is low-risk and just needs you to put in the work, find a buyer, and get a healthy profit margin. On the other hand, it can be difficult to run a wholesaling business because you need to be able to find properties that want to be sold for less than their market values. But it doesn't end there. You must also know how to negotiate with buyers and sellers, and identify cash buyers who want to close deals as quickly as possible.

There's also the point of taking your time to develop a list of leads, finding buyers who are willing and capable of buying your offerings, and networking to stay on top of your game. If you are ready to put the work in, you will succeed in real estate wholesaling. You also need to be creative with your offers, as pricing is a crucial factor in wholesaling. If you offer a low price, sellers might suspect foul play and steer clear. On the other hand, going too high will scare off buyers and leave you with a stagnant contract. Especially in the case of distressed properties, buyers are less willing to spend high on a house they still have to fix.

To succeed, you need to find that sweet spot—one that allows you to leave a deal before it becomes stagnant or as the closing date on the contract starts to run out. This will prevent you from risks associated with the business.

Pros and Cons

Pros

- **Little to no funding necessary**: You won't have to purchase the property to fix and resell, like flipping or other niches in real estate. In fact, the only thing you have to invest is your time, skill set, and marketing know-how. There are only a few cases when you'll need some earnest money to be a wholesaler.

- **Higher earning potential within a short time**: Selling one property in wholesaling gives you profit without needing to pour in capital. What's more, this profit is substantial and can be earned in a couple of months. If you are able to sell more properties simultaneously, your earnings increase further.

- **Learning on the go**: Wholesaling is a good starting niche for beginners, because it allows you to trade the market without investing your capital—sort of like a demo to the buying and selling part of real estate. So, if you commit to it, you'll learn vital skills for your real estate journey, including negotiating, marketing, networking, legal documentation, and organizing.

  In a way, real estate wholesaling is a combination of little bits of other niches that you will deal with the longer you stay in the industry. And being the easiest niche, you can get the hang of wholesaling after a couple of deals, including knowing the do's and don'ts.

Cons

- **Low profits**: Even though your earning potentials might be high as a real estate wholesaler, your profit per deal won't always be substantial. Since you'll be looking for houses under the standard market pricing and trying to sell them at reasonable markups, there won't be much left for you at the end of a deal. Wholesaling has low profits because it is low-risk, compared to other niches like flipping.

- **Too many interdependent factors**: To make any profit, you need to find a willing seller and buyer. This can be challenging, and is one of the contributing reasons to the low profits rate.

- **Income isn't steady**: Unlike investing in REITs, which guarantee a steady income flow through dividends, wholesaling real estate doesn't guarantee fixed profits or regular flow of income. Contracts may run out before you close a deal, and buyers may back out last second. You may even go through dry spells, when you won't find a willing seller to strike a deal with.

- **Buyers aren't easy to come by**: One half of your success as a real estate wholesaler depends on your ability to find buyers. But sometimes, buyers are hard to come by. And even when they aren't, not all of them will agree to your pricing—so you may have to further reduce your profit to make a sale. And depending on the amount you put on the contract as escrow, you could end up losing money without profits. The best way to avoid this problem is to have a buyer on standby. Also, you have to regularly make and close deals. Otherwise, sellers won't want you selling their properties.

Usually, in most real estate markets, the number of people who want to buy properties are more than the properties available for sale. Real estate wholesalers fill this gap by finding property owners willing to sell and bringing them to buyers and investors. Like any other business, real estate wholesaling isn't without its risks. But it also comes with some decent rewards. For instance, real estate wholesalers stand to gain healthy profits on each successful deal. Also, they don't have to deal with the property directly, and are more like a middleman for bringing sellers and buyers together.

This makes wholesaling properties one of the most straightforward methods of earning a living in real estate. But that doesn't mean you should go in unprepared. Instead, take the time to learn how it works, research the market, and create a strong network of buyers and sellers. Doing so will make you more successful in wholesaling, and you won't have to deal with contracts running out before you find a buyer. The best part of wholesaling is that it's a good foundation for starting your career in real estate. This is because it doesn't require huge capital or inventory of any sort. You don't even need a huge working space to be a real estate wholesaler.

Chapter 16:

The Importance of a Business Plan

Real estate is a business like any other. So, if you must succeed, you need a plan. Business plans are the foundation for healthy, sustainable businesses. In fact, 75% of business owners are more likely to get funding and loans when they have a plan than when they don't.

As we find that plans are important to the growth and continuity of your business in real estate, it wouldn't be too much to ask you to put time and effort into making one. However, business plans are easier said than done. There are too many details to include, and dragging it out may be more expensive over time.

According to Harvard Business Review, business owners who spend less than three months developing their business plans are 12% more likely to succeed than others. On the other hand, business owners who spend beyond this time are usually worse off. This raises the question: How do you write a business plan as a real estate investor without losing sight of the details or adding too much?

What Makes up a Business Plan?

A business plan is a document you write containing your plans and future vision for the business you're about to start and how you expect to go about them. More specifically, the document contains your strategies, goals, and tactics for achieving your plans and handling any problem that comes your way. It also talks about your measurement strategies, responsibilities, roles, and SWOT analysis.

A business plan will help you figure out the answers to some operational and strategic questions, such as:

- your target audience or ideal clients

- the number of sales needed to cover your expenditures over a specific time

- how much you expect to make over a particular time

- the main opportunities and threats to your business

While your business plan must be professional, it shouldn't be rigid. Make room so that you can be flexible with both external and internal factors. Remember, contingencies can happen at any time.

How Long Should a Business Plan Be?

Usually, there isn't a fixed length as to how much time your business plan should cover. But the go-to time frame for many people is three years, and some prefer to use five. Just try to keep it between these two.

Why Not Longer?

Only a few people can plan for a business up to five years in the future. The reason why people try not to go above five years is that the future is up for speculation most of the time. For instance, we can only guess what will happen in the future. Even the trends we see today may not be around tomorrow. This is why most agents prefer three years, because it seems more predictable and plannable, and you can achieve some of your set goals within that time.

How to Write a Winning Business Plan

Writing a business plan isn't as hard as it sounds. The process is straightforward once you have all your details in hand. Here is a seven part step-by-step guide you can use to come up with a plan for your real estate business:

Mission Statement

You've seen this in every business' plan. Otherwise known as the executive summary, your mission statement should be about the goals and purpose of your business. It is the foundation that sets the pace for the rest of the plan, so you have to get it right.

Here are some tips to help:

- **Keep things short, simple, and direct**: No one wants to read your biography in your business plan, so limit your mission statement to a few sentences.

- **Define the time frame**: Set a specific time for staying on track. One year is enough to get started.

- **Don't get too comfortable**: Don't make your mission statement about things you can achieve in your sleep. You want to challenge yourself to leave your comfort zone.

- **Review**: Get your mentor, peers, and partners to review your mission statement and ensure it's on point.

SWOT Analysis

Strengths, Weaknesses, Opportunities, and Threats (SWOT) analysis should be done before going into a business. Doing so will help you figure out the factors that will affect your business and decide how you go about things. When starting your SWOT analysis, begin by going through your internal weaknesses and strengths to know what you have been doing and if it's working as planned or needs changing. Internal factors are within your control, so you can be more forward with these.

On the other hand, external factors that may influence your business are beyond your control. However, that shouldn't stop you from noting them in your business plan. Doing so allows you to find room around them and correctly evaluate the potential of your business.

Strengths

Your business' strengths are the qualities that give you an edge over the competition, like having a dedicated team or better knowledge of an area. In this section, detail your real estate skills and know-how, such as being able to wholesale or flip properties.

Weaknesses

Find out what your business is lacking and include it here. For instance, lack of capital or an incomplete team. You need to find out the things that other businesses have over you.

Opportunities

Find out about new markets that haven't been taken over by competitors. Also, talk about how you can better take advantage of your business' reputation or use word-of-mouth. Finally, add areas or markets with increase in demand that aren't already part of your already existing target market.

Threats

Threats to your business come in many forms, like a direct competitor. It could also be your business model. Perhaps your target market is heavily saturated or too broad to benefit you. Instead, you could do better by going into a niche sector. Additionally, take note of important changes happening in the current market. You can also add events outside your control here, such as bad reviews on social networks, natural events, and so on.

Goals

After your SWOT analysis, the next step is to go into the tactics and goals for achieving success in the business. When setting goals, ensure that your goals are specific, straightforward, reasonable, and measurable. Don't be vague or unreasonable with your goals. Include an action plan that shows a step-by-step plan for how you expect to accomplish them. Finally, diversify the types of goals you set. Go for a mixture of long- and short-term goals. Using this method will help you complete your goals better, as both goal types complement one another.

Here are some tips for setting specific and straightforward goals:

- Define success. It's up to you to explain your perspective of success.

- Avoid using negatives like, "I won't," or, "I can't." Instead, use positives like, "I feel," "I will," "I am," and "I can."

- Choose a particular time for achieving your goals.

Marketing Strategy

With your goals in place, it's time to move on to creating a road map for achieving them. This section is the most fun part, as you can personalize it. For instance, some people use checklists. The idea of putting pen to paper for ideas works wonders for them. Find your thing and roll with it. The idea is to look into different parts of your mind and psyche up the parts that fuel your drive to be successful.

Here are some handy tips for creating your marketing strategy or roadmap:

- identify your target audience

- find out where you can find your target market

- identify what makes you unique

- highlight tested strategies that you can use to appeal to your audience

- decide on the amount you are willing to part with

Lead Generation and Nurturing

After getting the facts and figures right for your marketing strategy, it's time to come up with processes to aid you on the journey to success. To do this, you have to determine how to go about generating leads, identify processes and tools for nurturing already existing leads, and how to use outbound and inbound lead generation techniques. However, as time goes by and your business grows, you may need more processes to deal with growing numbers of transactions and how to keep up with back-office processes.

Revision

As a real estate investor, you should know that a deal is only as good as the benchmarks that you have reached. So, the success or failure of your business plan is based on the valuation of your benchmarks or steps. It also helps you to recalibrate and ensure that you haven't strayed from your path.

And if the outcomes you're getting don't align with your goals and objectives, it's time to make corrections. Outcomes to expect would be increased income generation, more business, and an increased client database. So set a time to go through your business plan and evaluate how far you've come. It could be quarterly or biannually—just enough time to make updates and changes and see results.

In conclusion, think of writing and following up a business plan like creating a new recipe. At the beginning, you will have to follow the directions verbatim, stick to the timing, and include everything as said. Missing any of these steps or doing them in the wrong order may lead to a different outcome from what you want.

Bear in mind that just because your real estate business plan has to be prim and proper doesn't mean it should be drab and boring. You want to look at it in the future and be informed and inspired about why you began in the first place. So, when writing your business plan, ensure to add more than just goals and dreams. Also, include steps for how to achieve those things. It's a plan, after all.

It's important, because regardless of where you might be in your career in the future, a well-thought-out business plan can offer guidance on how to move your career forward. The goal of the plan was to give you the best road to success, was it not? So, try to give it your best shot.

And if you still feel like it isn't time to start a business plan, you are wrong. There's no better time to start than now. And it doesn't matter if your plan doesn't look like much at the start. Remember, a business plan isn't cut in stone. It's there to be adjusted and tweaked until you achieve all your goals and dreams.

With the real estate industry always changing, it makes sense why your business plan should be flexible. That way, you can keep up with the latest trends in your niche and the industry in general.

Chapter 17:

Tips for Successful Real Estate

Partnerships

Real estate partnerships is a form of investing that combines the skills and strengths of investors (two or more) into one property. Usually, partnerships are active or passive. In active partnerships, everyone does their part in managing the investment every day. But for passive partnerships, the investors don't have to be involved in the running of the investment.

Additionally, real estate partnerships work as a passthrough body. Meaning, they don't get taxed for the income they bring in. Instead, each investor gets taxed for their returns on investment based on how much they earn.

Whether you are in an active or passive partnership, you can't afford to take it for granted. Not only is it important to your success in the industry, but it can also go a long way in keeping your skills up-to-date. So, at the least, you owe yourself the right partner and a partnership to be taken seriously. It would be your best decision yet.

On the other hand, joining a bad real estate partnership would be bad for your career. So, when choosing potential candidates for the partnership, make sure you do your homework. Look for people who bring value to the partnership—ones who complement your shortcomings. Only then would you get the most out of the arrangement.

Real Estate Partnership Entities

There are many passthrough entities for forming a real estate partnership. The three most common ones used in real estate are S Corporation, Limited Liability Partnership (LLP), and Limited Liability Company (LLC). Whichever one you use, you can be sure that every investor gets the same dual benefits. Both as an individual investor and as a corporate entity (the partnership), you won't need to worry about taxes because your revenue and losses aren't yours to keep, they flow to the investors. So, it's they who must report it on their personal tax returns.

Another upside of real estate partnerships is that they are legally protected from claims against the personal assets or businesses belonging to other investors. As long as these third-party assets aren't part of the partnership, you are not liable.

Commercial Real Estate Partnerships

Partnerships are one of the easiest ways to get into commercial real estate. When compared, commercial real estate has higher requirements than residential investments. This difference can be traced to the size, responsibility, and financing needs. Residential investments require less funding, less responsibility, and the properties are much smaller than commercial real estate. However, the right partnership of two or more investors will help get properties to provide profit on the highest level.

Also, since there is more than one person involved, risk is shared equally between the partners, including: workload, equity, debt, and other requirements to get the property up and going. With this, partners can now look forward to the benefits their investment brings.

Pros And Cons of Partnerships

Pros

- Partnerships depend on balance, allowing everyone involved to share responsibilities and conquer them separately or collectively, easier and faster.

- Since multiple people are involved in partnerships, there is room for different perspectives when analyzing investments and deals.

- The right partner(s) can be a source of extra resources, such as network, capital, or business know-how.

- The collective portfolios of partners can give them an edge in meetings with other investors and in the market.

- The way a partnership is built allows all parties involved more workroom for sharing risks, losses, and profits.

Cons

- Partnerships may sometimes lead to relationship strain on an otherwise perfect friendship.

- The total profit from investments reduces significantly when shared across the board.

- Partnerships could lead to conflict, especially when everyone involved has different approach styles, management tactics, and perspectives.

- It's not unlikely for one partner to have a higher skill set or better portfolio than others. This may lead to disparity in skills and equity.

- Partnership agreements may not always be clear, and could lead to issues with bearing risks and responsibilities.

The Do's and Don'ts of Partnerships

- **Determine if a partnership is for you**: You need to be sure, beyond all reasonable doubts, that you have to partner up with others. Often, real estate investors are too giddy to join up with someone else before they weigh the risks involved or check out other alternatives. And while it'd be a flat-out lie to say partnerships aren't beneficial, they also need to be thoroughly considered.

- **Goal-setting**: In a partnership, don't turn a blind eye to the long- and short-term goals of your potential partners. In fact, understanding what the next person wants to get out of the business is important not just to you, but also to the business you want to build together. At the very least, it should help you better figure out the needs and wants of your partner(s) and if that would be an aid or a problem in the days to come.

- **Simplicity is key**: Once you start building a partnership structure, don't try to make things more complicated. You can go ahead and plan for business operations, but it might be too soon to start planning for lunch breaks. Be simple, yet thorough in your negotiations. Stay focused on the goal and mutual benefits. When talking to potential partners, speak in simple but firm words and avoid legal jargon to ensure everyone is on the same page. Other partners also need to know and evaluate the partnership before agreeing to it.

- **Self-evaluate**: When building a real estate partnership, you should be more concerned with getting qualified investors than anything else. However, while you may spend your time evaluating everyone else, you could skip yourself. And that isn't something you should do. Self-evaluation is important. And not just any run-of-the-mill assessment, but an unbiased one using the same metrics used for judging other potential candidates.

- **Get protection**: After finding your ideal candidates and building a partnership together, you might think that your work is done. But it isn't. In fact, setting up a partnership is only one-half of the challenges. Partners still need protection from future risks that could affect the business. This means creating a business structure that safeguards personal assets, either through an LLC or another means.

Getting protection also means allotting time to talk about solutions to probable issues, such as disagreements or conflicts. You want to be clear on how risks and losses are shared, how to deal with the exit of a partner, and what to do when trying to dissolve the business.

Real estate partnerships are good opportunities to get started in real estate, combine your strengths with those of others, and get your business up and running. Since all of these are important to the success of your career, it's important that your partner is the right person for the job. Having a bad partner can ruin any chance of your business making it, and also your ability to develop a good portfolio. So, before agreeing to a partnership or starting one, do your homework. But above all else, ensure that there are proper structures and boundaries in place.

In the end, the key to a strong and successful partnership in real estate is a sense of unity and good communication. Also, don't get too excited about the partnership that you forget to plan, set goals, and discuss your expectations for other partners. Further, assess the weaknesses and strengths of your partners before giving them responsibilities.

Finally, as a member of a real estate partnership, try to have an open mind. Not only will it help with honest communication, but you can also tackle problems together. And if at the end of the day, partnerships still don't work for you, it's fine. Instead, consider crowdfunding or becoming an angel investor.

Chapter 18:

Types of Businesses

From what we have talked about so far, it should be clear that real estate is a business like any other. And as a business built around a plan, it should also have a structure. The type of structure used for setting up your business will determine the type of paperwork you'll be stuck with, your ability to generate revenue, and how you will be taxed.

But to choose the right business type, you need to do your homework. In this section, we'll be going through some of the most common business types and structures. And while factors like taxing, requirements, rules, and liability can be found in all the different types of businesses, they aren't the same everywhere.

Sole Proprietorship

In a sole proprietorship, you own and run the business or company. It is the simplest type or structure of business, and also requires the least legal and financial protection to set up. Also, unlike the other types, sole proprietorships don't separate the legal identity of the owner from that of the business. This means that as the owner of the business, you and your business share the same identity. As a result, you are responsible for all the ups and downs the business faces.

Going for a sole proprietorship will help you maintain complete control over your business. This business structure is simple and cheap to set up, with tax benefits. Since the owner and the business share the same identity, income is taxed once. Lastly, the requirements for opening a sole proprietorship are few and easy to achieve.

Pros

- You have the flexibility you need to run the business as you see fit.

- Every profit is yours to use as you want.

- There are only a few necessities for starting a sole proprietorship. Most times, all you need is a business license.

- There are little to no rules for running a sole proprietorship.

Cons

- You can't tell apart your personal income and the income your business generates.

- Your equity is determined by your personal resources.

- You are responsible for every debt the business takes.

- It's difficult to transfer ownership of this type of business.

Partnership

Partnerships are the best choice for people who want others to join in opening and running the business. Usually, there are two forms of partnerships: limited and general partnerships. With limited partnerships, no partner is involved in running the business and they are not responsible for any troubles along the way. Meanwhile, for general partners, they see to the running of the business and are responsible for any liabilities that happen.

Unless you want to build a business with a lot of passive investors or partners, starting a limited partnership business as a newbie in real estate is a bad idea. It is made up of many complicated administrative activities that need to be filled out. Otherwise, if you will only be joined by two partners who will be involved and help you run the business, then go for a general partnership. One great upside to using a general partnership is that it helps with tax. The business allows you to pass both losses and profits to the investors. But they are often more expensive to set up, and require more legal services.

Pros

- Partnerships use the same simple design and flexibility found in sole proprietorship.

- Since more people are involved, everyone can contribute to raising capital.

- Whether the partnership is formal or informal, it's easy to create a partnership.

- Every partner is given a share of the profits of the business.

Cons

- A partnership can only go as far as the partners want to.

- Every one takes responsibility for the losses and debts of the business.

- It's difficult to talk others into a partnership, so you may not meet your ideal partners right away.

Types of Corporations

- **S Corporation**: This corporation is a type of business that is protected from liabilities and has some tax benefits. It also has a shareholder limit of 75 people, which means more capital can be generated for the business. The shareholders can also use the cash method of accounting when they don't have to deal with inventory.

  However, S corporations are still corporate outfits. So, they still need shareholder and director meetings and are required to file paperwork for incorporation. The shareholders in S corporations must be allowed to vote during decision-making.

Also, the business can only issue common stock, which affects its ability to get funding.

- **B Corporation**: These corporations, also known as benefit corporations, are businesses that are run for profit and mission. They pay taxes like regular C corporations, but their focus is more on being transparent and accountable to shareholders.

- **C Corporation**: Corporations hold the highest form of liability protection for all people involved. However, it's also the most expensive type of business to start. Corporations also need more in-depth operational processes, recordkeeping, and reporting. The investors in a corporation are called shareholders, and they have separate identities from the business.

  This means that they may have to pay taxes twice sometimes on their income from the business. But while they may be taxed higher, they have the benefit of raising capital by selling their stock. And stock options are one of the best ways of getting the best employees for the business.

Nonprofit

Nonprofit corporations are set up for philanthropic work. Since what they do benefits the public, they don't have to pay taxes—both on their income and on profits. But they must also follow the rules of a C corporation, except for profits and funding.

Close Corporation

This form of corporation is similar to B corps, but differs in that it doesn't have a formal corporate structure. Close corporations don't use many formalities used for running traditional corporations and small companies. The rules for this type of business are different in every state, but one thing is common to all of them: the company can't sell shares to the public. Close corporations don't use a board of directors, and are often run by a small group of shareholders.

Pros

- In close corporations, the assets of shareholders can't be used to pay for debts in the business.

- The business bears all the losses, risks, and profits.

- The owner of the business has limited liability to losses or debts.

- Corporations can be easily transferred to new owners.

Cons

- Corporate income receives two taxes, although there are some exceptions to this rule.

- Starting a close corporation is expensive.

- You need to file a lot of complicated paperwork.

Limited Liability Company

Limited liability companies (LLC) have the most flexibility of all the types of businesses mentioned so far. They are made by combining the strengths of a corporation, partnership, and some proprietorship. How does this work? LLCs get the limited liability of a corporation and the tax benefits of a sole proprietorship. The business can also choose the type of taxing it wants. So, as long as it doesn't show off as a C corporation, it gets to keep the flow-through taxation rate.

In addition, LLCs get more from having reduced liability because the company is seen as an entity of its own. This means that the people involved in the business aren't personally responsible for how the business operates or the debts it takes on.

Pros

- In an LLC, every profit generated by the business is shared to everyone involved without paying tax twice.

- The owners have reduced liability to the losses or debts of the business.

Cons

- Setting up an LLC is expensive because of the many filing and legal fees you must pay.

- The agreement between owners is complicated and extensive.

- In some states, there are laws limiting ownership in LLCs.

Cooperative

This form of business is owned, set up, and run to benefit everyone involved in the business. The income and profits generated by cooperatives are split between the members, who are also called user-owners. The business usually has an elected board of officers and directors who run the day-to-day affairs of the outfit. But these elected members don't have all the power, because floor members vote to control the decisions of the business. To become a part of a cooperative, you must get their shares. The upside of becoming a floor member is that the amount of shares you own doesn't affect your voting power.

Pros

- Cooperatives don't have a size limit, so members can be as many as the business can afford.

- The business structure encourages members to share responsibilities and contributions.

- Every member has equal voting rights and power.

- There is limited liability for members.

Cons

- The legal limits for paying dividends to members may not be suitable for every investor.

- Whether their investment is small or large, members have the same voting power—which may not be the best idea for a business driven by investors.

Best Business Structure for Real Estate Investors

Knowing about the different types of businesses isn't enough to decide the best one for your real estate business. It's best for you to consult an accountant and attorney. They will help you decide the structure that gives you the best risk-to-profit margin depending on your area, capital, and other factors.

The attorney will show you the options that give you the best flexibility depending on the state, as well as the cons and legal benefits of each business structure. On the other hand, the accountant will help you meet the requirements of your chosen business type and leverage tax benefits.

They will also help you track expenses in the business, and prepare your tax statements for your chosen business type. You can rest assured that you are on the side of the law and not bringing risk to your business.

Deciding on a business structure isn't something you want to take lightly. You must think it through, because the success of your real estate career depends on it. Don't forget to make your business plan according to the structure you have chosen. Also, outline it in the plan together with details of why you think the structure will work well for your business.

The importance of this stage of developing your own business can't be overstated. Be cautious, deliberate, and listen to expert advice.

The type of business you choose to set up is a crucial one—not just for your interests, but for your career as well. Not only does your choice of business determine how people will see you, but it also affects the type of financial and legal treatments you will get.

In all, here are some tips to keep in mind about the different types of businesses we have talked about so far:

Sole proprietorships and partnerships are the best types of business to start when going into real estate for the first time. And as your business starts to grow, draw attention, and bring in income, you can now upgrade to the status of a corporation or a limited liability company (LLC).

But don't be in a hurry to scale your business to an LLC or corporation without first thinking of the pros and cons involved. Remember, they all have their upsides and downsides, and not all types of businesses are good fits for every small business just starting out. So, you just want to go with the one that aligns with your goals the most. To do that, you will need the expertise of an accountant and a lawyer, who know about your industry.

Chapter 19:

The Importance of Money

Management

Money isn't wealth. Making wealth is more than just having money. You need to manage money to get wealth. So, without any discipline and money management plan in place, you will merely be chasing money without feeling fulfilled, missing out on opportunities, and never really getting anywhere. You need money to get more money, and you will find that merely spending money won't bring you closer to where you want to be. The fulfillment and success is in growing an income bigger than you and what you could ever want without letting go of your goals and ambitions. Money shouldn't make you less shallow; it should cement your legacy.

But it's easier to talk big about managing money than it is to actually do it. If you want to make wealth rather than just have money, money management is something you cannot understate. Not only is this crucial to your personal finances, but it also determines the success of your business.

Having a decent income flow without any form of money management will leave you spending money impulsively, without rhyme or reason. Remember that money is a current. It flows in and out, and how you deal with that current determines your movement—forward, stagnant, or backward.

Meanwhile, people who have mastered money management tend to be wealthy and have a more grounded approach. They don't want money to be fulfilled, and they never have to struggle to meet their needs.

Money management refers to financial practices that safeguard your finances and help you create security and wealth. And not just knowing how to create wealth, but also understanding how to maintain it. There isn't a one-size-fits-all approach to managing money. Your system will depend on your decision-making, risks, goals, habits, and needs. Essentially, everything that can help or ruin your chances of success. Money management also deals with situations beyond your control, like market volatility, taxes, inflation, and debt.

Learning to manage money will teach you the importance of not giving into impulses and help you make intelligent, well-thought-out decisions.

Tips for Money Management

Here are some tips for money management that are crucial to your financial literacy and journey into real estate:

- **Set clear and reasonable goals**: Building wealth and succeeding in real estate requires you to have a clear conviction about your decision-making. You need to be sure of the decisions that could make-or-break your business. To do this, you need to set goals with clear definitions and reasonable standards. Your goals should be practical and within a specific time frame that gives you enough flexibility to achieve them.

  Goals also act as benchmarks to track your journey and how far you have come. And this is important, because knowing your progress makes you less likely to give up along the way. To remain proactive, you can even break your goals down into short-term milestones. This way they won't seem unachievable, and you can easily monitor your progress.

  Lastly, clear and measurable goals help with decision-making. This way, you can easily weigh issues and decide on ones that best align with your progress. So, for instance, if a particular decision will take you away from your goals, it makes sense to let it go. Doing so gives you clarity of purpose, and encourages you to remain driven.

- **Control your cash flow**: Whether you're managing your money for wealth creation or something else, the goal is to accumulate more than you spend. Most people fail to see that wealth doesn't come by earning a lot, but by having enough left every time. If you spend just as much as you earn, you'll be as broke as the average Joe without a job.

This explains why you must take charge of your cash flow and decide how to use your money. You want to know where your money goes and how it comes in. You can draw up a budget or use an app. Knowing the inflow and outflow of your income is important to coming up with a strategy for using, investing, and saving more effectively.

For a business to be more profitable over time, it has to focus on managing money. It's why people get jail time for misappropriation of funds. Earning more than last month isn't the goal of a business. Otherwise, many businesses would be satisfied by just raising prices and sticking to the same consumers. The main goal is to create financial growth with the profit made, and only a good money management plan can do this. One that involves investing and seeking more profit.

So, whether you want to manage your own money or that of your business, you need a solid plan for money management. The better the plan, the better you control your flow of income, and the closer you get to your goals.

- **Investing**: Studies show that investors who stick to a good long-term investment tend to get more positive returns in the long run. On one hand, this outcome is due to the confidence the investors have in their strategy, as well as other factors like avoiding herd mentality by chasing market performance. On the other hand, a great money management plan helps to maintain focus on personal goals instead of movements in the market. This way, they don't give in to short-term events in the market.

- **Dealing with risks**: One of the main reasons investments fail is because investors can't manage risks. When dealing with risks, you can't afford to slack. You must be proactive and understand the relationship between risk and return, and use that to your advantage. In fact, being proactive with risks helps with investment performance in the long run, and could help with short- and long-term goals.

  With a sound money management plan, you will better understand the risks in the market and know how to avoid negative returns. By holding a long-term portfolio, you know that it has the potential for negative returns, but the extended period gives room for positive returns.

- **Deal with taxes**: Taxes are a big part of how you manage your money. We all know that we pay taxes, but not everyone is sure how or the amount. What we don't all know is that there are unnecessary taxes, which can be bad for money management.

  In money management, income isn't all the monies that come into your account. It's the total amount left after taxes. This amount is a much better system for planning your finances. When planning for investments, you want to look into the situation of your account and invest your income based on taxes. The same goes for every other investment you plan to make. Doing so will help you understand your wealth status, as well as other options for distributing wealth. It also increases the accumulation of wealth.

- **Checking for risks**: The more money you accumulate, the higher your risk potential in many ways. A single risk is enough to ruin all or some part of everything you've built. It would be a nice thing if wealth could protect you from every risk, but that isn't the case. As much as your life can improve by accumulating more money, it can also become way more complex. It's why people get round-the-clock security once they come into some money, even though they lived their lives never needing this before. Their identities are harder to keep out of the public now, everyone wants to know about them, the paparazzi won't stop stalking them, and now they have to follow a security routine.

The bottom line of money management is that the wealth it creates brings an equal amount of risk and reward. The amount of wealth created weighs similarly to the potential of losing it. This is why risk assessment and management is a crucial part of money management. You need to be aware of your financial exposures and make plan for contingencies, such as accidents ending in disability or demise, illnesses, loss of income, death, acts of God that lead to huge losses, fraud, identity theft, the risk of liability claims, and other factors that could interrupt or shut down your business.

Everybody wants to be financially free, but not everyone has the financial literacy to pull it off. Some people think that having the money to buy everything they want is financial freedom. Others think that if they have enough jobs, they just might save some more. But that's not the case. Buying everything you could ever want takes out of your money, it doesn't add to it. And even if you make top dollar at all your 15 jobs, it's not a guarantee that you won't die broke and miserable.

To have money, you need to be able to manage your finances properly. Only then will you know how and what your money is going into. With the right money management skills, you can improve your savings, create wealth, and help with budgeting. Furthermore, you will achieve your financial needs and have different sources of income while also knowing how to get more from your income.

The first and most important step in money management is to become financially literate. Once you do that, you will make better financial decisions for the security of your future. It's impossible to become financially literate and start managing your money properly overnight, but it's not impossible. Once you get the hang of it, you have solved one-half of your financial troubles.

Chapter 20:

Marketing Your Properties

Your place as a real estate agent is an important one. No buying or selling can take place without you in the picture. However, that doesn't mean buyers and sellers have to settle for less when dealing with real estate. More people are now doing their homework both online and offline, before seeking your expertise. The National Association of Realtors (NAR) conducted a study in 2020, which showed that 88% of buyers got their homes from a real estate broker or agent.

The study also showed that 73% of buyers only contacted an agent when searching for properties to buy. This figure tells us that awareness is important in selling yourself to buyers. As the market grows more competitive and cutthroat, you must have a sound understanding of marketing in real estate.

The NAR put out another study that found that 92% of property buyers go on the Internet when searching for properties to buy. This statistic proves that you can't afford to limit your presence to offline markets alone. Without a steady online presence and network, you will miss out on the new generation of the real estate market.

However, as much as an online presence is the solution, it isn't the easiest thing to set up. Unless you have a large platform as a real estate property owner, agent, or investor, it could take a while to draw the attention of audiences.

Tips for Improving Your Marketing

Getting a thriving marketing strategy may be hard, but it's not impossible. There are many tips and tricks that other real estate agents have used over the years to different levels of success. They will help you market your goods and services to a wider audience, and with better chances of success:

- **Get an online presence**: Technological advancements have pushed businesses online, and real estate is no different. People are taking to the Internet when looking to buy anything, and are more trusting of businesses with online presence than those without. The foundation of every online presence is a website. Currently, it's essential to have one. But not just any website will do. A bad website will harm your business more than having none at all.

  After setting up a website, the next step is to list your services and inventory for all to see. Ensure to update the listings on your site regularly, otherwise customers may start to view you as a scam. It will also help drive traffic. Another aspect to add to your website is video marketing. Merely listing a property with some pictures doesn't convince buyers. They want a video walk-through of the house to make up their minds about the property before contacting you. They would hate to waste their time and yours commuting to see a property they don't like.

  Studies also show that listings with videos attract 403% more inquiries than ones without. The videos used should be professional, appealing to potential buyers, and contain the best features of the property.

- **Get complementary businesses**: Two shops sitting side by side will make more profits from selling complementary goods and services than selling the same things. For instance, a shoe shop with a cafe next door will benefit both businesses more than if they were both shoe shops or cafes. The same thing goes for a pastry shop next to a drink store.

  You should be familiar with the businesses in your area and know how to pick ones that complement your trade—like coffee shops, clothing stores, hardware stores, and home decor showrooms—for your listings. And when you organize an open house, consider setting up pop-up shops around the property.

This will keep visitors looking around longer and allow you time to convert leads.

- **Get a real estate agent profile**: There are several websites you can join to get a free real estate profile that will expose you to the housing market. Once you claim these profiles, you can now proceed to enter your details like name, contact information, markets covered, brokerage, niche, expertise, etc. On some websites, you are also given the option of sharing blog posts and other types of content.

Agent profiles help you take advantage of the traffic and credibility of websites without having to spend on advertising. What's more, most of these platforms rank high on search engines, so you don't have to worry about being seen. Before creating an agent profile, though, make sure that the website is available and used in your area. There's no point having awareness on platforms that don't cover your area. The free exposure can do a lot for your business, expertise, and experience.

The Best Places to List Real Estate

The National Association of Realtors Profile of Home Buyers and Sellers revealed some statistics in 2020, showing that 51% of property buyers found the home they bought online. For scale, only 7% of buyers bought a house due to a yard sign, and 28% went to a realtor to get a property.

That said, it's time to jump on these platforms to sell your properties and services:

Realtor

The Realtor.com website is connected to the National Association of Realtors, and has more than 580 regional Multiple Listing Services (MLS). Realtor.com is the best online space to list properties as a real estate agent. And since it's regularly updated by agents on there, it's the most accurate depiction of the real estate market out there.

Pros

- There's a well-developed "find a realtor" feature that could improve business for you.

- You can easily look for homes depending on the areas of their listing.

- The database contains 99% of every property listed in the MLS.

- It connects you to financial calculators and pre-qualified financial buyers.

Cons

- There isn't an option for sellers to display their properties on the platform.

- There isn't a "for sale by owner" listing type.

Zillow

Zillow.com is the brainchild of two ex-Microsoft executives. Created in 2006, it contains the best tools for everyone in the real estate market, like: agents, landlords, buyers, renters, sellers, and other professionals in the business. Zillow towers over many real estate platforms because of its flexibility and power.

Pros

- It has lots of "how-to" guides for selling and buying property.

- It has an in-depth sorting criteria.

- It has the biggest database with more than 135 million properties.

- It connects to pre-qualified financing.

Cons

- Apart from listing agents, the other agents listed on property records don't always know about the property.

- Lenders and realtors have to pay for leads. So, if you don't wish to contact any agents, don't go signing out every form on the website.

- The Zestimate algorithm used on the platform only works with the data fed into its database.

Trulia

Trulia.com excels at having a transparent system on both their mobile application and website. The platform was created in 2005. Trulia has managed to create an app that is simple to use, yet powerful. This decision is due to many renters and buyers using their smartphones to check for properties online.

Pros

- It connects you to pre-qualified financing calculators built into the app.

- You can customize alerts to fit your needs.

- There is enough information on the locales of properties on the app and website.

Cons

- Home sellers don't have a platform to put their properties up for sale.

- You must register or sign in to save your search details.

Chapter 21:

How to Promote Real Estate With

Social Media Ads

It's possible that you already have a business account on one or more social media platforms. But it's not enough to have an account or make a post once in a while. Doing so won't give you a huge, steady flow of customers. What you need is a social media advertising strategy to get your message out to interested persons and increase your online presence.

We can't forget that every social media platform comes with a unique type of lead. Also, content doesn't perform the same way on every channel; so you must adapt your content to fit the social media platform and your target audience. For instance, after putting up an infographic on your website, you might want to save different formats to use on your social media handles.

It also helps to make your brand feel warm and welcoming. People don't want to interact with a brand that seems more mechanical than human. Also, instead of just bombarding your viewers with content incessantly, take out time to engage with active users. Go through your comments and respond to messages every other day. Social media should be a middle ground with which potential clients can contact you, not just a billboard to display your business and be closed off.

To improve the traffic coming to your social media posts, make sure to add hashtags to all of them. Apart from regular hashtags like #housing and #realestate, use other ones that are relevant to your area and niche. Do your research to be sure what's trending at a particular time. Doing so, you will attract more attention to your page and have more leads to convert.

Tips for Social Media Advertising

- **Use social media channels with receptive users**: What makes social media a good advertising space is that there are many demographics and data that you can use. There is a well-defined demographic for real estate. So, it's easier to find platforms that have more of this demographic. It would be a waste of effort if you took your business to a social media channel with the wrong market.

  Your target audience or demographic are older people, as younger demographics aren't in the market or can't afford to invest in real estate right now. So, you want to use platforms with lots of older generations within the stage of buying property. Some platforms you can find them on are Instagram, Facebook, and YouTube.

  Of course, you can still advertise on other platforms. But if you are just getting started with your business and want to get the best out of your social media ads, these three platforms will give you the best advantage. Once you are up and running on these three, you can now consider spreading to other social media channels.

- **Define your goals and audience**: When advertising on social media, you need a goal and target audience. What demographic are you reaching out to? Is it the ones buying their first property or renters looking for a yearlong lease? Maybe you're even looking for a unique market or want to draw attention to the location you are covering. Whatever your targets are, the first thing to do is to create well-defined social media ads.

It also helps to set clear goals ahead of your ad campaigns, as this will help you organize your first ads on social media, as well as the objectives to follow. Goals can also lead you through the remaining processes involved in creating ads, especially the format to use for each channel—whether its static ads, video ads, story ads, and other types.

Goals also help you stay on track and monitor your progress, whether it's for breaking into a new market or trying to sell off a property. If you can plan toward it by setting reasonable goals, there's no reason why you can't achieve it.

- **Go local**: The first time you try setting up an ad on social media, you will find that there are many options to choose from in terms of how the ads appear to your audience. These options are known as ad creatives. Sometimes, the difference between an ad creative that works well and one that performs poorly is location targeting.

Location targeting is a feature on social media ads that allows you to decide the area and people that get to see your ads. The great thing about social media, especially platforms like Instagram, is that it allows you to be very specific with your target location. With radius and zip code, you can easily highlight the area you want your ad to cover. Once that is done, only the people interested in what you're offering will see your ads and contact you.

This system can be limiting sometimes, so you may want to throw in other areas where your target market may move to or from. For example, if you sell properties to buyers from Harlem, about a 60-minute drive from New York City, then the audience you want are rentals who usually come from the city. So, you want to set your sights on not just the areas bringing you customers, but also the city they are moving to. This will help with lead generation for people moving in the other direction.

- **Video Ads**: Speaking of ad creatives or formats, one type that has been making waves recently is video ads. The fact that they are available on many social media platforms is an advantage that you can't overlook. Instead of using still frames in all your content, you can switch things up with attractive videos featuring great properties and stunning deals. The more interesting your videos are, the more people they will attract.

  Videos are better at attracting attention than any other ad creative used right now. When buying properties, people are making huge life decisions. So, it only makes sense why they would prefer videos so as to see and appreciate what they are getting out of the deal. Thankfully, videos aren't hard to make. You can have a professional photographer handle it, shoot and edit with your smartphone, or repurpose some video footage from other projects.

- **Use testimonials in your ads**: Testimonials are just as important to real estate as reviews are important to online shopping. People want to know that you have done business with others and how it went. So, sharing testimonials can make your business seem more legitimate and increase the effectiveness of your ads. It also helps to build trust between you and the potential customers that come along.

  If you have been doing your best and offering people good value for their money, there's no reason why their praises can't speak for you.

- **Schedule ads**: Every business has its season, even real estate. There are dry spells when deals are few and far between, and there are times when there's so many clients to deal with you wonder what door they came through. During this high season, it's easy to get caught up with potential buyers and forget to run your ads. You're busy after all, who can blame you?

Well, that's a mistake. You won't always close a deal with every interested buyer, so you might as well have your ads running still. Plus, it's better to have too many clients vying for a property than hoping the one who showed interest comes through. But how do you plan for the busy seasons?

- ○ **Simple**: Many social media platforms offer scheduled ads that allow you cycle when and for how long your ads run. So, with some funding, you can get the system to automate your ads, while you focus on closing deals.

- **Straightforward, short, and sweet**: Yes, you're the most experienced. Of course, you have a great portfolio. But no one wants to read your biography in an ad. People don't have the attention spans to indulge long ads, that's why ad copies tend to be catchy from the start. You don't want to lose them before you even get a chance to upsell.

So, keep your copies short, sweet, and to the point. This doesn't mean that you shouldn't put the work in to make your ad good. No. Instead, it means you should not waste the time of your readers. Show them what you can offer, including all the vital details like number of bedrooms, price, location, square footage, and so on. With this information, anyone that reaches out to you already has plans of striking a deal.

Chapter 22:

The Dangers of Doing Business

With Friends and Family

Business combined with friends and family remains one of the most controversial relationships to date. For many expert entrepreneurs, these three should not mix. And they aren't wrong, with the ton of soured relationships caused by deals turning bad. But on the other hand, there are many other expert entrepreneurs who swear by friends and familial relationships with business.

This brings us to the big question: *Should* you do business with friends and family?

The answer is more nuanced than yes or no. In fact, it's a matter of perspective. There are patterns that show that friends and family would or wouldn't be great for business. These patterns show the important factors in a regular relationship, and how that could play out in a business. That brings us to the two viewpoints. There are real reasons why your family and friends are the best people to be in a business with. Conversely, there are also reasons why you should deal with strangers.

So, should you?

On your part, you must realize that your relationship with and feelings about these people is a key factor in deciding if they are worth the bother. For instance, if you are scared of formalizing financial transactions with a friend or family member, that's your cue to get out of any business situation with them. If you can't find the words to tell them about a bad situation, you really shouldn't be considering business.

You'd be surprised how many people go out of their way to loan family members and friends, or bring them into a business without due procedures. They are afraid to bring in a lawyer to ensure both parties hold up their end of the bargain for fear that they could upset them. So, the friend or family member ends up defaulting on the loan, and they never do anything about it. Instead, they make up excuses. The same for when the friend or family member performs badly in the business. They would rather pick up the dead weight than call out the defaulting party.

Doesn't that sound like too much work?

You must remember that the streets are filled with dead and dying relationships. Sometimes, things are beyond anybody's control. But in business, except if it's an act of God or forces beyond you, someone has to be responsible for it.

Your business goals and aspirations shouldn't be stifled by the relationship of a friend or family member. Demand from them what you would of anyone else. The success of your business depends on your ability to make crucial and logical decisions that aren't born from sentiments and dreams of family. Even Dominic Toretto rides solo sometimes, and he never shuts up about family.

If you can't criticize or be candid with your family and friends, don't bother dragging them into a business. It doesn't bode well for both parties. Essentially, you're holding a cracked wall together with sellotape; it won't hold up forever. And if they hate to be criticized, told what to do, or delegated responsibility, then why are you considering business with them in the first place?

Tips for Doing Business With Your Loved Ones

- **Have a conversation**: The first mistake you can make in a business with friends and family is to believe that they know what to do. Never assume that your relationship automatically makes them sensitive to your needs and desire for the business. This is why you need to talk to them. Discuss your goals and dreams for the business, where they fit in, and how they can contribute to its growth. Talk about what happens when they show up late or don't come at all. Or when they miss deadlines or want extra leave days. Talk about everything and anything that could lead to conflict.

- **Decide on their responsibilities and roles in the business**: Defining what your friends and family bring to the table is important to the success of the business. Everyone has a unique skill they can provide, even if it doesn't incline with the business. For instance, if you'd rather be buried in numbers and calculations than talk to customers, that shows you prefer to handle back-office processes. And if your friend or family member has their finger on the market's pulse and enjoys talking to people, they would be better off in customer relations.

Take your time to find out the passions, strengths, and weaknesses of everyone, and assign them to areas where they would most likely make an impact. Also, make time to review your business plan and ensure that everything is as you want it to be. If adjustments are needed, make as necessary. Updating your business plan will help you adjust to new scenarios that may affect your goals and plans.

- **Keep your personal life away from work**: You know how you shouldn't mix business with pleasure? Well, the same goes for your work and business lives. Both should be as far apart as the North and South poles. Many business owners tend to mix their work and business life, especially when family and friends are involved. But this can lead to problems. For the best work-life balance, you need to be able to tell your work life from your home life. Your business hours should be well-defined and not spill into your personal life, and vice versa.

It's enough hard work going into business with loved ones, you don't want to also lose your home life to work or have no work ethic. You can have a great work relationship with friends and family as long as you set and respect boundaries and know when to work and when to kick back and unwind. Like every other thing in life, balance is crucial and important.

- **Make exit plans**: If your house has a fire escape or emergency exit, why doesn't your business have an exit strategy? We often overlook this part of business, because we expect that things will always work out as planned. The optimism is lovely, but things aren't always so black and white. Just as you planned for your entry into the business, you should also work out a way to leave when necessary. An exit plan is all the more important for businesses run by friends and family, because of emotions. Never underestimate how big a factor emotions are in business.

It's not easy to imagine all your hard work going down the drain, but an exit strategy isn't foreboding. It doesn't mean something bad will happen, just as a house with a fire escape isn't an invitation to start a fire. Your exit strategy should cover what you expect of your partners in different scenarios, like if a friend or family member opts out to pursue something else, if the business starts to fail and pulling out early would help prevent losses and debt, or when the business is liquidated or sold to a third-party.

- **Use different accounts**: You can easily mix accounts if the family member in your business is your spouse or partner. So, it's crucial that you keep your business finances away from your personal ones. This will save you confusion and heartaches over time.

With a business credit or checking account, you can easily track your expenditure and revenue, plan for the business, and evaluate your budget. This becomes a hassle when your business account and personal account are the same. You could be dipping into your business income or taking out of your personal income without knowing.

Also, having a separate business account can help build your credit profile and financial overview for potential investment opportunities in the future. This may not be possible with a personal account.

Chapter 23:

How to Find the Right Real Estate

Agent

Buying or selling a property isn't as easy as walking from door to door with Girl Scout cookies. It's a huge financial decision for sellers and buyers—one that a real estate agent has to facilitate. So, while the heavy lifting might be left to you, the process is just as important to those involved.

A quick look in a newspaper, on social media, and all over the Internet will reveal thousands of real estate agents, brokers, and realtors. Each of them promise a unique experience that gets the job done. But what does it mean for sellers and buyers who have to make a choice?

Any real estate agent that is contacted believes that you have made up your mind to sell or buy a property. So, here are some steps to prepare yourself in different situations:

For Buyers

- **Pre-approval**: You need a mortgage pre-approval before starting your search for a real estate agent. This will help set the price range for the property you want to buy. It'll also save you time on going through houses you can't afford or picking up debts.

- **Understand the process**: First-time property buyers may not know how mortgages work or the processes involved in the loan. Here's how it works: create a budget with down payment and earnest money. Your down payment should be at least 20%, while earnest money is the deposit you make once your bid is accepted. The money is used to fix closing costs or just added to the down payment. Other factors that must be considered as well are insurance costs and property tax, which are part of the monthly mortgage paid into an escrow account.

- **Have a priority list**: Buyers should know the type of property they are looking for in the market, including the features they need and ones they might want in the future. It also helps to know and be familiar with the area you might like to live in if it's different from your current one.

For Sellers

- **Prepare the property**: People will be coming to see the house you have on sale, so you might want to tidy up. Potential buyers will be more interested in a clean house, that way they can move around and inspect for damages. Take out the items that are taking up space and ones you haven't used in forever. Declutter everywhere and ensure its roomy and sellable by the time buyers arrive.

- **Begin the search early**: Getting a property ready for the market is no small task. It could take months or a year, because of repairs and reconstructions. But that shouldn't be a reason to wait before contacting a real estate agent. In fact, get in touch with one before you start the repair and tidying process. This way, you have time to budget and plan repairs so that they don't affect your personal resources, and it will help you get the most out of the sale.

Deciding on an Agent

- **Go for an agent you like**: It might sound like silly advice, but wouldn't it be better if your agent was likable? You want someone whose personality doesn't put you off. This will ensure that everything goes smoothly, whether you are a buyer or a seller. Also, with both parties on the same page, the risk of disagreement of pricing, marketing, and viewing of the property will be avoided.

- **Go for regional experts**: It would help a lot to get a real estate agent who is an expert in the region of the area you're selling or buying a property in. These agents will offer you insights into the cost and selling prices of properties better than others who don't work there.

- **Check for availability**: Availability is a huge part of buying and selling properties. While you can easily go through a part-time agent, you also want to look for someone who has flexible working hours. As a buyer, they should have time to take you to see the property. And as a seller, they should have time to take people to view your listing.

- **Contracts and commitment**: When hiring an agent to list your property, you must sign an agreement between two to six months. The commission the agent will receive depends, but is usually from five to six percent of the price of the property. But they don't keep it all—half of the commission goes to the agent of the buyer. If the rate is too much for you, some agents are willing to haggle for a more convenient deal.

After signing the contract, you have to be sure that your agent has your best interest at heart. Sometimes, your agent might have a buyer who is interested in your property. At that point, they become an agent to bother the seller and the buyer. On the buyer's part, this may be a problem because the agent might try to get a higher commission from the deal by inflating the price of the property.

For sellers, there isn't much cause for concern. If you don't mind the arrangement, you could get an even better deal on the commission since there isn't another agent involved.

The Importance of Finding the Right Agent

- **Stay on top of the goings-on in the market**: Knowing what is going on in the market or a particular area helps you to decide how best to deal with an agent as a seller or buyer. You don't want to sell a property for less or buy one for more than the market price. To avoid these pains, you need a good agent—one who knows how to balance the price and value of a property and help you get a good deal. It's why some listings stay up for ages and never sell, because the agent doesn't know how to balance the price and value of the listing to the acceptable market rate.

- **To make complicated processes simple**: Buying and selling properties isn't a simple process that only takes an agent, buyer, and seller. There are other parties you can't take out of the equation, like the governmental bodies (think HDB), the bank, and attorneys. If that isn't hard work enough, you also have to deal with a truckload of paperwork at different times before the deal is completed.

  A good agent is already aware of all the processes involved, and will easily guide you through them. They will also ensure that you don't make beginner mistakes and get good value for your time and resources.

- **Expertise and network**: Agents have spent a lot of their time working on property projects, whether it's buying, selling, flipping, wholesaling, etc. These things have built their portfolios and expertise in the industry, and their wealth of knowledge is more than anyone outside real estate can comprehend. This is why you need them, because they know their way around the market to help you achieve your goals.

  And since they have been in the industry for a while, they have built a network that allows them to make moves easily. With this knowledge, expertise, and network at their disposal, they can get you good deals—better than attempting to sell or buy properties yourself.

- **Financials**: For buyers, your ability to purchase a property largely depends on your financial health. You might feel ready to start the process of buying a house, but only an agent can confirm if proceeding will work out or end in debt.

Chapter 24:

Telltale Signs That It's Time to Sell

Your Property

Property remains one of the most valuable assets you could own. And if it's your home, then it's all the more priceless. But, sometimes, it could be time to move on to other things and sell off your home. So, how do you know that the time is right for that?

Unlike trading in the stock market, there are a lot of emotions tied to your home. You can't even pretend to not feel connected to that special place. So, it's not a matter of looking at the market and trying to sell high.

It's a lot of work to make up your mind about such a scary idea, or even know when to begin moving out, especially if you can't decide if the time is right or not. Whether you are looking for a bigger place, a change of scenery, or to move closer to family, there are many signs that show that it may be time to shut the door on your home.

That said, here are some signs that the time's up on your current home:

- **Your home doesn't meet your current needs**: It's not uncommon to outgrow your home, no matter how long you have lived there or the memories you've created there. Many homeowners buy their properties when starting families. So, usually, the home meets their familial needs. But once children grow and leave to find their way in the world, the house becomes a little too big to manage on their own. Or, it could be that they had a much larger family than planned for. In both cases, it's time to look for a new home that meets the immediate needs.

While it's only natural that you will outgrow your home at some point, it isn't always a sign for you to abandon ship and move. Sometimes, all you need is a plan to see if the time is right to get a new place. You have to look into other factors, like your finances, market trends, and the cost of moving houses.

So, whether you are starting a family and need a bigger house, trying to swap a bigger house for a smaller one, are satisfied and want a new adventure somewhere else, or want to move closer to family and friends—the time might be right to move. Just ensure that you have done your homework to make the process as straightforward as possible.

- **You have positive equity**: If you have been consistent with your mortgage payment for at least five years, you will have some built-up positive equity. This is an important part of the financial side of selling your property, because it decides whether or not the time is right to sell.

  Equity comes by how much you lose or gain when the current value of your home is subtracted from the balance on your mortgage. You can try to figure this out on your own, or speak to a professional for help. Usually, if your equity is good after selling your property, what you have left is enough to make a down payment on a new property, as well as the cost of the agent and moving. Don't sell if you have bad equity, because it would only make things harder on you.

- **The market is great for sellers**: If you are considering selling your house and want to make some profit from it, look out for a good seller's market. If the market is thriving, then that is the green light you need to list your property. But how do you know when the market is in swing? Start by reaching out to a real estate agent in the area or doing your research for some signs. Things to look out for include many for sale signs around the neighborhood, increasing price per square foot of real estate, if your neighbors got a good deal on their home, and if properties in your locale are sold quickly. You don't want to be left out of a great market.

- **Cost of upkeep is too much**: If by the time you finish evaluating all you need to do on your property (including repairs and maintenance) to make it into the home you want goes beyond your budget, it might be time to move. On average, homeowners spend up to $2,000 per year on maintenance alone, like septic service, landscaping, recycling, snow removal, and private trash. And this doesn't include repairs and replacement.

These costs and the additional money you need to pay for other outstanding fees, like mortgage and property tax, can become stressing. And while you can choose to not make any repairs and save money, the thing that needs repairing could get worse in the future. Once this becomes a recurring issue in your home, it's okay to start looking at other properties. You will be saving on recurring costs.

- **You are emotionally prepared**: Saying goodbye to the home that has all your memories is one of the hardest things to do. But if you find yourself looking at listings currently and imagine yourself trying to make a home in a new place, that could be the sign that you are ready to move on. Your emotions are an important part of the equation, because they can affect how you act. For instance, some people are slow to making the decision to move because of emotional attachments and end up selling late at less than market value. Others may give up too soon and act earlier than when a seller's market appears.

Take it slow. Prepare yourself to say goodbye, and take your time to get the house in shape before it's listed. Consider tidying up your final goodbye to the place that gave you so many memories. Once you are emotionally ready, it's time to face feedback from real estate agents, potential buyers, and home stagers.

- **Financial readiness**: Your emotions aren't the only thing that you must think about. Finances are a huge part of selling your home, because it determines where you go next and if you can afford to buy or rent a new property.

Before getting in touch with an agent, find out how your finances are doing. With equity and good finances, you just might be ready to sell. Finances are especially important if you hope to move to a bigger property or a more expensive neighborhood. Such upgrades come at higher costs, and you must be able to foot them without dipping into the income from selling your property. Also, you should be able to afford some basic comforts in the new place. No need selling and moving into a new house where you can't even afford a bed after making every necessary payment. When considering your finances, look into debt, emergency funds, and disposable income.

- **Lifestyle changes**: One part of this discussion that isn't talked about a lot is lifestyle changes. Sometimes, the factors that make you want a new place are about you and the things that have changed in your habits. For instance, say you and your partner created a remote business that you run from home. You're going to need a house with a home office. Or, say, you are almost at retirement age and want a comfier place in a slow-paced neighborhood, where you can relate to the goings on there.

There's a lot that can change in your life from the first time you moved into your current home. And those reasons are valid for why you might need a new house, especially if the current one doesn't meet the changes that occurred in your life.

Chapter 25:

Strategies to Avoid or Reduce

Capital Gains Taxes on Home Sales

Owning a property has to be the biggest bragging rights you can have, whether it's a country home, a vacation condo, or your primary residence. But what's more rewarding is when you get good value on your property during sales.

But there's a catch.

As much as you can enjoy staring at the figures—especially if you sold for higher and got decent profits—you now have to worry about something else: taxes. Properties are capital assets, and the profit you make on them is called capital gains, and can be taxed.

It's crucial to understand how this tax works, and how you can legally avoid sharing all of your loot with the government. In the United States, the federal capital gains tax can reach up to 37%, which doesn't leave you with much when you consider other costs that come with selling a property.

What Is Capital Gains Tax?

Just about everything you own is a capital asset, whether they are investments or personal effects. These include items like property, vehicles, bonds, stocks, etc. So, once you start selling these assets—like your house, for instance—the profit made after the completion of sale is taxable by the government under capital gains tax.

Capital gains typically apply in two ways. Short-term capital gains happen when you sell an asset that you owned for less than 365 days or a year. On the other hand, long-term capital gains happen after selling any capital asset that you owned for more than 365 days or a calendar year. The tax rates on these capital gains differ, with short-term capital gains taxed higher than their long-term counterparts.

To avoid the short-term capital gains tax, you should hold onto your property for over a year before selling. This will save you from forking over up to 37% of your gains, when you can be taxed between 0 to 20% as long-term capital gains tax if you own the property for longer.

Strategies for Reducing Capital Gains Tax

Apart from trying to qualify for long-term capital gains tax, there are other strategies that could help lessen the brunt of CGT. They include:

- **The 2-out-of-5-year rule**: Properties usually attract a use and ownership test, which comes by living in a house for a specific number of years (two to five years). If your property passes this test, you could get a tax exclusion of up to $500,000 as a joint filler, or $250,000 as the sole owner. The best part is that you don't have to live in the house for two to five years at once. It's a cumulative total, so as long as you live there from time to time, it adds up.

  The Section 121 exclusion states that the property has to be your primary residence for two out of the five years after you become the owner. But there's a catch here, too. You can't be eligible for the tax break if you have been excluded from capital gains tax on other capital assets you sold within two years of the current one. Also, since this technique only works for one property that has to be your primary residence, it's of no use to investors dealing with many properties. In addition, you must hold onto a property for at least two years and can't qualify for a tax exclusion for another two years. That's a long wait time for many investors.

- **Save receipts from home improvement**: The value of your property goes beyond the price you got it for. It also includes all the improvements you made over the years. If you spend more on home improvement, your capital gains tax will be lower to protect your costs.

- **Low income means go time**: Usually, the capital gains tax applied on your property sale is decided by your tax bracket. And since you are taxed based on how much you earn, having a low income at the time of sale can be a good strategy. For instance, if you recently retired, lost, or quit your job, you can wait until a low income year to begin the process of selling your property.

  The returns on the sale won't be considered as wealth, and you will receive a similar tax to what you pay on your income. Obviously, this isn't the most pleasant option, because no one is looking forward to a lean year. But if it happens, you can take the initiative.

- **Get a partial exclusion**: In the IRS Publication 523, there are some situations that can help you get an exclusion of capital gain tax. They include selling your home because of unforeseen contingencies, health, or work. If this is the case for you, don't hesitate to bring it up when calculating your taxes.

- **Don't sleep on the 1031 Exchange**: After selling your property, especially if it's an investment or rental, you can avoid paying capital gains tax by putting the proceeds back into another similar investment. This process is known as the 1031 exchange, and is mainly used by real estate investors trying to grow and accumulate wealth.

  But this strategy isn't as straightforward as the ones we have talked about so far. You still need to meet some eligibility requirements and fill out a lot of paperwork. You will need an expert to guide you through the process. So, unless you're into real estate investing, this option might be more expensive than beneficial.

- **Look for opportunity zone funds**: The United States government created the Opportunity Zones in 2017, which are made up of distressed areas. The idea was to improve infrastructure, small businesses, and housing in the areas.

After selling your property, investing in these Opportunity Zones with your capital gains will allow you to leverage certain tax benefits, such as:

- You can avoid capital gains taxes for up to eight years if you reinvest all your profits into an Opportunity Zone.

- If you hold the investment for 10 years at least, you won't have to pay capital gains tax on any future capital gains accrued from the funds you invested.

- If you invest and hold in an Opportunity Zone for five to seven years, you will reduce your capital gains tax by 10% and 15% respectively.

- If you don't want to invest in anything other than Opportunity Zone real estate, check for Opportunity Zone Funds that purchase and renovate old buildings in Opportunity Zones. These funds offer the properties at reinvestment costs and will help manage them as rentals.

    This strategy works best for real estate investors or people looking to buy and sell properties and get income that could increase their tax brackets. Regardless of your income level now, there's nothing stopping you from investing in these Funds or Zones. Not your state of residence or amount, either. Better still, Opportunity Zones won't leave you with a lot of paperwork. The process is simple, profitable, and versatile in lowering taxes on capital gains for a long time, giving you enough financial power to reinvest or buy new properties.

Chapter 26:

The Best 30 Ways to Increase the

Value of Your Investment Property

Your property is an asset, meaning it can increase or decrease in value. But that change in value depends on how you manage it. Here are 30 different ways to improve the value of your property, and get the best returns for it whether you are selling or renting:

- **Maintenance and renovation**: Even though we say never to judge a book by its cover, that's all we do. First impressions matter a lot, and affect how we value things. This goes for property, too. The easiest way to increase your property value is to keep it in good shape and aesthetically pleasing. Don't let maintenance issues go unchecked. Resolve them as quickly as you can. Real estate also obeys the laws of supply and demand in business. If your property is in good shape and stands out from other neighboring ones, you will get more when selling. And if you're renting out, you will always have tenants. You have created the supply, and the demand is going to come. Say hello to steady cash flow and high market value rents.

  Apart from regularly maintaining your property, another technique for improving property value is renovation. This doesn't mean tearing down one property to erect another. Instead, try to put in new things that will make the property more appealing to buyers or renters. That way, the item pays for itself. For instance, you could upgrade appliances in the property or submeter utilities.

- **Improve security**: One of the biggest issues renters face is the lack of security. Worse still, it's not the most expensive thing to add to your property. Installing insect screens on windows and doors, a security or alarm system, and some deadlocks should work just fine.

- **Take advantage of little spaces**: It's easy to not mind nooks and crannies around your property. But what if I told you that you're sleeping on some decent income? Yes, you may be getting rent, but other spaces around—like garages, broom closets, and sheds—are sitting idle and doing nothing. Instead, turn them into mini storages. You'd be surprised how big an industry this is. Add this income to your rent, and the value of your property just balloons.

- **Create built-in storage space**: If you don't have any mini storage spaces, you could create full-fledged ones instead. Consider adding backyard sheds and en suite wardrobes, you'll be glad you did.

- **Spend wisely**: This isn't a technical value booster, it's a cost-saving one. You don't necessarily have to buy or pay for something before your property value increases. In fact, this is the most important strategy on this list. And here is why: If you're buying a property to rent or resell, try your hardest to find good deals. For instance, if you get a $10,000 reduction on the value of a building, you have indirectly increased its value by $10,000, which is the actual market value. So, do your homework and try to get the most out of your purchases.

- **Reduce your running costs**: The first thing to do after buying a rental property is to check the running costs. The amount you arrive at will determine if you should increase or decrease it to improve value. If there is room for improvement that won't affect renters and would make things easier on your budget, by all means, indulge yourself. For instance, you could submeter utilities. Reach out to the utility company serving the property and ask for an audit. From there, you can find new ways to improve efficiency. Say, for instance, the lights in the property are regular bulbs. Changing them out for energy-conserving LED lights will freshen things up while helping to save costs on power bills. To the renters, it would be a renovation. But to you, it's cost saving.

Technological advancements make it possible to use hydronics heating systems and solar energy. In the case of solar energy, if your units generate enough to add to the power grid, you could get returns for it. How great is that! Now you no longer have to worry about energy consumption or increasing utility rates from service providers.

- **Fee increments**: Apart from taking advantage of physical spaces within and around your property, you can also improve the income your investment generates through fees. There are a lot of things you don't charge for that could improve your income and property value. For instance, charges for parking violations, late rent, background checks, missed maintenance appointments, etc. You could also throw in paid parking and charge for using in-house laundry facilities. You should get all the fees you deserve.

- **Increase rental income**: While you can have other sources of income outside collecting rent, it makes up the biggest chunk of your income. It's pretty straightforward that increasing rent will boost your income. But how does that affect property value?

First, you must understand that raising rent to market level and maintaining that structure could lead to tenant turnover, which is bad for your income and property value. This is why many owners would rather not raise rent, for fear that it will scare tenants away and ruin business for them. While this is something to be worried about, it shouldn't stop you from getting good value for your property. Remember, if they leave, they are still going to pay market value rates somewhere else. And if your property is worth it, they won't bother. So, instead of worrying about raising rent, consider improving your property to fit the value of the new rent.

- **Reduce your costs**: There are too many things to pay for and remember when you own a property, so you could be paying a little too much sometimes. But you can do something about it. Take the time to audit your expenses regularly and look for cheaper alternatives to some services. Take garbage, sewer, and water expenses, for instance. You can transfer them to your tenants or speak to utility and service companies for a cheaper deal. Check for leaky faucets and repair them to save on water costs. Your property value increases as your expenses decrease.

- **Lower turnover rates**: The most important factor that determines the cost of running your property is turnover. Whether you own a commercial or residential property, tenant turnover is bad for business and your bottom line. Because when a tenant moves out, they don't pay rent to you anymore. And that shortage in income will make your expenses seem even bigger. It gets worse when you have to keep maintaining the place until another tenant comes along. To even get another tenant, you need to spend more (tenant screening and background checks, marketing, and land leasing commissions among other things).

  The best way to avoid these issues is to offer leases instead. Long-term ones at that, with built-in rent increments. This will help with property maintenance, and you won't struggle with expenses even when a tenant moves out before their tenure runs out. In doing so, the value of your property increases, especially if you choose to upgrade to a property with more income, sell your current one, or use a 1031 tax-deferred exchange.

- **Don't forget the flooring**: A house with frayed and dirty carpets will be an instant turnoff to get a buyer or renter. The same goes for when the floorboards looked weathered and scuffed. It makes the property look old and tired, which may lead to bad deals. To avoid this, clean your carpets regularly and replace them when they become too bad to manage. For bad floorboards, consider having them sanded and recoated for a new shine.

- **Find a market niche**: There are properties for just about every demographic of renters and buyers. One popular demographic for rental properties right now is seniors, and they remain one of the most available renters on the market. This has made many property owners market their houses as seniors' homes, targeting older people who need special services like food and care, which may be difficult for regular property owners to provide. Another part of this market wants to bring in social programs and activities, which seniors properties aren't known for. This will sway the other half of the older renters who don't need special care or have huge capitals to rent.

Student housing is another great niche that you can explore, especially if your property is close to a university. Many college students don't want to live on campus or in dormitories, and would rather private rentals that give them privacy, convenience, and high-speed Internet connection. However, it's a seasonal market, so business can be slow sometimes. But there's a way to avoid that. You can opt for leases, which will help you control income.

- **Freshen up the paint**: The quickest makeover you can give your property is to repaint it. Not only is this cheaper, but it also draws attention to your property, making it more marketable to buyers and tenants. If you are unsure what color to go with, stick to neutral tones. They are less likely to clash with the tastes and styles of renters, which will save them the cost of repainting and make the property more appealing.

- **Check your property tax**: A quick study of the breakdown of the costs of owning and running a property will show you that the most expensive thing property owners pay for is property tax. In many areas in the United States, the tax on property is determined by the value of the property. If this rule applies in your area, and the real estate market declines, get in touch with a local assessor. You need to do a reassessment. If your house gets a lower assessment, your property tax will reduce, making more room for positive cash flow.

- **Improve the bathrooms**: Bathrooms are barely taken seriously in some properties, that's why we find houses with clunky and impractical washrooms and unideal toilet locations. There's even a case to be made for too little bathrooms in a house. Back in the day, it was okay to have a single bathroom. But now, two should be the least you should have. If you get the chance to remodel, you can throw in a half bath. It would cost you, but your property value will increase and it becomes even more marketable to renters or buyers.

- **Get better management**: Management is a key part of owning and running real estate. It gives you an added edge, unlike other forms of investment. For instance, it would take more than a call to get the CEO of a multinational company to change the pricing of their products or services, especially if you're not an important company member. However, your manager can ring you and offer advice on how to run your property for the best results and revenue.

And since you can easily control and use many management styles, your tenants will be more satisfied and you won't have to deal with frequent turnovers. Some owners usually outsource the day-to-day running of their properties to a professional, while others don't mind doing it themselves. Whatever the case, make sure to give the best. Good property value comes from good management.

- **Choose good renters**: One of the best ways to maintain the value of your property is to only allow renters that will treat the home well and keep it in shape throughout their tenure. That way, you will have lesser repairs and maintenance to do, which will save you on running costs. They will also be punctual with their rents, which will give you enough financial power to offset bills.

So, when selecting tenants, be sure to do your homework. Check their references thoroughly and learn more about them to decide if they are a good fit for your property. Doing so could also help create a relationship that could suit both parties.

- **Improve the look of your curb**: You can make a statement with your property and draw attention from everybody with some landscaping. Making little changes that don't cost much, like getting fresh mulch or changing out the plants, will increase the appeal of your environment. This will increase the value in the minds of renters and buyers before you even get a chance to talk.

- **Make your property pet-friendly**: Many property owners believe that allowing pets will lead to disasters: cats will claw the drywall and dogs may gnaw at the carpet. But that isn't always the case. And even if it were, you could make tenants with pets pay extra deposit for damages. Then, you won't have to bear the cost of repair and maintenance.

  Anyway, many people own pets and only a few rental properties allow them. So, giving tenants the option to own pets will help reduce turnover and keep them for longer.

- **Declutter and clean**: Before getting your property appraised, take the time out to clean and declutter the environment. That way, you can make a good first impression. And if it's a buyer, they will be more interested in a clean one than a dirty, stuffy one. And don't just do a routine clean. Mop the floors, dust high areas, clean up baseboards, and take out junk that you don't need.

- **Go for properties in areas with a huge renting demographic**: Unless you plan on selling your properties, you need to be careful when choosing the area for your property. Go for neighborhoods that have a strong demand for rentals, high rental yields, and low tenant turnover rates. These places are often growing regions, so the value of the real estate market is gradually rising. This way, you can get property for cheap and get a good return on your investment as the market ages and becomes stronger. Another thing to look out for are infrastructure, amenities, and job opportunities. It's best to go for areas with these factors, or ones that are developing with them. With these things in place, you can rest assured that you will have a steady flow of tenants and get good, steady returns from your property.

- **Add air conditioning**: The weather gets hotter every day, and we experience lots of heat waves each year. If your property is in an area that experiences less rainfall per year, you could make extra income by fitting the building with air conditioning units. This will be more beneficial if you run a rental property. And as split systems are cheaper now, you will get returns on your investment quickly. This addition will also make your property more appealing, especially if other rentals in the neighborhood don't have the same infrastructure. You will get more business, reduce tenant turnover, and be able to raise rent as needed to keep up with market standards.

- **Complete basements and unfinished areas**: One of the factors used in determining the market value of your property is finished square footage. So, even if you can't do an entire makeover or renovation on your property, there are simpler projects you can undertake, like adding carpets, putting up a drywall, or creating patios and barbeque spots. Doing this increases the footprint of your property, making every part of it useful to renters or buyers. Hence, its value would be higher.

- **Get a good team behind you**: Even if you put all your efforts into maintaining and repairing your property and your tenants are the best, emergencies and contingencies could happen at any time. What makes your house more valuable is the tenants being able to reach professionals for their problems and get them solved quickly. Getting a plumber or handyman for a quick fix can be difficult, especially as most of them are involved in projects of their own. This is why you need your own team of professionals that can handle every possible happenings around the property. That way, your renters can reach out to them, and save you from the exorbitant costs of hiring instant aid.

- **Improve the doors and windows**: Improving the doors and windows on your property helps with both noise reduction and aesthetics. But that's not all. You can also configure doors and windows to let in more natural light, improve ventilation and cooling, and help keep the heat in during cold weather.

You can further spice things up with French doors, for instance, that open to a backyard. This gives your property more pizzazz and space that many renters find attractive. Adding a skylight could help reduce utility bills by keeping the house brighter for longer. With uniquely structured windows, you could even create a stunning view that many will love to pay for, or tune out one that might disturb renters.

- **Create more living space**: You can get even more income from improving the living area of your property. Consider fitting in an extra bedroom to create a spacious plan, which more people will appreciate. Think families or roommates. These demographics are more likely to stay for longer than students or seniors.

You don't have to make a custom addition to the property by building something new or adding another floor. Inspect your floor plan and look for areas that could be repurposed. For instance, that walk-in closet could make another bedroom and bring you higher rent as a two-bedroom apartment than a one-bedroom suite that less renters are interested in. Don't be afraid to take down walls and make bigger space for sellable areas. Consider the attic, garage, dining room, and master suite. These are some common places that can be turned into living areas.

- **Noise reduction**: Homes are meant to be places of comfort where you return to after all of life's toils to enjoy serenity. Make your property an oasis for your renters by adding insulation, plants to absorb noise, doors and windows with double panes, and rugs and carpets to reduce footfalls.

- **Don't ignore appliances**: Many renters don't come with appliances and furniture, and tend to buy them over time. This could be a huge source of revenue if you fitted your rental property with appliances. These types of properties are known as furnished apartments. Invest in appliances like dryers, refrigerators, dishwashers, and washing machines. You'd be surprised how much people flock to rent from you.

You also don't have to worry about the cost of these appliances. You don't have to go to a showroom; simply use alternative sources such as surplus stores, ReStores, and outlet stores. You can even find great deals on thrift markets like Facebook Marketplace, eBay, Craigslist, etc. There are many ways to get appliances without breaking the bank. You could even take them on installments and have them pay for themselves.

- **Improve your floor plan for better functioning**: Creating a functional floor plan may have to do with tearing down a non-load bearing wall that separates the living room and kitchen, adding an en suite bathroom to the master bedroom to make it a full suite, or even redesigning the kitchen to make it more spacious and create room for extra furniture. It may also be swapping two rooms, like a dinning room and home office, to allow for a better dynamic. The idea is to make every space count and make the most of it. So, instead of sticking to a floor plan that wastes vital space, you put it to good use that makes the property more functional and appealing.

- **Know when to pack it up**: Many people think of real estate as an investment that brings income when value increases. So, as the property appreciates, it brings in more money. This does make sense, but real estate is more than just value increments. It also retains its value. For instance, if your property grows at a 5% appreciation rate per year, it could increase your income as time passes.

And this is where the problem is. Appreciation isn't something you can cause on your own. You can take all these steps, and your property could still perform poorly. Why? Because other factors affect the value of your property, like its location, other surrounding properties, and the present market situation in the area. So, if the real estate market around you starts to go downhill, don't try pumping in money to make your property more valuable. Cut your losses, sell the property, and move on to a better place with better growth potential.

Chapter 27:

Negotiating for Success in Real

Estate

Negotiating is more than a business procedure. It's an art you have to learn and master, especially in real estate. Knowing how to work your way around deals will help you get great commissions for yourself and good prices from your clients.

That said, here are some tips to help you become a master at negotiations:

- **Courtesy**: Negotiating won't always be as straightforward as you want. Sometimes, it can get frustrating and you may find yourself getting angry. But the negotiation table is no place for impoliteness. As much as possible, begin on a positive note and try to steer from negative tones, even if the next person is being problematic. Maintain a respectful and polite tone, and try to guide the conversation forward until all parties are satisfied.

- **Limit your excitement**: Treat every deal as important. In doing so, you may sometimes happen on interesting deals that give you butterflies in your stomach. But don't show it, though. Never show your excitement during negotiations, as it could ruin all your hard work. Instead, keep silent when you have nothing to contribute and allow the other parties to express their excitement instead. Sometimes, silence can even help your cause, as the person might feel like they are losing you or you're rethinking the deal. This will make them more agreeable to your demands.

- **Patience**: Don't be in a hurry to close a deal. Bad deals are made in a hurry, so take your time. By showing no desire to close a deal quickly, you could wear down the other party's resolve and get them to agree with you. It gets even better if they want to conclude the deal quickly. You just sit back and watch them find new common grounds to agree on. The patient dog might yet get the juiciest bone.

- **Do your homework**: Never go into a negotiation unprepared. That's just a recipe for disaster. Anytime you find yourself at the table, ensure that you have learned everything you need to know about the deal. Otherwise, you will miss important details and end up with a bad deal.

As a rule of thumb, here are a few questions you need to ask and answer before you start negotiating:

- What does my client need?

- Are they under pressure to buy or sell? If yes, how can I help?

- Is the client a first-time home buyer?

- What if they can't make any decisions due to stress or sentiments?

- Do they have other options if this one doesn't work out?

These questions aren't meant to make you stressed, but to keep you grounded. You must understand what is at stake, so you can know when to dig in and grind out results or let go and look for something else. Your decision-making at the negotiating table must be accurate and in line with all your client wants. The more informed you are, the better your negotiations will turn out and you won't have to leave money on the table. Here are some tips to be aware of:

- **Assert your needs**: The key to successful negotiations is to be assertive and know when to challenge and counteroffer. Everything that comes to the table can be negotiated, and you can get away with what your client wants if you put your mind to it. Being assertive means informing the other party of what you want out of the deal and sticking to it. No, it doesn't mean to be rude or aggressive. You still need to be polite and show respect to the other party, for the best interests of your client.

Instead, focus on getting a great deal that contains everything your client wants. And if there is room for compromise, get the go-ahead nod from your client first.

- **It's not your last deal; act like it**: Don't be the agent who takes every deal as their last; it really isn't that serious. And it can be bad business if the other party suspects that you want the deal badly. Approach negotiations with an open and clear mind, not like you're going into a battle for the ages. Show empathy and humility, and don't let things get heated up. If you go in too hard, you will make a bad impression on the other side and things will only sour from there. Instead, look to find a situation that benefits both sides and try to hear them out and provide solutions to any problems they have.

- **Be in the know**: Besides doing your homework on the deal, you also need to be knowledgeable. Find out more about investors in the area and try to get a rapport with city planners in the area you're buying into. Also, find out more about land uses and zoning in the area. You will find this knowledge handy when negotiating, as it will help you avoid legal troubles and pitfalls that could make the deal bad for your client.

- **Understand market dynamics**: Before you begin negotiating, you should be well aware of the situation of the real estate market. Sometimes, rates could be up or down depending on what's happening in an area. So, knowing these facts will be helpful for getting a good deal that won't overcharge your client or leave them with properties in a dwindling neighborhood. And don't just use the data from your previous negotiations—new deal, new check.

Furthermore, you should find out about the factors that affect the value of properties in an area. For instance, the influx of job creation to an area will improve the value of properties in the neighborhood. The best part is that you don't have to dig deep. Just a brief overview of the market in the area should get you sorted. You should also find out about the climate there. If you can't do it yourself, you can always seek out a professional.

- **Hear out the needs of the other party**: Your needs aren't the only important thing at the negotiating table. You must also see things from the perspective of the next person. Everyone sees the process differently and hopes for different outcomes. But if you'd just switch sides, you could better understand the other party and find a way that works for everyone.

  If it were you on the other side, how would you go about achieving your goals? Follow your thoughts and see where they lead, and intimate the other party on common grounds you might share.

- **Have reasonable expectations**: Don't go into a negotiation expecting to conquer the world, especially if you're representing a seller. Most sellers think they can get huge profits on their properties during a seller's market, but are often disappointed when the offers pouring in are market value rates. Sometimes, it could be that many buyers want extra items after inspection. As the presiding agent, it's best to help your client know that things won't always go their way, and they should expect offers lower than their asking price. This doesn't mean you'll accept lowball deals, but their expectations will be within reasonable reach.

- **Get in touch with sellers**: You'd be surprised how much of a difference meeting the seller beforehand makes during negotiations. Just take out the time to schedule a meeting, say on the morning or evening of a weekend. Do this before the open house or negotiations. Not only will it make them feel closer to you, but you could also get a better deal than most.

  Remember, sellers only look at the highest price offers when they have nothing else to decide on. But if their first choice is someone they like and have bonded with, chances are they won't look at price offers alone. Now, instead of just being another offer among many, yours will stand out because they can identify the face behind it.

Chapter 28:

How to Identify Your Target

Market in Real Estate

If there is one thing we have successfully done in the world, it's create a lot of options. For instance, the Internet alone is filled with many different websites and several billion active users. Just about everything has a website and can be found online. Even traditionally physical industries like real estate can now be found online now. What makes options a problem is that there can be too many of them. Presently, the real estate industry is oversaturated. In the United States alone, there are more than 1.5 million active realtors and many more will join in the foreseeable future. All of these people are looking to sell or rent property to the rest of the population and do their best to be appealing.

What this means is that you can't simply spread your net and hope to get lucrative business. Whether you use an online or offline approach, you can't just pitch yourself to the big market and expect the best. You must play to a particular audience—a niche. Otherwise, you will become one of the many options and won't stand out.

Currently, it's imperative that you find a specific market or demographic that you can thrive in. Not only will you get better business this way, but you will also face less competition than taking on the remaining 1.499 million realtors across the country. Also, modern customers find specificity appealing. They have seen just about every ad and heard every catchphrase. But they want to be targeted as a collective niche, and that's the most effective way to market to them and convert leads.

But knowing it is the easiest part, and the more trickier side is knowing how to effectively narrow down your audience. Before implementing a marketing strategy, ensure to get in touch with your team. Once you have identified an audience that pairs well with your skill set, area of knowledge, and availability, it's time to ingrain it into your brand. A strong brand identity should promote the audience you stand for.

What Is a Target Audience?

Target audiences refer to the demographic that you intend to sell your services and products to. As a real estate agent, your demographic are people who are interested in the type of properties you offer, and are willing to rent or buy them.

Of course, sometimes, your clients may not fit into this mold—but knowing how to identify the majority of your customers, as well as what they are looking for, makes all the difference in how effective your marketing will be. When deciding on your target audience, many factors will come into play, such as financial background, gender, age, and ethnicity.

The Factors That Drive the Real Estate Market

Real estate usually makes up the biggest chunk of many people's wealth. This is especially the case for many U.S. homeowners. The Federal Reserve carried out a Survey of Consumer Finances in 2019, which showed that 64.9% of American households were owners of their primary residences. The scale and size of such a real estate market makes it a lucrative and appealing industry for many. But that number didn't come overnight. There are many things that drive the real estate market and make it a worthwhile investment, they are:

The Economy

This factor is the most crucial of the lot. How a country performs economically affects how much people will invest in properties. Stable economies will attract investors, who will drive the real estate market for both buyers and sellers. On the other hand, if the country has good job security, high purchasing power, good GDP, and financial stability, more people will be willing and able to invest in real estate.

Conversely, if a country's economy is poor and it has a bad GDP, poor job security, and lack of employment opportunities, people are less likely to invest in properties there. For one, they don't have the purchasing power. Secondly, it is bad business as property value will only fall with the economy. So, essentially, a good and stable economy is the backbone of a promising real estate industry.

Demographics

Demographics refers to the data that shows the type of people that make up a population, including migration patterns, age, income, population growth, race, and gender. While these statistics are usually overlooked, they are a major part of how real estate is valued and the type of properties needed in the market. If there is a huge shift in a nation's demographics, the impact will be felt on real estate and its trends for many years.

For instance, people born between 1945 and 1964 (known as baby boomers), are one of the most important demographics in the United States real estate market. They also greatly influence the market, as many of them are now seniors and moving into the retirement phase. But within their lifetime, they successfully created one of the biggest real estate trends in the past century. And since their retirement that began in 2010, they will continue to affect the real estate market for another decade or more.

Other demographics based on income power, like the elite class, upper-middle class, and middle class, have huge effects on the real estate and market trends in the country. And positive ones at that. The reason for this influence can be traced to their socioeconomic standing and higher purchasing power, which lead to high sales in the market.

Supply and Demand

The flow of supply and demand is another important factor in real estate. While these depend on a particular place, the effects can be astounding. They affect the market locally and nationally, and can't be taken lightly. For instance, if the price of or tariffs on lumber and other building materials increase, the prices of new homes are going to change to deal with the increase in production costs. And if prices continue to climb, demand is going to reduce as buyers opt out or take a time-out to increase their purchasing power. In turn, builders won't have much to do, and supply will fall as well.

Governmental Policies

The government also has a hand in how the real estate market develops. If there are friendly policies, the real estate market will grow well, and more people will be willing to invest in properties. Government can help by creating deductions, subsidiaries, and tax credits for developers and investors. Not only will this go toward improving infrastructure in the country, but it would also attract foreign investors to join the residential and commercial real estate market.

However, if the government sets rigid rules and policies, investors will be scared off and would rather put their money into other industries that guarantee cost efficiency and good return value.

Interest Rates

Interest rates are the icing on the cake of what drives the real estate market. Low interest rates make people more eager to buy properties, because they can borrow without running into crippling debt. However, when interest rates start to increase, it doesn't reflect on the real estate market at first. One one hand, this is because interest rates increase slowly and buyers can lock into rates and avoid increments. On the other hand, if there is a dramatic increase to interest rates, the market will begin to slow down and buyers will look for other alternatives to avoid breaking the bank.

Chapter 29:

Insurance in Real Estate

Insurance in real estate is a term used to describe several policies that protect or cover property, property owners, and liabilities. How it works is that insurance financially reimburses a renter or property owner and its contents, should things go awry due to theft or damages. Insurance also covers people beside renters or owners who get injured on a property.

What many people don't know is that insurance doesn't just cover one thing. There are multiple policies in real estate insurance, like earthquake insurance, flood insurance, homeowner's insurance, and renters insurance. Renter or homeowner policies usually cover personal property, except when the personal property is expensive and of high value. For that, you will need an additional policy known as a rider. When you make a claim, the property insurance policy will reimburse you for replacement cost if the problem cannot be fixed. Otherwise, you will be given the full value of the damages.

Why Insurance Matters

Owning or renting a property without insurance is bad business because there are many things to worry about. Essentially, it's a gamble you shouldn't take if you can help it. You have to see insurance as more than money you pay for what you don't expect to happen. See it up as a backup that kicks in when things don't go according to plan. And we all need that sort of backup. Here are some vital reasons why insurance matters:

- **Dwelling coverage**: Dwelling coverage pays for any damages to your home or surrounding structures, like a garage or patio, caused by a peril in the policy. The dwelling coverage value of your property is determined by the square footage of your house and how much it would cost to rebuild. That doesn't make it the actual market value of your property.

- **Personal liability coverage**: Say you or someone related to you accidentally injures someone or damages their property; paying out of pocket may not be good for your financial health. Liability insurance covers this likelihood by paying legal fees, repair costs, and medical bills.

- **Structural coverage**: Insurance typically includes a policy for other structures, which helps pay for replacement or repair costs for structures detached from your property—like a shed or fence—when they are ruined by a peril in the arrangement.

- **Extra living expenses coverage**: If your property becomes unlivable after a covered claim, like a fire or flood, a homeowner's insurance company can help you sort out temporary living situations and its costs—like hotels and bills.

- **Personal property coverage**: Personal property coverage goes into replacing some belongings that were damaged or stolen, such as electronics and furniture.

- **Guest medical protection**: This is for when a guest on your property is injured. The guest medical protection policy on your insurance covers their medical bills.

Types of Insurance for Real Estate Investors

There are different types of insurance you can get as a real estate investor. Here are a few, including additional coverage options:

- **Liability insurance**: Liability insurance is a policy that deals with accidents that happen on your premises. It's usually for visitors at your property, such as guests, handymen, service personnel, or tenants. Liability coverage will protect you in situations like these:

- if an accident happens on your grounds that requires rehabilitation and hospital bills

- if something gets stolen or someone is hurt

- if someone sues you and you have to pay for damages

- **Sewer and water line backup**: You can add the costs of sewer and water line backups or breaks to your insurance coverage. There are simpler repairs you can make on your own to your plumbing system, like clearing clogged lines. However, if there is a break, the expenses will increase by a lot and you'd have to pay for other damages it may cause to surrounding properties. In many municipalities, if there is a burglary in your area of the property line, the city would not be responsible for the repair cost. Instead, you will have to contact a licensed contractor to get it fixed.

- **Tenant rent default insurance**: This type of insurance is also called rent guarantee insurance. Companies like Steady and Rent Rescue can save you from drops in rent due to a tenant skipping out or defaulting on rent. How it works is that this insurance steps in and pays you in the stead of the defaulting tenant. That way, your income flow remains intact.

- **Loss of income coverage**: This type of insurance protects you in cases when your rental property is unsafe for renters for a long period, like when a natural disaster or fire occurs. If your mortgage is affordable and you have a single rental property, even if there are no tenants in it, you can sufficiently foot your own bills for a while until things return to normal. However, if you have a bigger rental property portfolio and your expenses depend on the income you make through rent, the loss of income insurance is practical and can save you from losing your livelihood.

- **Fire and hazard insurance**: Usually, basic insurance policies cover fire and hazards, such as theft, fire damage, and structural damages caused by storms. With this insurance, many investors prefer to go for policies that cover the replacement cost of the property instead of the cash value at the time.

- **Partnership insurance**: As investors grow and increase their portfolios, they may start a real estate partnership or invest in a joint venture. When this happens, they could get partnership insurance to protect them against other partners in the business. That way, when things go awry, like the death of a partner, they can easily buy the investment of the deceased from the family and continue running the business on their own. This protects them from having to do business with a new and unknown partner used to replace the former.

- **Landlord insurance**: This type of insurance is also called rental property insurance. In this package, investors get different forms of insurance coverage that is essential to the well-being of their investments. For instance, a landlord insurance policy comes with loss of income, hazard, and liability coverages. The only thing that it may not cover is the properties of the renters. That is up to the tenants to decide. In many states, landlords can make it mandatory for tenants to get and foot their own insurance policies.

- **Pet coverage**: Allowing pets on your premises can increase its appeal to renters, reduce the rate of tenants leaving, and help you get competitive rent. However, if you must allow pets on your property, you should ensure that your tenants are insured against damages caused to and by their pets. In some areas, the local laws for property owners allow you to make it compulsory. That way you won't be responsible for any injuries or damages that the pet may cause.

- **Builder's risk insurance**: Investors only need builder's risk insurance for when they purchase a vacant property or are renovating one. Since contractor injuries, vandalism, and property damage could happen at this time, it's best that they aren't liable for it. This insurance exists because regular insurance that covers fire, liabilities, and hazards doesn't extend to vacant and nearly vacant properties, or ones under renovation. An insurance broker or agent will typically source this insurance from secondary markets for the investor. An example of a company that deals in secondary insurance is Lloyds of London. Just bear in mind that this insurance is more expensive, at up to four times the amount of regular liability, fire, and hazard policies.

Chapter 30:

Writing a Winning Purchase Offer

Purchase offers are one of the staples of seller's markets—a time when there are more buyers than there are property listings. And if a property has all the appealing factors, it will get the most interest and offers from buyers. When this happens, the property is usually sold for more than the original asking price. But profit isn't everything sellers are after. There are certain factors in a purchase that makes it stand out from the rest.

So, before you draft and send your offer, here are a few tips to give you an edge over other offers:

- **Get a great real estate agent**: An agent is the middle ground between buyers and sellers. But what makes an agent better than others is their expertise of going through the market and their networks to get a lead on a property before others. Getting a head start gives you enough time and flexibility to close a deal.

- **Send your offer with a pre-approval letter**: A letter proving that your credit rating has been checked and you have the ability to purchase the property is a trump card that you should use. It shows the seller that you have the intention to buy and can put your money where your mouth is. If your offer is the highest of the lot and comes with a pre-approval letter, there is no reason why you won't be considered for the sale.

- **Include the seller's preferred closing time**: In a seller's market, you will be up against a lot of competition, and some of them will try to extend the arrangement beyond the preferred closing date of the seller. Try to make sure your offer falls within that window or earlier. Doing so will show the seller that you take their time seriously and are keen on the deal. This little factor could be the key deciding factor in helping you close the deal.

- **Make sure your offer is friendly**: That you are giving cash for a property isn't an excuse to be rude. Your offer should be polite and respectful, and without unnecessary demands that may anger or irritate the seller. To do this, you must be aware of the do's and don'ts of the property area. For instance, in some places, it's not unusual for buyers to cover the cost of title insurance. So, asking the seller to bear this additional cost could be a turnoff. Most buyers demand to possess the property by a specific time on the day of closing the deal. If you're not in a hurry, you can write in two to three days into the offer, allowing the seller enough time to move their belongings and cut emotional ties.

- **Your offer shouldn't depend on the sale of another property**: Don't make an offer that will be financed by the sale of another property. That will send your offer to the trash with others. When your listed property sells, you can offset your debt and build equity. Or, you can get an agent to ensure your current property is sold quickly, with the proceeds going into the new one. It's a plus if you sell for cash.

- **Prepare for contingencies**: Sometimes, the appraisal value of the property you want to buy might be below the contract price. When this happens, offer a modified appraisal contingency that won't ruin the seller's expected outcome.

- **Don't hold back on your best offer**: Your first offer should be your best offer, because you may not always get room to negotiate. Sellers make decisions based on the best offers they receive, so don't try to lowball on the first try and expect to get a second chance with a counteroffer. If the property is a hot sell, always imagine that only the best and highest will be considered. Anything outside these may not even get the time of day. So, before making an offer, decide on the top dollar you are willing to part with and include it in your offer.

- **Don't try to make sellers pay for home warranty**: There's nothing wrong with wanting some insurance for repair costs in the future. But that shouldn't be something you try to fit into the offer. Get a good inspector to verify the property and decide if it's a worthwhile investment. Then, you can negotiate any repair costs into the inspection contingency of the property.

- **Don't go after every contingency**: If you are determined to get a property, speak to your legal advisor about risking your deposit to get rid of contingencies for inspections, appraisals, and loans. But this tactic isn't without its downsides. Waging an appraisal contingency means that if the property is appraised for less than the sales price, you will have to fork over the price difference to the sellers. So, with this drawback in mind, only waive contingencies if you're absolutely sure it will give you an edge over other offers.

- **Improve the value of your offer by offering cash**: Even if you use a mortgage to finance the deal, offering cash from the get-go will make your offer stand out. If you have some accounts with enough cash to close the deal, you can use them as proof of funds in your offer. If the seller accepts your offer, you can then change to financing with a mortgage instead.

- **Reduce inspection time line**: A standard purchase contract allows a buyer to take several days to inspect the property before they can go ahead to close the deal. The default in many purchase offers is 17 days, but you can decrease it to 10 days. According to Federal law, unless you waive your Lead Paint Disclosure right, 10 days is enough to check the property for any signs of contamination due to lead paint.

- **Deal with inspection contingencies**: You could modify the inspection contingency in your offer to lower the requests or credits for repairs caused by the home inspection. But before doing this, make sure to talk to your agent or legal adviser.

- **Put down a substantial amount as a healthy deposit**: Putting down a large and earnest deposit tells the seller that you are serious about the purchase and want to close the deal quickly. That way, they will put you down as one of their leads. And you don't even have to go overboard with it. Instead of, say, a 1% deposit, try 3% to 5%. So, if a property is on sale for $500,000, offer more than $500,000. That way the seller will feel that you want the deal and won't have to worry about you backing out halfway. So, instead, go in with $5,000 or more. That will show them you are serious.

- **Use your earnest money**: You could include in your offer that a percentage of your earnest money is nonrefundable. Now, this tactic should be used sparingly and only for cases when competition is high.

Chapter 31:

Foreclosure and Real Estate

Owned Properties

The possibility of facing foreclosure is one reason why property buyers are not encouraged (in this book, at least) to choose Interest-based funding. Loans often include down payments and interest rates which may be too much financial load for many willing real estate investors to bear. However, many homeowners do lose their properties to lenders. This chapter serves to educate people who've already taken mortgages and those thinking about purchasing Real Estate Owned (REO) properties.

Foreclosure refers to the processes involved when a property owner cannot continue their mortgage payments and has no other means of stopping the process. When this happens, the lender takes the property away and tries to sell it to get back the part of the loan (mortgage) that hasn't been paid.

You might wonder if this is even legal—and yes, it is. If you miss your mortgage payments a couple of times, the lender will send you a reminder called a Notice of Default. They may even give you a period of grace to get your affairs in order before they start foreclosing the property. If you're wondering why they don't immediately seize the property after the first default, that's because mortgage lenders don't like the foreclosure process any better than the defaulter does.

Not only does it take a long time, but it's also very expensive—and all the cost is on them. As if that's not enough, it's not certain that they will be able to sell the property. So, you can see it's not doing them any favors, either. It's why many mortgage lenders will go the extra mile to try to make other arrangements with the property owner. They would rather modify the loan and repayment plan for the other payments missed. Some would even organize a short sale.

But if nothing works and the owner still can't do anything to pay back the mortgage, the lender starts the long and expensive process of the foreclosure. Unlike a short sale, during a foreclosure, the property owner no longer has any rights to the property. Ownership has now gone to the lender, so they won't even be involved in the auction process. If the lender can't sell the property at auction, they will just hold onto it, not as a foreclosed property again, but as an REO property.

Short Sales

Short sales happen during foreclosure, just before the owner forfeits their rights and the property goes to auction. In a short sale, the lender agrees to sell the property for less than the amount of debt owed. Unlike during a proper foreclosure, investors can negotiate the price of the property for less because they aren't responsible for back payments or paying off the loan. Instead, they are making a deal with the lender to accept less than what the lender would typically accept to avoid the cost of foreclosure.

How Mortgage Lenders Sell Off Real Estate Owned Properties

Most of the time, mortgage lenders are banks. And properties, especially ones that aren't commercial, are huge risks on their books. So, they try to get them off as soon as possible so that properties don't pile up. This saves them from poor markets when there are less buyers than sellers.

Speaking of the properties, they are often sold at discounted rates because banks just want to recover the balance left on the mortgage, including payments that the property owner may have missed. If they are unable to secure a buyer even at less than market rate, it means that the value of the property has decreased between the time the loan was issued and when the property was foreclosed.

Having a foreclosure auction for one property is too much work, so banks prefer to sell a bunch of them at the same time. It also helps with sales, as investors may be willing to buy more than one property. Properties that aren't sold after the auction are put up for rent to help the bank recoup some money.

Benefits of REOs and Profiting off Foreclosure

- **Liens issues and taxes are out of the picture**: When you buy a property from a seller, you still have to deal with the unpaid mortgages and property taxes from the first owner, which can put off a lot of buyers. However, in the case of a foreclosure or REO, you don't have to worry about these things because it all ends at the negotiation table with the lender. Once you make the payment for the property, all liens and property taxes are cleared.

- **Good return on investment (ROI)**: REOs are a good source of return from both real estate flippers and landlords. For instance, flippers get REO properties at cheap rates, renovate, and resell at a higher price. On the other hand, landlords can also buy an REO property for less than market rate and rent or lease it to tenants for standard market rates. Over time, the landlord will get back their capital and a steady source of income.

- **Cheaper price**: Lenders are always eager, if not desperate, to dump their REOs and foreclosures on someone else. They are only interested in getting back the rest of the loan that the borrower couldn't pay. Profit isn't their biggest concern, and so you can expect some great deals, especially if a significant chunk of the debt has already been paid.

Also, lenders don't cover the entire value of a property. That's why borrowers still need to make down payments. This helps the lender maintain a price margin that allows them to sell the property should things not go as planned.

- **Terms are negotiable**: Unlike with property sellers who have outright terms of agreement, you can negotiate with the lender. Their desperation to sell makes it easier to haggle over down payment, rehab costs, loan amount, closing costs, etc.

- **Inspections are allowed**: Even though REO properties are sold without any work done to improve value, lenders allow buyers to access and inspect the property. This is good for negotiations.

REO or Foreclosure: Which Is the Better Investment?

Both foreclosures and REO properties come at heavily discounted prices compared to standard property listings. However, when buying distress sales, most investors tend to go for REO properties. From a general perspective, the negative aspects of foreclosures are more than the positives, which makes them a sensitive purchase. But that doesn't make it bad for investment. In fact, the answer to which is better between REOs and foreclosures isn't so straightforward. It depends on your perspective.

You have to decide between the pros and cons of both types of properties and decide on the one that works best for you. Beyond that, you also need to look into the specifics of foreclosures and REOs. Approach these properties with caution and do your homework thoroughly. Finding great REO or foreclosed properties can be a profitable investment. But you must know how to pick them, because some are time- and resource-consuming without providing any decent returns.

The Potential Drawbacks of REOs and Foreclosures

Just because Real Estate Owned properties and foreclosures are sold for cheap or owned by lenders (banks) doesn't make them the best properties on the market. They can also have negatives that can affect the time it takes to break even. Worse case scenario, they might need extensive and expensive repairs to get in shape. And if you have limited capital to invest into preparing the property for sale or rent, your returns could be greatly affected. At this point, the property will cost more money to fix than it could possibly bring in.

REOs are no better with problems, either. Some of them may come with problems with the title, which you may not notice until the deal has been finalized. The only way to tackle this problem is to get a separate owner's title insurance, as well as a lender's insurance to prevent any other problems that may come up. But solving this problem only ends up creating another: increasing the cost of owning the property.

Chapter 32:

Different Ways to Make Money in

Real Estate

Real estate is one of the biggest wealth-creating industries right now. But many are still skeptical about joining. And for good reasons, too. Whether it's the investment potentials peddled by gurus or the millionth infomercial going on about how real estate can get you the big bucks in little time, things can get noisy at some point and lose their meaning. But there's actual money to be made in real estate, and it's not nearly as shiny or quick as it's sold to be.

In this chapter, we will delve into money-making strategies in real estate, including basic means that have been used for centuries and newer opportunities created by the real estate landscape in recent times.

- **Income-based real estate**: One of the biggest ways real estate generates money is through regular income payments known as rent. Generally, rental income in real estate comes through different means and in several forms, such as:

    - **Commercial property income**: Commercial properties generate income from rent, rights to the land, and a niche agreement called option income. Commercial tenants will often buy contractual options like the right of first refusal on the office next door. These positions cost a premium, which tenants can pay to own the option whether or not they use it.
    - **Residential property income**: A huge percentage of income from residential properties comes from rent. Tenants are required to pay a certain amount weekly, monthly, quarterly, or yearly. But the amount isn't fixed and could grow to reflect demand, inflation, and the current state of the real estate market. After running costs have been subtracted from the income, the rest is the profit generated by the property.

    - **Raw land income**: If you have the rights to a piece of land, companies or the government could pay premiums to erect structures on it. And should they discover valuable materials in it, you could be entitled to royalties.

- **Lease options**: Lease options are one of the simplest ways to get into real estate and make money without needing to have great credit or a huge chunk or capital. The idea is leasing with an option to buy. This strategy works best when the real estate market in an area is growing, because it allows you to agree on a set price to purchase the property at a later time regardless of its new value at that point.

For instance, if the market does well, you would buy the property at a huge discount, which would be impossible without this option. But you don't have to buy the property yourself. You could also sell the rights of purchase to someone else and leave with your profits without needing to invest lots of capital. Why is that? Because of the 'option' in the arrangement. Having the option to do something also means you can choose not to. And since you have the rights of purchase by the end of the lease period, you could turn it into a profit, too. This strategy bets on the real estate market performing well to work.

- **Contract flipping**: Another means of making money in real estate without good credit or a lot of capital is by flipping contracts. Mind you, this isn't about flipping houses. Instead, all you have to do is find an eager buyer and a distressed seller and help them find each other. It's like Tinder for real estate.

Distressed sellers aren't uncommon in the market, but finding them can be stressful—not impossible, though. The trick is to look for properties that are vacant, losing tenants, or behind on mortgage payments. If the property is already vacant, that increases your chances of finding a distressed seller. Once you locate them, you should have a buyer ready to go at once.

- **Buy and hold**: This is one of the oldest strategies used for earning money in real estate. Buying and holding can be done in different ways, such as:

  - purchasing a single-family home and renting it out to demographics that fit the bill

  - buying a multifamily unit, moving into one, and renting out the remaining units to other families to help offset your own expenses and mortgage

  - getting a multifamily property and renting out all the units, then working as the property manager or hiring a professional to deal with repairs, maintenance, tenant checks, rent, and damages

- **Buying land**: Buying land isn't so different from the buy and hold strategy. The only difference is that you aren't purchasing a property. Instead, you look for undeveloped lands in areas with booming or up-and-coming real estate markets. After getting the land, you don't have to develop it. Instead, you hold until its value increases and sell for a profit. Alternatively, you could build on it and sell for an even bigger profit over time.

- **Home-renovation flips**: Fixing and flipping is basically pop culture in real estate. We have tons of home renovation shows over the years to thank for that. Currently, the industry is experiencing a surge in the traditional renovation flip sector. While renovation flips may sound interesting, considering the huge transformation that happens to houses on those shows, it's more technical than just waving a magic wand. Navigating the sector is risky in the beginning, which it more than makes up for with huge income generation.

If you have no experience or understanding of how renovation flips work, you may find yourself losing funds on bad deals, especially when it comes to picking the right home. You see, just because every home can be renovated and flipped doesn't mean they are all worth the effort and resources. This strategy is only profitable when the property and the cost of renovation is below its market value and can give you a decent profit for your troubles. Otherwise, it could turn into a huge loss on your part.

To avoid this, you need an expert contractor and on-site inspection of the property before buying. While it's much easier to buy properties at auctions before seeing them, unless you are absolutely sure of the potential of the market in that area, you may risk losing money. However, the money-making part is relatively simple once you know the costs of getting the property back to market value.

- **Vacation and short-term rentals**: More people are interested in homes away from home now than at any other point in our history. Like cutting the cord, the demand for short-stay rentals has ballooned, allowing just about any property owner to share in the market. You could either rent out the entire property as a short-let home, or rent out a room. And if your property is close to a tourist destination, then you're in luck.

However, the market has been slow as of late; and it's unclear when things will pick up again. But when it does pick up, don't just jump in. Short-term rentals are frowned upon in some areas and heavily regulated in others. So, be sure of the legal backing in your state and city. Look up the bylaws before listing your property on sites like HomeAway, VRBO, or Airbnb. Also, factor in running costs like cleaning, repairs, and maintenance after each guest stay.

Chapter 33:

Some Mistakes Made by First-

Time Investors

Real estate remains one of the most timeless and most guaranteed investments globally. However, just because it's a profitable industry doesn't make it foolproof. Many have lost investment and resources in real estate due to silly errors.

If you are a newbie to the world of real estate investing, one thing you should learn is patience. You won't reap from the market in a heartbeat, unless you have been fooled into a get-rich-quick scheme. And like any other business of buying and selling, you need to be skilled, determined, and knowledgeable. These qualities will keep you from making rookie mistakes such as the following:

- **Going in without a plan**: You're not invincible, and real estate doesn't care about your pedigree. If you go in without a plan, you will feel the burn of your carelessness.

  The last thing you want to do is buy a property without any prior due diligence. You should know if a property will be a liability or an asset from the get-go. But you may sometimes miss this when the real estate market is bubbling and everyone is in a buying frenzy. But resist the urge of FOMO, step back, and make plans according to your capital, budget, and expectations—as well as exit plans for when things go awry and your assumptions don't work out.

  Don't get a mortgage first and throw cash on a random deal before deciding on how to proceed. Start by identifying the type of property you want to invest in. For instance, are you looking for a commercial or residential property? If so, what niche are you considering: lease, mixed-use, rental, or short-term rentals? Afterward, draw up a purchase plan and fund properties that fit the bill.

- **Don't ignore the numbers**: Investing in real estate is one of the leading sources of wealth creation, and has made more millionaires than most asset classes. But the industry is a death trap for an uninformed and inexperienced investor. Why is this? Because most of these people tend to miss or underestimate the costs involved in investing in the market. Worse still, many new investors are optimistic about their numbers.

  In real estate investing, numbers are your favorite thing. Because how else would you know if a project is going to bring in money or fail?

  The best thing to do is to create a cash flow calculation showing your potential income if you get a property, depending on how you want to manage it: flip or rent out. Whichever one you try will give you good returns, but not before planning for it.

  In fact, you will find that some properties are not worth the time and effort even if you end up getting decent returns on them. This is why you can't sleep on the numbers. Run them before you buy, sell, flip, or rent.

- **Property location**: A property's location is one of the most important factors about it that determines whether or not it would be a profitable investment. In fact, you could say it's the most crucial factor that you can't overlook when buying a property. Because, for every other component, there is a work-around and an upgrade that can bring them to speed with current realities. But if you buy a house in a rainforest, there's no convincing an entire city to move in with you.

  So, how do you avoid the bad location mistake?

- In real estate, a good location is one that has the potential to grow in the future. And there are signs to be aware of such places, like:

- infrastructure and facilities in the area are up-to-date and attract traffic, such as commercial centers, recreational facilities, etc.

- proximity to basic amenities such as airports, hospitals, good road networks, schools, banks, etc.

- **Flying solo**: Real estate isn't a stunt plane fair, so you don't have to fly solo. Many first-time buyers and investors think that all they have learned about real estate is enough to carry them through. And while that is partly true, it's also false because they don't have all the knowledge. Just because you can negotiate a deal on your own doesn't mean you should. Even if you have done several deals before, changes in the market means the outcome of your negotiations isn't fixed. Things could get out of hand or not go your way, and you would have only yourself to turn to.

You should be willing and open to leveraging all the resources around you. Make friends with experts who can guide your purchases and lead you in the right path. By all means, get a team of experts behind you, including a competent property inspector, a professional attorney, a savvy real estate broker or agent, a creative handyman, and a good insurance agent.

These experts from different fields will alert you to potential problems or opportunities in their own sphere of the market. In the case of any attorney, they could help you stay on the side of the law and avoid properties or deals that could spell trouble in the future.

- **Ignoring the needs of renters**: If you want to get a rental property, you must have a particular demographic in mind as a target audience—for instance, college students, seniors, young families, etc. Family renters will typically prefer neighborhoods with schools, good road networks, and low crime rates. Singles, on the other hand, will prefer neighborhoods with a great nightlife and access to mass transit.

Meanwhile, if you prefer a vacation rental, then your property must be located within a tourist destination, like a beach, local attraction, etc. The idea is to get a property that fits the type of tenants an area is most likely to attract.

- **Ignoring or overlooking maintenance and repairs**: The cost of maintaining a property isn't the first thing that comes to mind for many investors, and that can be a bad thing. Every property you buy, even the ones in perfect condition, will require maintenance over time. As a rule of thumb, you should always set aside about 2% of your property value each year to cover potential maintenance costs.

  New investors and buyers often forget to account for repair and maintenance expenses until it's too late. Then they are surprised that it's expensive, and they can't tackle it due to lack of funds. Instead, every time you're in the market for a property, remember that you're about to make a long-term investment, even if you won't hold onto the property forever. There will always be something to fix or replace, and you must be ready.

  Even if you are financially prepared to deal with maintenance and repairs, not paying attention to when they are needed can be costly. If you plan to rent out the property or flip for sale, you need to see to everything that needs to be fixed or replaced. Not only will the value of the property improve, but it will also save you the cost of getting a quick fix at odd times.

- **Don't forget the local side of real estate**: You can't do much with your property if you don't understand the local market and the neighborhood. Not only do these factors contribute to the value of your property, but they are crucial if you want to turn a profit. So, you must learn and drill down on levels of inventory, land issues, demand and supply problems, and property values. Understanding these parameters puts you in better standing to decide if a property for sale is worth the time, effort, and resources before committing to it.

Chapter 34:

The Importance of Location in

Real Estate

During a big real estate market, many investors and buyers will be eager to buy any property that is listed. While that is all well and good, when the market returns to normal, only those who invested in good properties in great areas will be left with properties that gain more value than they lose. Why is this the case? Location is the reason why.

Every detail of a property can be changed. A house coming apart can be renovated or torn down and replaced with a new one. If it's too small, with some work, a property can be increased. But the one thing that stays with you forever, though, is the location of your property. One great location is enough to transform a neighborhood as quickly as overnight. Take Downtown Raleigh, North Carolina, for instance.

Supply and demand are some key factors in how real estate grows in value over time. And if there's anything we know about the finest areas, it's that the properties there are limited. And since they're such desirable places, the demand for properties there is high. And with such a fixed and limited supply, the values of properties in the area continue to grow.

Why Is Location Important?

A real estate cliche states that the three most crucial factors for buying properties are location, location, and location. Usually, many people base their decisions to buy a property on how well they like the place, forgetting that they are getting more than just a building in the deal.

They are also getting land, and—in turn—a chunk of the neighborhood. The house erected on the land can be rebuilt, remodeled, or renovated—but there's no moving that land to someplace else. The clearest depiction of this situation is in suburban neighborhoods, where properties have defined limits.

But bad locations aren't limited to places outside of cities alone. Even when buying properties in a city, you would still be investing in a particular location. And a city block could be a bad or good investment similar to buying property in a suburban neighborhood. This means that the single most important factor affecting the price of real estate is location. And as we covered earlier, the importance of location boils down to supply and demand. High demands for homes in desirable locations meet a fixed and limited supply.

Factors Influencing Location

Proximity to transportation networks and amenities are influencing factors: The value of a location is important to buyers and investors for many reasons, one of which is the desire to be close to transportation facilities and other amenities. This could mean proximity to grocery stores, important roads, subway stations, restaurants, bus stops, dry cleaners, and shopping and entertainment. People don't want to travel for miles to reach these amenities. Additionally, the presence of these amenities in an area make the place appealing—thereby driving up property value.

- **School zones**: School districts determine the quality of schools you get in an area, whether private-owned or public. They also influence other factors, like bus stops and surrounding properties. As a result, the value of a location is tied to its school zone, and with it, the properties located there. This is especially the case for areas that are more family-oriented and occupied by people with kids of school age.

  But don't buy properties in every school zone whether or not you have school-age kids. What you want to look out for is the quality of schools in that zone. If you buy a property within a school district with good schools, your property will maintain and grow in value over time.

- **Neighbors**: Like location, you can't change your neighbors once you buy a property—unless you get fed up and leave or they move by some miracle. If your neighbors aren't the most desirable—like neighbors with loud, nocturnal, or dangerous pets, or a fraternity house—the value of your property will take a huge hit during resale. So, before finalizing the deal on a house, take your time to go through the neighborhood. If possible, meet up with some neighbors and try to get a rapport going. They should help you better understand the street and potential pet peeves you could encounter. But besides looking out for the profitability of your investment, you also want to make sure your neighbors are people you can be safe living next to.

- **Crime rate**: It goes without saying that crime rate and safety are important factors to look for in a location. It's not like anyone goes out of their way to look for dangerous and crime-ridden neighborhoods. So, do your research. Check online for local crime rates and reports in the area you want to invest in.

How to Find the Right Location

Lifestyle Preferences

Lifestyle preferences is a recurring theme in recent years, especially among millennial buyers and investors. More people want to purchase properties that reflect or complement their habits and lifestyle choices. And for good reasons, too.

When deciding on a location based on your lifestyle preferences, here are a few questions to answer:

- Do you want to live in a small, quiet town or a large, bustling city?

- How do you wish to live your life and what habits and hobbies take up your time?

- Would you like to try sporting activities like kayaking, surfing, snowboarding, surfing, skiing, biking, skating, etc.?

- Do you want to live close to a body of water or the view of the area?

Create a list of things you need and draw up a budget. Doing so will give you a template to narrow down properties, saving you time and effort. Instead, you will channel your resources into checking out properties that meet your taste.

Budget

Budgeting is the first thing you ought to figure out when choosing a location. If you plan on using cash, go through your financials to be sure of your outflow during the process. On the other hand, if you want to get a mortgage, speak with a loan agent to get a pre-approval. You will get a fixed loan amount based on your assets, credits, and income. With this in mind, you can begin trimming down listings to fit your budget.

Necessities

Don't get too hung up on the financials and forget about other necessary things. For instance, if you have school-age kids, you should go for properties in districts with good schools. You also want to get a property close to businesses that sell day-to-day goods and services, such as grocery stores, hardware stores, clothing stores, playgrounds, etc.

Sources of Income

Another crucial factor to bear in mind is your source of income. If you aren't a remote worker and need to commute to work to earn a living, you should only go for locations that make it easy to go to work, offer jobs peculiar to your skills, or allow you to start and run a business. A rural location may not be the most lucrative in terms of career opportunities needed to keep the property running and up to market standards. And even in places with job opportunities, you want to make sure that the cost of living doesn't overshadow the wages. Otherwise, you could run into debt.

Chapter 35:

Building a Real Estate Team

So you are no longer a newbie to real estate. You have been navigating the market for some years now, establishing a professional brand, great portfolio, and good returns. Business is coming in regularly and you are starting to stretch thin with responsibilities. That's the telltale sign that it's time to get a real estate team behind you.

Those who went through this phase know that it's the beginning of all the fun real estate promises. But how would you know you are ready to run a team and it's not just the stress getting to you?

Let's find out, in this step-by-step guide to creating the ultimate real estate team (insert superhero explosion background).

Have a Business

It's silly that this has to be mentioned, but it's important, too. To get a team, you need a business. And not just something you started as a hobby last night. You need a business and related responsibilities to justify why you need extra hands on deck.

Your responsibilities are enormous as a real estate agent, from dealing with mortgage brokers, running ad campaigns, running open houses and property tours, prospecting new leads, and more. Your hands are full of things to do more than half the time, and you can't let go or postpone, because these tasks are crucial to your career and business success. And as you grow into a more reputable brand, business also increases. That means more responsibilities to deal with and even bigger shoes to grow into.

You are only human at the end of the day, and you will reach your limit at some point. Whether it's sleepless nights or missing meals or having to multitask; sooner or later, something is going to give and you will begin turning down clients or defaulting on responsibilities. While this can be seen as a good problem, because it's a sign of booming business, it's still a problem. And that isn't a good thing to have.

It makes sense to assemble a team and begin your crusade throughout the real estate industry. But are you prepared for the leadership requirements that come with it?

Leading a real estate team isn't a walk in the park. It's not something you can wing—you must be ready professionally, financially, and mentally to have any chance of pulling it off. If there were any magic strings to pull, I'd tell you. But there are none. You manage your team according to the people you have.

Prepare your Underlying Systems

Every winning team is built on a game plan. When putting together a real estate team, first, you must set revenue goals. Then, you can decide on the amount of leads to target and the team members necessary for meeting these targets. As the head of the team, you automatically become the Chief Lead Generator. And while it's important to have enough team members on ground to deal with multiple leads, you also need a good system in place for when the volume of leads increases.

Here are some necessary systems that would provide a sturdy backbone for your team:

- **Business plan, vision, and goals**: What financial goals did you set, and how do you aim to attain them? Have you any plans on navigating these goals? Are there good qualities motivating your business?

- **Branding guidelines**: What slogan, color palette, logos, and fonts will be used by your team? What look will your listing packages, business cards, signs, and website carry?

- **Client database growth and maintenance plans**: What's your plan for growing and maintaining your customer base? Do you have a working follow-up system? Do you have software for managing contacts?

- **Online presence and content marketing**: Do you have a real estate website for your business? What's your plan for marketing properties online? Are there any plans for growing your business' online presence going forward? What type of content do you have in mind?

- **Transaction management systems**: What software will you use for processing business transactions in real estate?

- **Tools and software**: Will you need some tools and productivity software for real estate?

- **Identifying your ideal team members**: Sometimes, you could hit a productivity patch, in which you go through business tasks and activities in a blur. Everything is going smoothly and the world becomes your oyster. But just as you start running at peak productivity, you are suddenly behind on a million tasks that should have been completed the day before. At this point, it makes sense to shake the hand of the first person that walks into your office and decides to be a part of your team.

But that's not the smartest thing to do. The wrong team member can turn a day's work into a month's, if not more. Instead, go for team members with the right personality and mindset for your team and not just any rookie eager to prove themselves. A bad hire will have you spending mental energy and time on all the wrong things. And a team member with a poor attitude will stink up the place and ruin the morale of other team members. You also want to avoid disruptive people, as they are prone to causing workplace conflict and attempting underhanded business practices.

Personality assessment tools can help you get started on identifying the right people for your job.

Using a Practical Team Structure

Having the right people on your team isn't going to solve all your problems if you don't know how to use them correctly. You need to position them just right with an organizational structure that works. This also goes for the compensation model.

There are several methods of structuring your real estate team. To decide on a model that best suits your business and plans, you need to work based on your goals, preferences, and experience.

Here are a few of the best real estate models to consider for your team:

- **The mentor-mentee model**: In this model, the team members you recruit will be under your mentorship to mature into successful real estate agents. After the mentorship period, they grow out of the mentee status and relocate to another part of the system—as a downline. There, they can be committed to other things or begin mentoring the next generation of team members. This model works if you like teaching others. It's also a means of getting some passive income outside of your business.

- **The team lead model**: This model takes on a more traditional approach that focuses on your personal brand as the team leader. If you already have a strong and established personal brand or want to create one, this model is the best for you.

- **The lead team model**: Unlike the team lead model, this structure is focused on getting inbound leads. The only thing that might make this model unsuitable for everybody is that it's expensive. But that is only because it guarantees the highest growth rate compared to others. To succeed in this model, you need a great marketing and lead generation system. If that sounds like your thing, go for the lead team model.

  Finally, the expectations you set for your team members, as well as how much support you provide them, determines their compensation at the end of the day.

- **Get an administrative assistant**: If you are unsure of who to hire first when building a real estate team, you are not alone. Real estate team leaders are divided on the subject, too. Some believe that hiring a buyer's agent first is best because these team members don't work for salary. Instead, they earn commissions based on deals they help close. So, hiring them won't start costing you money from the start, and will help to bring in income through lead conversion while you are busy with other things.

  However, on another hand, it's a wiser choice to get an assistant as your first hire. And it makes sense why. For one, assistants are better off as your first hires, long before you even start considering buyer's agents. With an assistant, you will have another pair of hands that will see to the smooth running of your business' systems until team members are hired to fill specific roles.

  In addition, an administrative assistant will also help manage contracts from the first stage of drafting to the end when the deal is finalized. Doing so will free up time for you or a buyer's agent, which would otherwise have been spent on paperwork.

Chapter 36:

Due Diligence and How to Do It

Right

Due diligence is a term that we have heard many times. It's even been mentioned several times in this book so far. But what does it mean?

Due diligence is an important aspect of business, especially the buying and selling of real estate. To make sure due diligence is performed on a property, all the parties involved must look into the situation and confirm that every aspect of the deal is coveted, including legal, contracts, conditions, and provisions, among other concerns.

The process involved in due diligence might be the most crucial part of a real estate transaction, especially after the commercial aspect has been finalized. The process can influence the proceedings of the transaction, including the commercial aspect and if the deal will go through. Although the commercial side of the transaction is focused on concluding the deal as quickly as possible, it's in the best interest of every party involved to make time for and pay attention to due diligence.

By doing so, they can find out more about issues that could affect the nature of the property and determine if the commercials will be renegotiated, such as legality of construction, title, encumbrances and easements, and permitted use.

How Due Diligence Works

Usually, many residential real estate contracts come with a due diligence period built into the details. In some states, you can have as many as 10 days, while others allow for 15 or more days. Sometimes, the period of due diligence begins from when the contract is agreed on by the seller and buyer. On the other hand, the due diligence period can also be started by an escrow.

Of course, it's not compulsory for the parties involved to stick to the rules in the contract. There is room to negotiate a more convenient time for everyone involved.

However, as a rule of thumb, you shouldn't agree to a short time line for due diligence because it won't give you enough time to completely go over the property and be assured of its value. Granted, you can ask for an extension on the time line—but there's also a possibility that the seller could refuse. If you take the refusal as a red flag and pass on the property, you could risk losing your earnest money deposit.

Remember, when investing in properties—especially ones that will generate income in the future—you should look beyond physical appeal.

Types of Due Diligence

Due diligence reports come in two main forms. They are:

- **Limited search report**: This type of due diligence report is often used for property deals involving leases. They are often limited to a time frame of 15 years.

- **Full search report**: A full search due diligence report is more in-depth than the limited search report. It is mostly used in deals for property sales, and involves a title period beginning from a 30-year period from the date when the seller first came to be. The report provides more details about every aspect of a property's history.

Why Due Diligence Is Necessary

Due diligence is the only way to find out and confirm all the facts about a property, including its title, history, deeds, etc.

The 'title' of a property means the right one has it. This doesn't necessarily mean that one is the owner of the property. On the other hand, it also means one has control over the property as a possessor, permanent lessee, or owner. For a title to be marketable, it must be valid and free of doubts. The title documents must contain papers about an agreed plan layout. In turn, the plan should be verified by the land records officer.

The aim of due diligence is to confirm the ownership of title of a property, as well as potential encumbrances that may exist. As such, it protects you from preexisting claims on a property that could be bad for business in the future. These claims may affect the transfer of ownership of the property from the seller to the buyer. Alternatively, it could still be attached to a property even after the transfer of ownership.

As a result, the primary concern of due diligence is information gathering. But the type of due diligence that will be applied in a deal, as well as how long it will take, falls to the lawyer of the buyer and depends on certain factors, such as the following:

The Type of Real Estate Assets

- the business goals of the lessee of buyer and their risk profile

- the type of real estate transaction (i.e., whether it's a mortgage or financing, cash purchase, or short-term or long-term lease of the property)

- whether or not the buyer will be financed by a third-party before or after the transaction

- the time taken to complete the deal

Meanwhile, for a likely purchase, lease, or financing of a property, due diligence is done on the title to answer three main questions:

- What types of restrictions on the use of the property will the buyer or lessee have to deal with?

- Does the property lessor or owner have the power, right, or interest to go into negotiations involving the said property?

- Are there any liens on the property that must be met before negotiations can be completed and the deal finalized? These liens would take the form of easements, unpaid taxes, mortgages, litigation, acquisitions, and charges, among other assessments.

Besides performing due diligence when buying or leasing properties, the procedure also applies for mortgaging properties with a lender or financial institution like banks. In this case, the borrower will perform due diligence on its own or require the property owner to provide a due diligence report of the said property.

Here is a breakdown of the steps used in conducting a due diligence report. For the report to be valid, the following areas of the property must be looked into:

Encumbrances on the Property

- the nature of the right of the present owner over the property (and whether or not the right can be transferred)

- the legal capacity of the current property owner (whether the person has the legal standing to enter into an irreversible contract for leasing, selling, or mortgaging the property)

- the source of the right of the present owner

- if the property has any acquisition process in its history

- the legality of the property

Chapter 37:

The Entrepreneurial Mindset

An entrepreneurial mindset is an important ingredient for real estate success, because it contains strong motivation and an eager to learn mentality. Generally, the right mindset is just as crucial as your ability to take action. For perspective: Every year, more than one million people in the United States try to start a business. Within the first year, about 40% of these new businesses will fall flat and never return. In five years, the number jumps to 80% that never survive. And even if this 80% tries hard enough to stay afloat, they will most likely not reach their potential.

As a fresh face in real estate, you will make mistakes—it's a given. In fact, you might wind up making a truckload of errors. But it's not making the mistakes that will affect your career, it's the mindset to overcome the hurdles. It also determines how your experience in the industry will turn out, as well as your development over time.

Investing in real estate is as much about specific skill sets as it is about having the mindset of an entrepreneur—at the very least, having the clarity to invest wisely and the ability to be logical when making deals. You can't run a real estate business successfully if you don't even have the skill set to compete in the market. And you most certainly can't meet your true potential if your mindset is anything but entrepreneurial. Although these traits go hand in hand for success as a real estate investor, one is more important than the other: the entrepreneurial mindset.

Knowing how to invest will make you one of the best in the industry, without a doubt. However, not having the proper mindset will only take you so far. As great as your skills might be, not knowing how to apply them makes you no different from someone without skills. That said, the most powerful tool you can use in real estate is an entrepreneurial mindset. Not only will it help to kickstart your ideas and goals, but it will also boost the skills you already have. Put simply, an entrepreneurial mindset is the foundation of everything you want to build in real estate. If you make it deep and sturdy, you will be able to build your career as high and mighty as you like and vice versa.

Why and How to Sharpen Your Entrepreneurial Skills

- **For meaningful relationships with other entrepreneurs**: Social media platforms like LinkedIn and Twitter are great places for meeting key people in the industry and finding out what they are up to. Better still, you can create a list filter to decide the type of content that is on your feed.

  To create a list filter, enter the hashtags of subjects that are important to you. Another list should focus on the entrepreneurs that you relate to or admire, and another one could help you identify key figures.

  Finally, you can become a member of an entrepreneur organization. There are both paid-for and free ones that offer upskilling programs. Doing this will bring you in close contact with many entrepreneurs on the same stage as you. You are one Internet search away from finding the closest entrepreneur organizations near you.

- **Upgrade your skills**: Real estate and entrepreneurship are two fields with markets that change frequently, so it's important to not believe that you know it all. Instead, be willing to learn and grow. Understand that the changes may sometimes be above your skill set or knowledge. But as long as you are willing to learn, there's no stopping you. In fact, it makes you a leader by example to your team, who will then be driven to emulate your attitude.

  If you don't know how to go about improving your skills, consider working on your soft skills first, like communication skills, empathy, public speaking, and active listening.

- **Connect with a business coach**: Learning from others' experiences is a great way to improve your entrepreneurial skills. To do this, you will need a seasoned business coach. These people are often expert entrepreneurs, small business owners, and business executives who can guide and advise you on your journey. It works best if the person is an expert in real estate too. Now, you can learn certain concepts that will evolve your business.

A business coach will help with informed decision-making, problem-solving, working on weaknesses and shortcomings, and defining your vision.

- **Make time to chill**: Between working on your business, leading a team, and being proactive as an entrepreneur, you are going to have a lot of responsibilities. You also have talks to prepare for, elevator pitches to finish, events to attend, and meetings to host. While your skills will improve, no doubt, you will also run out of time for yourself.

Instead, take the time out to catch a film, read a book (not one about work), go for a swim, go for a run, or get a massage. Just relax and de-stress for a bit.

- **Grow the people around you**: As a team leader, you can improve your entrepreneurial skills by developing your team members and guiding them to successful careers. You should be proactive about their welfare and actively contribute resources to helping them achieve their objectives on both professional and personal levels. Additionally, look for new and exciting ways to empower those around you to push beyond their limits, look for opportunities to establish themselves, and take responsibility for situations.

To do this, create a system that allows for flexibility in working hours, training opportunities, and a channel for feedback and active communication.

- **Practice self-awareness**: Self-awareness is the sense of knowing yourself, including your personality. It also involves finding out your weaknesses and strengths to be able to draw upon your skills, lead your business, and grow your team successfully.

The best way to practice self-awareness is to be aware of your emotions at every moment, because knowing how to keep your emotions in check will improve your decision-making and help you avoid irrational decisions. You should also learn to take healthy risks, as they will put you in a position to think quickly and logically with all you have learned.

In all you do, remember: patience. Taking things one step at a time will allow you to pace yourself and identify problems in time to make good decisions. Look for new means of improving your creativity and personal growth. Finally, be aware of your mistakes and learn from them. It takes a lot of discipline to pull this off, but when you do, you won't be stuck in the past and can use your errors to fuel your growth.

- **Test your limits**: Challenges are the best test of skills. And the best way to keep your skills sharp at all times is to leave your comfort zone regularly. This will give you a chance to learn a lot. So, set a goal that tests your limits and creates a sensible deadline, and try to accomplish that said goal.

  For instance, say, you improve your client base. You can set a goal to get five new and regular clients within a year. The success of this challenge isn't in meeting this goal, but your attempt to do so. The effort made to get new clients will improve your acquisition skills, making it easier to close leads in the future. And if you do meet the goal, then it's time to review your weaknesses, strengths, and efforts and begin working to improve yourself ahead of your next responsibility or goal.

Many of the entrepreneurial skills you need to succeed in real estate are already a part of you. They come naturally, and just need to be sharpened. Others can be learned and improved upon with education, training, and experience. There are many channels that can help you improve your entrepreneurial skills, whether it's entrepreneur-related platforms like Marketing and Entrepreneurship, Gary Vaynerchuk's

Blog, Small Business Trends, Harvard Business Review, or MBA programs.

MBA programs are common routes for many people who wish to work with financial institutions in real estate. These programs also help teach them about starting up businesses and leading in management positions.

As you develop the entrepreneurial mindset, bear in mind that things won't always go as expected. Even great plans and perfect executions can sometimes fail because of bad luck, competition, and market factors. Of course, the numbers don't look good for new businesses. But for every 8 out of 10 businesses that fail, 2 more succeed. Even if the odds are one in a million, someone has to be that one. And that could be you. It just depends on how much you want it.

Chapter 38:

How to Determine Property Value

It's normal for people to think about the value of the property they own or want to buy. But how do you know the value of a property? The short answer is relatively straightforward: The value of a property is the amount a seller and buyer have agreed upon.

The long answer, however, is more complex. The value of a property depends on many factors, like the state of the market, the financing details (is it through cash or a loan), and the seller (is it a lender, a foreclosure, or an REO?).

It's important to know how to calculate a property's value, because it puts you in a better position for refinancing, selling, buying, using built-up equity, and negotiating for a reduced property tax rate. This knowledge also helps you know how in-shape you are financially, if you are a property owner. The Harris Poll conducted an online survey in 2028, which found that 73% of Americans think that the value of their homes is a crucial detail in their finances.

Why Property Value Is Important

Having an estimated property value is important in real estate for many reasons, such as taxation, investment analysis, financing, property insurance, and sales listing. But in terms of selling and buying properties as a business, the first step is usually to find out the worth of a property.

While it might seem like a simple process, it's far more complex, and requires a lot of factors. It gets even worse when the property is commercial and brings in revenue. How hard can it get? Just remember that we have professional appraisals for a reason. And no, it's not a fancy job.

Concepts Used in Property Valuation

From a technical angle, the value of a property is the current worth of all the future benefits that you can get by owning the property. And unlike other consumer goods that can be used up quickly, like toothpaste or food, real estate lasts a long time—which means the benefits can change hands from one generation to the next. As a result, the estimated worth of a property has to consider social and economic factors, as well as environmental conditions and governmental regulations and controls.

These factors are important details, because they affect the four main value points of a property:

- **Transferability**: This refers to how easy it is to transfer the rights of ownership of a property from the seller to buyer.

- **Demand**: This refers to the need to own property, and is backed up by the financial power to meet this need.

- **Scarcity**: There is a limited number of competing properties. So, supply is fixed. And when demand is greater than supply, scarcity is created.

- **Utility**: This concerns the ability of the property to meet the needs and desires of its future owners.

That said, here are some concepts that are important during property valuation:

- **Market value**: Market value refers to a professional opinion about the likely price a property can be sold for without any kickbacks or concessions from a buyer. A property's market value is based on factors such as the value of similar properties in an area, supply and demand, benefits of the property, the local real estate industry, and unique features in the property.

  While market value and market price are sometimes used interchangeably, they don't mean the same thing. A property's market price may be higher or lower than the market value. Why? Because the price of a property is the amount the seller wishes to exchange for ownership. So, it could be the same as market value or it might be higher or lower. For example, in distress sales, where sellers want money quickly, they are less likely to stick to market value and will sell for cheaper.

- **Value versus cost and price**: As mentioned above, property value isn't always the same as property price. The same also gives for costs. The cost of a property involves all the expenses that went into the property, such as labor, materials, etc.

  Of course, though price and cost are considered when valuing a property, they do not decide the value. For instance, while the selling price of a house might be $300,000, the value could be lower ($150,000) or higher ($500,000). So, if the property is actually valued at $500,000, but is located near an industrial area, the pricing could increase or decrease.

Formulas for Determining Property Value

The process of determining the value of a property is known as appraisal. For an appraisal to be accurate, it needs to collect data methodically—and not just any type of data. It needs certain data that concern the details of the property itself, as well as other general data like the neighborhood, city, region, and country of location. All of this data is for deciding on property value.

There are several methods used in appraisals, including the following:

The Income Capitalization Method

This method is also known as the income approach. It's all about finding the connection between the net income brought in by a property and the rate of return an investor is looking for. This method is often used to find the value of properties that produce income, such as shopping centers, apartment complexes, and office buildings.

Using the income capitalization method for appraisals is simple, especially if the property is still expected to bring in income in the future. It also helps when the cost of running the property is steady and predictable.

Direct Capitalization

Here are some steps used during appraisals when determining the value of a property using direct capitalization:

- Find the total income the property is expected to generate each year. Consider factors like rent collection losses and vacancy when calculating the effective gross income. Subtract the cost of running the property each year to find the yearly total operating income. Determine a rough estimate of how much an investor might be willing to pay for the income produced by the property of specific class and type. To do this, find an estimate of the capitalization or return rate.

- Add the capitalization rate to the net operating income of the property to get an estimate of the property's worth.

The Gross Income Multiplier Method

This method is mostly used for appraising properties that aren't bought to generate income, although they can be used as a rental. An example of such properties are one-family or two-family homes. In this case, the gross income multiplier (GIM) method connects the income expected as rent to the selling price of the property.

When dealing with industrial or commercial properties, the total income per year is used. But for residential properties, the total monthly income is preferred. Here is how the gross income multiplier method is used for finding the value of properties:

Gross Income Multiplier = Sales Price / Rental Income

You can also collect data from recent rentals and sales from three properties of the same stature to get a more accurate GIM. Once you have found the GIM, you can use it on the estimated fair market rental of the property to figure out its real market value. To calculate, use the formula:

Rental Income x GIM = Estimated Market Value

The Cost Method

The cost method is used for finding the estimated property value when one or more buildings have been improved. This method uses two different estates of the land and the building, and considers depreciation value, too. Then, the estimates are added to find the value of the property from an improved point of view.

The cost method assumes that any reasonable buyer won't want to spend more on an improved property when they can spend less on buying a land and erecting the same property. This method is best used to value properties that aren't sold regularly and don't bring in income, such as government buildings, churches, schools, and hospitals.

The cost of the building is determined in several ways, such as:

- **The quantity-survey method**: This finds the amount of raw materials needed for replacing the property, as well as the present cost of these materials and how much would be required to install them.

- **The unit-in-place method**: Here, costs are calculated using the cost of constructing every unit in the different parts of the property, including materials and labor.

- **The square-foot method**: This approach uses the cost per square foot of a newly-built property, similar to the one being sold to multiply the amount of square feet in the property being sold.

Depreciation

Depreciation during appraisals means conditions that could negatively affect the value of a property, thereby reducing it. This factor must be looked into during every appraisal.

Depreciation comes in many forms, such as the following:

- **Economic obsolescence**: This is caused by external factors that affect the value and desirableness of a property, like being close to a polluting factory, noisy railway, or busy intersection.

- **Functional obsolescence**: This involves features in the design and physical aspect of a property that aren't appealing to a property buyer, like a property with multiple bedrooms but just one toilet, outdated fixtures, and out-of-style appliances.

- **Physical wear and tear**: This concerns physical breakdown, including ones that can be solved—like roof replacement and painting—or unsolvable ones like problems in the structure.

How to measure property value with depreciation

- Find a rough estimated value of the land, like if it was vacant and ready for sale. Since land cannot depreciate, the sales comparison method will give you a better calculation method.

- Find the estimated cost of erecting a building and doing site improvements presently.

- Determine the cost of depreciation on the improvements made due to economic obsolescence, functional obsolescence, and general deterioration.

- Subtract the cost of depreciation from the estimated cost of construction.

- Find the sum of the depreciated cost of construction and site improvements and the estimated land value. The amount you get is the current value of the property.

The Sales Comparison Method

This method of appraisal is often used for finding the value of land and single-family properties. It is also known as the market data approach, and is obtained by comparing the value of recent properties sold in an area with the property to be sold or bought. For this to work, the properties involved must have similar features, called comparables.

There are other factors comparables must reach to be valid, such as:

- There must be three to four comparables in during the appraisal process.

- The comparable properties have to have been sold under regular market conditions.

- The properties must be as similar as possible in size and features.

- The comparable properties have to have been sold in an open and competitive market within the last year.

- The main factors used for selecting comparables are location, similar features, and size. However, location is the most important factor, as it affects the value of properties more than size and features.

Comparables' Qualities

If you are wondering how two properties can be very similar, it's not always the case. Properties may share some things in common, but they are never exactly alike. To make up for these differences, the selling prices of other comparable properties will be adjusted to consider factors like dissimilar features, which could affect the value of the property. Other factors include:

- terms and conditions of sale—this factor works for when the comparables were sold under duress or between friends and family (where discount might be applied)

- history and condition of the properties

- location, because the same property will have different prices depending on the neighborhood it is in

- physical features, such as type and number of rooms, landscaping, hardwood floors, lot size, a garage, construction type and quality, central air, square feet of living space, a fireplace, kitchen upgrades, a pool, and so on

- time of sale—this applies for when economic changes occur between when comparable properties are sold and the time of appraisal of the current property

Often, the market value of the property you want to buy will be around the amount calculated from adjusting the selling price of other comparable properties. Also, because some adjustments are more from a personal point of view than others, the estimated value of the property to be sold or bought will fall between the comparables with little to no price adjustments.

The Absolute and Relative Valuation Methods

The absolute valuation method is used to find the current value of cash flow that a property will generate in the future. This data is then used to find the internal value of the property. The most common approaches used in the valuation method are the discounted cash flow (DCF) and dividend discount model (DDM) techniques.

On another hand, relative value methods show that two comparable properties should have a similar price based on how much money they create. This brings us to ratios like price-to-sales and price-to-earnings (P/E), which are used to compare properties in the same area to find out which has the highest or lowest value.

Discounting Future Net Operating Income

Here's a formula for finding the value of a property using its discounted net operating income:

$$Market\ Value = NOI1\ /\ r-g = NOI1\ /\ R$$

where,

- the net operating income is NOI

- r is the required rate of return on real estate assets

- g is the growth rate of NOI

- R is the capitalization rate $(r-g)$

The NOI shows the amount a property will bring in after its running costs have been removed, but just before interest payments and taxes are removed. However, before all these expenses are removed, we must first find the total revenue gained by the property.

The revenue generated from rent can be determined using other comparable properties in the area. With enough research, investors can easily find out the prices that tenants pay as rent in an area and use the same figure on the property. Of course, the process also takes note of potential rent increments in the future, under growth rate, as we see in the formula (g).

For a rental property, we can't forget that high tenant turnover or vacancy rate can be bad for business. So, this is also taken into consideration in this method using a realistic conservative estimate or a sensitivity analysis. With these tools, we can now figure out the income that won't come in when the property isn't used to its full potential.

The operating expenses considered are usually the ones that happen directly every other day in the property, like cost of utilities, management fees, property insurance, and maintenance fees. Keep in mind that when calculating for total expense, the process doesn't concern depreciation. As a result, the net running cost of a property is similar to the amount it generates before expenses like depreciation, interest, amortization, and taxes.

When the NOI is taken away from the equation through cap rate, this is similar to removing a future source of income through the appropriate required rate of return, with adjustments made for income growth.

The Capitalization Rate Method

Choosing a good capitalization rate (or cap rate) is one of the major assumptions you have to make when finding the value of a property.

So, What Is Capitalization Rate?

It is the rate of return a property is expected to produce, including depreciation and net of value appreciation. In simpler terms, it is the rate used in net operating income (NOI) to find out the current value of a property.

For instance, say, you believe that a property will generate an NOI of $5 million within the next decade (10 years). If a discounted cap rate of 25% is used, the property will currently be valued in the market in the ways described below.

For example, assume a property is expected to generate NOI of $1 million over the next 10 years. If it were discounted at a capitalization rate of 14%, the market value of the property would be:

20,000,000 ($5,000,000 / 0.25); where the market value is equal to the net operating income (NOI) divided by the capitalization rate.

But how do we figure out the capitalization rate to use? We can't value a property that brings in income without it. And it's not like we can pick a number at random. The process is a little more complex than finding the weighted average cost of capital (WACC) of an organization, but there are a couple of methods we could try before settling on the best cap rate. They are:

The Band-of-Investment Method

When using this method, we can find the cap rate on a property from the interest rates on properties using both equity and debt financing. One of the best things about this method is that it gives you the most correct cap rate for financed properties.

To use this method, you first have to find the sinking fund factor. This refers to a certain percentage that you must set aside every time you have a specific amount of money in the future.

Let's take an example. Say, a property is 50% financed at an 11% interest rate for a period of 17 years, and has an NOI of $2,500,000. Then the other 50% is covered by equity given a rate of return of 20%. To find the sinking fund factor, we will use the formula below:

$$SFF = i \:/\: (1+r)^n - 1$$

where,

- SFF is the sinking fund factor

- i is the periodic interest rate

- r is also the annual percentage rate

- n is the number of periods, often expressed in years

When we put the numbers in, we get:

$$0.11 \;/\; (1 + 0.11)^{17} - 1$$

Let's say the value we get is 3.98%. Then, to find the rate for settling the lender, we will add the interest rate to the sinking fund factor. For this instance, it will be (0.11 + 0.0398), which is 14.98%.

That said, we have to find the overall cap rate, or the weighted average rate, using the 50% weights for both equity and debt. This leads us to the following:

$$14.98\% \; [(0.5 \times 0.1498) + (0.5 \times 0.20)]$$

Once this is calculated, we get the real market value of the property, which is:

$$(\$\,2,500,000 \;/\; 0.1498) = 16,688,919$$

The Market-Extraction Method

In the market-extraction method, we assume that the NOI is current and available, as well as the data on the selling price of other comparable properties that bring in income. The upside of using this method is that the direct income capitalization is more useful because of the cap rate.

Here, we will still try to figure out the cap rate. But it's more straightforward. Take, for instance, a buyer purchases a parking lot with the expectation that it will rake in an NOI of $ 1,000,000. In that neighborhood, we can use three other comparable parking lots that generate money as follows:

Let's call these lots Parking Lot A, Parking Lot B, and Parking Lot C

- Parking Lot A has a $500,000 NOI, and sold for $6 million. Thus, the cap rate on this property is 8.33%, as calculated using ($500,000 / $6,000,000).

- Parking Lot B has an $800,000 NOI, with a selling price of $7.35 million. The cap rate is thus 10.88% ($800,000 / $7,350,000).

- Parking Lot C has $370,000 in NOI and a selling price of $4 million. The cap rate is therefore 9.25% ($370,000 / $4,000,000).

To get the overall cap rate, we will find the average of all three cap rates from the comparable properties. The value is 9.30%, which is a fairly accurate sign of what's happening in the market. With this capitalization rate, investors can safely find the market value of the property they intend to buy.

The calculation for this property is as follows:

$$(\$1,000,000 \ / \ 0.0930) = \$10,752,688.2$$

The Build-up Method

Another common method for funding the capitalization rate of a property is using the build-up approach. To begin, we need the interest rate. Then, we can start adding other things such as:

- **Risk premium**: This shows the general risk exposure in the present market.

- **Recapture premium**: This deals with the total appreciation in the value of land.

- **Appropriate liquidity premium**: This comes about because real estate isn't very liquid.

For instance, using an interest rate of 5%, a non-liquidity rate of 2%, a risk rate of 3%, and a recapture premium of 2%, we can determine the cap rate of a property as follows:

$$(5\% + 2\% + 3\% + 2\%) = 12\%$$

So, if the property's net operating income (NOI) is $500,000, it's market value can be calculated as so:

$$(\$500,000 \ / \ 12\%) = \$4,166,667$$

This method is one of the easiest to use, because the calculation process is straightforward. However, where it becomes complex is when we try to find the accurate values of everything that goes into the cap rate. That can be a real challenge. The upside of using the build-up method is that it accurately identifies all the parts of a discount rate.

How to Find the Value of a Property

Search Online for Valuation Tools

A simple search about the value of your house will bring up tons of results about how to value your property. You aren't the first person with this question, and many people have come up with several answers over the years. In fact, about 22% of American homeowners who wanted to find out about their property's worth used one or more online estimators. These tools are known as automated valuation models (AVMs). They are often designed by real estate platforms and lending agencies—two bodies that use them the most.

The AVMs use some mathematical models and data from tax assessments, property transfers, and deeds of ownership to predict the value of properties using other data from the property's area, including the recent prices of listings and sales.

Here are some common automated valuation models that you can use on a property:

- **PropertyShark**: This tool contains well detailed data of residential property listings in New York City.

- **Just Sold by Realtor.com**: This tool from one of the biggest real estate platforms allows you to look up the prices and values of properties that were listed or sold in your area recently.

- **Homesnap**: This tool comes with a search portal that contains tons of data about property listings for different homes nationwide. It also contains photos and detailed information about the sales history of each property listing.

- **Federal Housing Finance Agency's (FHFA) House Price Index (HPI) Calculator**: This tool will be discussed in full below. But for now, just know that it can help you track the movement of prices in your area.

- **Neighborhood Scout**: Although real estate investors are the main users of this tool, anyone can use it to check property value. The platform provides custom study points that offer you information about different properties nationwide. Unlike the others, it's a paid-for tool.

How to Use the FHFA HPI Calculator

If you don't trust AVMs with your data or are not sure about their accuracy, but still want to easily value your property, the house price index by the Federal Housing Financing Agency is all you need.

It uses the repeat sales method and contains a lot of data about mortgage deals from the 1970s. Since the tool is run by a government agency and the government is aware of every detail of every property sale, it has one of the most accurate valuation systems of any other AVM.

The tool also monitors the changes in the value of a house every time it is sold, using this information to predict the change in value in the market at any one time.

Get a Real Estate Agent or Broker

Real estate agents and brokers have a unique skill set for telling the value of a property. So, having their expert opinion alongside your findings from AVMs can help you be sure of your property value. Often, realtors use Comparative Market Analysis (CMA) to determine the values of properties.

CMAs contain data about comparable properties (or comps) in a specific area. And as we discussed earlier, these properties can be used to figure out how much your property is worth. It shows details about the selling prices of similar properties in your area, as well as the time taken to sell them and if the selling price was lower or higher than the original listing price.

Realtors use CMAs to determine certain factors in recently bought properties, such as current selling price, property view and style, location, size, and property type (townhome, vacation home, condo, single-family unit, and so on).

In addition, real estate agents and brokers also take data from the Multiple Listing Service (MLS) in an area when preparing their CMA. The MLS is a property database for a specific area that contains all the properties that have been listed or pending sales.

But, sometimes, realtors may not use a CMA. Instead, they could use a Broker Price Opinion (BPO). This is another property valuation tool, but it requires a license to use in some states. CMAs, on the other hand, don't need a license. To find out more about BPO regulations in your state, check out the Appraisal Institute in your area.

That said, BPOs are typically shorter than CMAs and are mostly used for checking the value of foreclosed and short sale properties rather than regular property sales. Also, unlike CMAs, BPOs may not be free to use.

However, whether your realtor uses a BPO or a CMA, they can still misjudge the value of your property. Because they wouldn't be able to track all the property features that may influence value. But this doesn't mean that realtors aren't any good at valuing properties. There is simply an error percentage with their tools is all.

Get an Appraisal

Before you can convince a lender to finance a loan, they will need an appraisal of the property. Only then will they approve the mortgage. But as a property owner, you can get your property appraised whenever you want. Surveys show that over a fourth (28%) of American homeowners used an appraisal for determining the value of their property. That's 6% more than those who use AVMs.

The job of an appraiser is to value your property according to your needs. Sometimes, property owners may want to know the value of their property at a past date or any other random time. Other times, they want to know the market value currently to decide whether to sell or refinance.

Unlike realtors, the tool of choice for many appraisers is the Fannie Mae's Uniform Residential Appraisal Report. It's used as a guide during the appraising process. Think of it as a checklist of things that appraisers have to look for to decide the value of your property.

Here are some things you might find in the report:

- **Foundation**: What type of foundation is the building erected on?

- **Location**: What state, area, and neighborhood is the property located in?

- **Time**: When was the property erected?

- **Amenities**: Are there any amenities on the property, like a fireplace, deck, or pool?

- **Improvements and repair**: What's the improvement and repair history of the property?

- **Market**: What is the state of the current real estate market in the property's neighborhood?

- **Fixtures and utilities**: What is the state of fixtures and utilities on the property?

- **Appliances**: Are there any appliances in the property? If yes, what condition are they in?

- **Comparable properties**: This concerns factors like depreciation, listings, cost price, sales, and vacancies in other similar properties in the same area.

- **Damages**: Are there signs of damages that may affect the structural integrity of the property?

- **Repairs and maintenance**: Will the property require repair or maintenance to be livable?

- **Extra spaces and systems**: What is the state of the doors, windows, heating and cooling systems, basement, walls, and attic?

- **Area**: Is the property located within or outside a Federal Emergency Management Agency (FEMA) flood zone?

- **Features**: What are the features of the property, including the land that it's erected on?

All these details (and others) are then combined to form the appraiser's opinion on the value of your home. It will be sent to you as an official report.

It's much easier to negotiate and close a deal when you are well aware of the value of a property through careful research and calculations. You can even go with reports from realtors and appraisers to improve your chances of a decent deal.

However, don't forget that the idea behind valuing a property is to know the right time and price to buy or sell that meets your needs.

Chapter 39:

Understanding Market

Segmentation

The real estate market is divided into three major segments, namely: industrial, commercial, and residential real estate. Without further ado, let's get into them:

Industrial Real Estate

The industrial segment of the real estate market is made up of properties used in production and manufacturing processes. Think warehouses, factories, and plants. Utility companies also fit in here, as they usually own and run several real estate assets, such as power plants, landed properties, and other things that contribute to power generation.

Commercial Real Estate

The commercial real estate segment deals with properties that are mainly used for business, including but not limited to hotels, shopping centers, office spaces, retail stores, and massage parlors, among other business enterprises. As of 2018, the estimated value of the commercial real estate sector was around $16 trillion. However, as the global economy continues to show price fluctuations, many investors aren't so eager to keep investing in the market.

Deloitte published an outlook of the commercial real estate segment in 2021. According to the report, up to 47% of commercial real estate businesses in North America expect rentals to fall, with 49% expecting vacancy to increase.

Residential Real Estate

The residential aspect of real estate deals with selling or buying properties used for non-professional purposes, like homes. This segment of the market is very diverse, and is made up of planned units, single-family homes, condominiums, multifamily units, apartments, etc. As of 2021, the residential real estate market was the fastest growing of the lot, with a steady increase in value over the years.

By May 2021, the median prices of residential properties climbed to about $337,400, while the general market was worth over $33.8 trillion. Although there have been many debates about the demographic buying properties recently between Gen Z and millennials, the price of residential real estate in the years to come will generally depend on the growth of large cities and urbanization.

While these real estate segments are the main divides in the market, there are other segments that further explain what happens in the market. This time, we will be considering real estate segmentation from a who, where, why, and how perspective.

Psychographic Segmentation (The Why Factor)

The psychographic segment of the real estate market involves the personalities, interests, and lifestyles of customers. Here, the reason properties are bought, sold, or rented depend on factors such as beliefs, values, hobbies, lifestyles, life goals, and personality traits.

In comparison to other segments in this section, it's much harder to identify this segment of the market. When dealing with this group, it's important to do your homework properly. Since they are intrinsically motivated, finding the right marketing strategy that speaks to them on a personal level is key.

Demographic Segmentation (The Who Factor)

Many people instantly think of demographic segmentation when they hear the term market segmentation. And for good reasons, too. This is definitely one of the easiest ways to divide the market. For example, baby boomers remain one of the major sectors in the real estate market to date.

Demographic segmentation deals with features that can be identified, unlike psychographic segmentation that deals with character. So, for this segment, the real estate market is chosen based on ethnicity, religion, age, income bracket, gender, profession, educational level, and religion.

Another example of demographic segmentation in real estate is targeting customers based on their professions. It's why we have housing plans for military veterans and service people. Or, homes for seniors, who are retiring or have retired. These properties will not fly with millennial property buyers.

Behavioral Segmentation (The How Factor)

Behavioral segmentation is one of the most useful and easiest techniques for segmenting the market, even more so for businesses. Like in psychographic segmentation, behavioral segmentation needs little to no data to work effectively, because it can be easily done online.

In e-commerce, for instance, the market is divided behaviorally based on browsing habits, brand loyalty, spending habits, brand interaction, purchasing habits, and prior product feedback. Some of these habits also apply in real estate, especially when you have a steady online presence. You can easily collect these datasets to find out the type of audiences you are attracting.

In addition, you can use the data to create relevant ad campaigns that appeal to your target market based on several behaviors they exhibit, such as the number of pages visited, how long they spent browsing your listings, other real estate sites visited, ad history, number of sessions on your platform, inactivity, etc.

For instance, you can easily tell first-time visitors apart from the regulars on your website, as well as people who have bought or sold properties through you. Using this data, you can easily prepare different messages for your audiences.

- **First-time visitor**: Browse our properties, complete with pictorial and video walk-throughs and property history.

- **Returning visitor**: Join our loyalty program and get massive savings on your next deal!

Geographic Segmentation (The Where Factor)

This form of market segmentation is the easiest to recognize, since it requires grouping the market based on its current physical location. In simple terms, it divides the market based on the most important factor in real estate: location.

There are several ways for defining geographical segmentation, such as postal code, region, country, city, state, district, etc. For instance, you can group potential clients within a specific neighborhood, making it easier to guide them on property tours, organize open houses, and close several deals in the same day. Geographical segmentation also helps with advertising, because you can appeal to your customers using the appealing factors a location offers.

Technographic Segmentation

Technographic segmentation is all about identifying and grouping the market based on their closeness to technology and the roles it takes on in their lives. This could mean picking out early adopters when creating new marketing campaigns or improving your medium of outreach. Technographic segmentation can be as easy as finding out the devices people use to look for when valuing properties, accessing real estate information, and looking for realtors.

This way, you can better position yourself to capture this tech-savvy group, and improve your brand image. For instance, many property owners go online to value their properties. Others go online to look for realtors and property deals near them. So, creating a good online presence that puts your business and services in their view increases your chances of closing leads.

Transactional Segmentation

Transactional segmentation has to do with previous interactions between a business and customer. Although behavioral segmentation can also work here, transactional segmentation has a much bigger scope of the market. It deals with how your business first came in contact with the customer (online or offline), how long ago they needed your services (for buying, selling, or appeasing property), and how much business they have brought to you.

Generational and Life Stage Segmentation

This market segmentation can also be seen as a part of demographic segmentation, because it's all about identifying customers based on factors like age. The only difference is that generational segmentation deals with a wider and more unique approach to age.

Life stage segmentation uses a similar strategy, but removes life experiences from age. Instead, here, the market is grouped based on factors like home ownership, marital status, with children or child-free (it also considers the age of the kids).

Firmographic Segmentation

The marketing segmentations we have talked about so far usually focus on business to customer (B2C) transactions. Firmographic segmentation, on the other hand, focuses on the world of business to business (B2B) transactions.

This form of market segmentation deals with analyzing and grouping business to business customers according to their features, attributes, and shared companies. Firmographic segmentation allows B2B companies to find out more about marketing strategies that work when targeting a specific audience. The process is just similar to how B2C marketing uses demographic segmentation.

In firmographic segmentation, there are eight main factors used to group customers. These are: location, executive title, status, company size, sales cycles stage, industry, number of employees, and performance.

Why Market Segmentation Is Important

- **Improved focus**: Knowing the right market segmentation will help your business meet its target audiences better. Because, instead of spreading your efforts and resources across the market, you can find your niche and give it your all. This way, your marketing goes beyond the surface and relates to the needs of your customers, and your research and efforts will go into meeting those needs.

  By doing so, your ad campaigns will be more effective and relatable, leads will close faster because clients get what they want, and demand for your services will be high. In the end, you will get good returns on your marketing campaign, and an extensive and diverse portfolio.

- **Improved customer base**: Real estate isn't like other businesses where you might have repeat customers. Usually, most buyers and sellers may never contact you again. Even if they do, it won't be as frequent as going to their favorite restaurant.

  But that's not a problem. As long as you do a good job of meeting their needs, rest assured, they have become unofficial marketers for you. They will most likely send their friends and family your way, making more business for you. And if your client is an investor with a huge property portfolio, you could get frequent business from them in the form of management or negotiations.

- **High-end leads**: As we discussed in chapter 15, it's easier to conquer a niche than to take on the entire market. The same applies here. You will be more successful targeting a specific segment of the market than attempting all the segments. That way, you can easily build up a solid base before going up against other established faces in the market.

- **Setting your brand apart**: Apart from allowing you to reach your target audience easily, market segmentation also allows your customers to see the value of your business and what you bring to the table. This will give you an edge over your rivals in the market, as you would have better lead conversion and word-of-mouth advertising.

- **Identifying niche markets**: If you do your homework on market segmentation, you may find new and up-and-coming niches in the market that are yet to explode into the limelight. Then, you can begin developing new products and services with the aim of capturing these niches and their respective markets.

- **Cost efficiency**: The idea of market segmentation is to help you decide on a segment of the market, where you can pour in your resources and skills. Not only does it make for better return on investment, but it also improves your cost efficiency, as resources go toward your target audiences alone.

- **Marketing efficiency**: An effective marketing strategy is one of the biggest benefits of market segmentation. Since you have settled on a segment of the market, you will be able to figure out the most effective strategies for meeting their needs, and improving their experiences and interactions with your brand.

Market segmentation shows the divides in the market, allowing you to see the real estate world as different parts that contribute to a much bigger whole. And while it might be difficult trying to fit its entirety into your palms, it's much easier to pick a piece and hold onto it.

Think of real estate as a pot of noodles. Of course, you can finish the meal, no problem. But do you just tilt your head back and dump the entire pot into your mouth? Of course you don't. Instead, you have one bowl after another. Each bowl of noodles represents a section of the market. Not only is it easier to manage, but it also helps you decide if the meal is to your taste.

Your success in real estate is tied to how your business relates with customers, and whether or not they end up with their needs met. Market segmentation helps you see these rules clearly and more directly, because you are much closer to that segment of the market than you'd be looking at the entire industry.

So, whether it's introducing your investor clients to up-and-coming locations, negotiating great deals for first-time homebuyers, or helping a cash-strapped client with a distress sale, market segmentation allows you to see the wants and needs of your target audience and position yourself as the solution.

Chapter 40:

Closing Deals

For many people in real estate, closing deals is the biggest challenge of their careers. And it makes sense, because many real estate realtors, brokers, and investors are trained to excel at the paperwork side of the industry, not how to buy or sell easily. And this is wrong, because real estate is all about closing deals. You want to get renters into a house as quickly as possible, find the right buyer for sellers, and help your buyer choose the right property.

But having little to no closing skills leaves you with no career, no money, and zero paperwork to be done. It doesn't matter how much you like paperwork, this won't close a deal.

It gets even more difficult to make regular deals when you learn that the industry is currently filled with unoriginal and fake responses. You don't need to follow the same old trick as everyone in the industry. Instead, dig deep into your instincts for fresh inspiration.

We get too focused on how hard closing deals can be, that we forget just how exciting the process can get. Of course, it can also be long and confusing. In fact, there is a long line of people new to real estate who have no idea how to close their first deal. It'd be a shame if you were to join that queue.

To ensure you are not, we will cover some simple steps that will give you a handle on how to close deals. With the right mindset and application, you will find that closing deals is an important part of your career in real estate.

How Long Does Closing on a Property Take?

There isn't a fixed time line for the processes involved in closing a property deal, but that is usually due to the importance of the steps involved in the process. Every decision you make when closing a deal, as well as the activities that fall to you, are crucial and shouldn't be rushed. As a result, it's best to not expect to close a deal in a heartbeat. Since each step has huge consequences if done wrongly, why rush through it at all?

But even though it makes sense why the closing process can take a while, it doesn't mean that it drags on forever. Instead, it should last as long as the time needed by everyone involved to fulfill their requirements. So, really, the slower party during the closing process determines how quickly or slowly a deal is made. If the parties are more experienced or have done business before, the process will be easier, faster, and less demanding.

But even for new parties doing business together for the first time, there is a time line they can look forward to. Usually, applying for a mortgage, for instance, takes between 30 to 45 days. It's impossible to close on a property without financing, so the success of your loan application determines when the closing starts. Once everyone has done their part and made it to the closing table, the idea is to finish the deal as quickly as possible. So, it could take an hour or several days. Again, experience and history come into play here. While some deals will be concluded in record time, others can take a long time due to negotiations.

The Changing Dynamics of Closing on Properties

Like most parts of the real estate industry, the time frame for closing isn't fixed and has been regularly changing. These changes are often tied to some regular factors like the state of the market, the season, financing, etc. But these are small factors. There are some large factors that affect how property deals are closed as well, such as changes in market direction, changes in interest rates, and new governmental regulations.

Usually, sellers and sellers' agents are the most eager to close deals as quickly as possible, while buyers and buyers' agents tend to take longer to close deals due to several reasons. The National Association of Realtors also believe that closing on property should take as long as it takes both sides to get ready.

How to Close Deals

- **Don't hurry the negotiating process**: Closing a property deal is as much about getting a result in the end as it is about protecting yourself and your client. And for good reasons, too. You should be prepared to roll out safety measures when necessary to ensure that you don't get burned. More on this in a subsequent section of this chapter.

  However, the primary reason you are negotiating in the first place is to get a done deal. As a result, you should evaluate all the processes involved in the closing so far and see whether or not to negotiate the price. For instance, if the inspection report comes back with bad news or unforeseen contingencies happen, you could be in a much better place to get a better deal. But this won't be possible if you hurry through the negotiating process.

- **Get insured and perform a title search**: Like in the previous step, you need a safety measure to be sure that you aren't wasting your time on a deal going nowhere. With a title search and title insurance, you will be protecting the property from anyone else who might rise up to claim ownership. While it sounds bizarre considering you are about to close the deal, you can't be too safe at this juncture.

  Start by getting in touch with a title officer to do due diligence on the property and confirm whether or not the seller has the right to ownership and to transfer it to someone else. If it turns out that the property isn't within the seller's right to sell, you will have dodged a legal problem.

The title officer helps to identify the real owner of a property through clear and in-depth research. Also, they are better able to tell you if some other third-party lays claim to the property you want to buy. It's a bad idea to ignore this step, because you will only be putting yourself at risk of someone else doubting the legality of your ownership once the deal is completed. So, as long as everything checks out and there is no shady business going on, you can move ahead with the deal. Also, if there are some problems found from the title search, you could have the seller resolve them before buying the property.

- **Don't forget to inspect the property**: You need a physical inspection of the property to find out if there are any problems, and to learn more about the surroundings. If your report comes back with problems in the home—whether it's an internal situation like a faulty foundation, or an external situation like closeness to an industrial dump site—then you are in a good position to negotiate better. You can either pull out of the deal or contact the seller to fix the problem. Alternatively, the seller can also pay you to deal with it. Just remember to include a home inspection contingency in your negotiations.

- **Simple is better**: Closing a deal isn't the best time to show off your knowledge of trivia. Don't start giving your clients unnecessary figures, data, and information that have nothing to do with the decision at hand. Treat them as you would prefer to be treated: clearly, directly, and personably. They might already be anxious about the deal, so there is no need contributing to their nerves.

If the clients still want to go through with the deal, then you can give them all of your findings about the property to help them make up their minds. You can also advise them on the best course of action from all you have learned. But, the key is to wait for them to show interest before offering the information.

- **Get an escrow account**: Opening an escrow account is a step you can't miss when closing deals in real estate. So, before coming to the negotiating table with your deal, ensure that you have a running escrow account that will take care of things as time passes.

  If you don't know what an escrow account is or how it works, here you go:

  An escrow account is held and managed by a third-party for all the parties involved in closing a deal. The idea is for a trusted and unbiased third-party to hold all the money and documents from the deal until things are finalized or fall through. This way, the documents can be transferred to the new owner, while the seller gets the money. This makes it impossible for any underhanded acts to take place. In fact, an escrow account is the safest way to exchange documents and money between the parties involved.

- **Stay confident**: Confidence is a crucial part of closing a deal. Believing in your skills and the deal itself is enough to make it happen. And you have to make sure that your confidence never wanes, from the first time you saw and inspected the property until the last time your pen touches paper to finalize the deal. Your client could benefit from your positive energy and enthusiasm.

  Remember, real estate is hard work, and closing deals is one of those parts that can drag on forever. Sometimes, you may not even be in favor of the property, but the client wants it all the same. Other times, you may have to deal with difficult clients. But as long as you remain confident in your abilities to identify, negotiate, and close the deal, you are unstoppable!

  Try not to get too cocky, though. Confidence is what you want—a sense of positivity and self-assurance, which will do good for your closing sales.

- **Get a legal representative**: Not every realtor, broker, or agent takes a lawyer with them to close a deal. And that's fine. But it's never a bad idea to get professional legal advice when going through the closing documents. Sometimes, the paperwork is filled with complex jargon that can make you doubt your education. An attorney can help you simplify it for the right fee, and offer you legal advice from an experienced point of view. This will come in handy to help you avoid potential problems and decide whether or not to go on with the deal.

- **Don't forget contingencies**: Any real estate investor that is worth their stuff knows better than to make a deal without contingencies. So, what are contingencies? They are clauses you add in a contract to allow you to get out of a deal if things go bad. It's also important to note that any contingencies you might have should already be taken care of before the closing process. Otherwise, why are you even here?

In addition, it's important that you write off the contingencies that have been met. That is, the contingencies in your purchase order must be removed in writing by a specific time to allow the deal to move forward.

- **Deal with closing costs**: From getting a legal representative to opening an escrow account, these third-parties cost money for their services. And the costs can grow over time into a lot of money if you aren't careful enough. For example, you need to inspect the home and check for pests before agreeing to a property deal. This will help you avoid huge and expensive problems in the future. However, buyers or investors who don't know about the costs of these services may sometimes be charged higher than normal. Even the closing fees on your deals can be increased for no reason.

There are also junk fees, which are charged by lenders when buyers close mortgage deals. Usually, these fees come out of the blue with no clear explanations from the lender. In worse cases, they can grow into huge bills. Junk fees are made up of settlement charges, ancillary fees, the appraisal review fee, processing fees, application fees, and administrative charges.

- **Get the property inspected for pests**: Doing a home inspection doesn't mean that a property is free of pests. You still need a pest inspection, in which a specialist comes to make sure there aren't any insects that destroy wood in the property, like carpenter ants or termites. These pests are bad for structural integrity and property value, especially if there is a lot of wooden materials around.

Even the smallest infestation is bad, because it can spread across the property. Not only does the property become more unhealthy to live in, but it would cost a fortune to fix the situation. While destroying these pests seems like a lot of work—and it is—that's not enough reason to pay more than what's reasonable. Better still, you can get the seller to deal with the pest problem before you conclude the deal. In some states, pest inspections are a legal requirement. Other states make it optional.

- **The final walk-through**: A final walk-through is important when closing a deal. In fact, there's no closing without it. At this point, you should already know whether or not you still want to continue the deal. If yes, then you need a final walk-through of the property to be sure all the demands you made (if any, like pest control) are in place, and if the property is as promised. Confirm that there are no damages to the property while other situations are being handled.

- **Put pen to paper**: It's fairly obvious that the only point in which a deal is closed is when you sign the paperwork. Once you have confirmed on the final walk-through that everything is good to go, feel free to deal with the paperwork. Don't expect to be done in two signatures, though, because there is a ton of work to go through here. Expect around 100 pages at the very least.

Just because your signature is required in multiple places doesn't mean you should go on a signing spree. You still have to go through the details and be sure of each page you sign on. If you can't figure out what a page is all about, meet with your lawyer for advice. You don't want to agree to an underhanded demand, especially those written in fine print.

Stalled Closing: What Causes It?

Not every closing process will end in handshakes and smiles between the parties involved. Sometimes, it can stall and drag on forever. But you don't want to be caught in stalled proceedings. It's like an overdue task that won't go away.

To avoid this, you can encourage the seller and their agents to be more committed to you through a large deposit. If it seems like closing a deal won't be happening any time soon, sellers may try to negotiate for huge deposits. In some cases, they may even want to extend the time. But be warned, this could cost more.

This isn't the case for buyers. For them, putting down less deposits means they have less to lose if things go bad. But things could stall. So, instead, break up your large deposit into several parts to be deposited after every milestone in the closing process. For instance, make a second deposit after the property and pest inspection, and a third one after appraisals and title insurance.

But you can't just make deposits to the seller. You have to choose an unbiased or independent third-party. It's why you need an escrow account.

Common Costs in Closing Real Estate Deals

The cost of the property won't be the last thing you pay for after closing a deal. There are other extra costs you must also deal with. And since these costs come from different sources, it's best we outline them individually instead of grouping them as after closing costs.

Here are the bills you won't be looking forward to after closing a deal:

- prepaid costs
- title insurance
- appraisal fees

- recording fees and taxes

- discount points

- real estate agent/broker fees

- private mortgage insurance

- escrow fees

- attorney fees

- miscellaneous costs

Slow Closing: What Causes It?

There are many factors that can affect the time taken to close on a property. These factors may be within or outside of your control. They are

- the parties involved don't have the property IDs to close the deal

- certificates of occupancy are needed

- agents are slow or unresponsive

- waiting for approvals for condos or the homeowners association

- problems with producing underwriting conditions

- lien and title problems

- method of financing

- unfinished work from appraisers and inspectors

To prevent the closing process from slowing down, try to start early and avoid as many of these problems as possible. For instance, you can develop a rapport with all the parties involved to ensure that no one is slacking off and slowing things down. You can do this by replying to all communications quickly and being in good standing with everyone involved in closing the deal.

Fast Closing: How to Speed Things Up?

The first thing about being quick is being prepared. So, if you want the closing process to be fast, make plans for all the steps involved.

Here are some steps you can follow to keep things moving smoothly until you sign the paperwork:

- Begin your search for properties early.

- Get all the important documents and some more before moving in to make the deal permanent.

- Form relationships with the other agent or broker, so that they will prioritize negotiations with you.

- Avoid periods like holidays and ends of the months, as it's much harder to close deals within these times.

- Inquire about important documents, such as condo docs, title searches, and so on.

- Double-check valid IDs and keep some cash in hand to speed up the closing process.

- Use incentives to encourage all the parties involved to close your deal faster.

- Avoid using your credit or taking loans that could affect your credit rating.

Closing Techniques

- **The summary close**: This closing technique works because it focuses on the benefits and values of the packages or components in the deal, such as the property coming fully furnished or having a backyard space for grilling and lounging. The idea is to summarize all the best features of the property to make it more appealing to customers, and make them see why the asking price is worth it.

- **The soft close**: Also known as the trial close, this closing technique can be used at any time during the negotiation process. As the name goes, it is more relaxed, and allows you to see how the seller feels before moving along with the negotiation. The goal is to get positive feedback from the other party. So, you want to warm up to them to get a yes.

  To do that, you could ask simple questions that require positive responses, such as: "Can I have a minute of your time, please?" They are almost always going to say yes to this, and listen intently to what you have to say. The more they reply positively, the better your chances of getting a good response.

- **The question close**: Question closes uses questions to hook a potential buyer and give them something to think about. The question might be about their opinions of a relatable problem in their present home, and whether or not the same problem exists in the current property. The idea is to return their attention to why they took an interest in the property in the first place. With the right questions, you can get good answers that let you know how the other side is feeling. In the end, you could get better commitment from them.

- **The hammer close**: The hammer close is usually used as a follow-up to a soft or trial close. Think of it as the more direct version of the soft closing technique. It's best used when the trial closing technique fails to get the other party to close the deal. If the seller is still interested in the deal and wants to resolve the negotiations quickly, it might be time to pull out the hammer close. It uses a strong call to action that makes or breaks the deal.

You could say something like, "Let's quit beating around the bush and shake hands on this deal already. It's a great deal: you know it; I know it, too. Give me an email address, so I can send you the details on my end."

Bear in mind that the hammer close is more aggressive and demanding. So, you have to ensure that your timing is right, otherwise it could ruin the deal for you.

- **The take-away close**: Here's a scenario: you take away a child's favorite toy. Now watch them throw a tantrum until you give it back. This is the idea for the take-away close. It's best used by sellers, although buyers can also try it. So, say a buyer finds your asking price too steep. Remove one of the impressive features in the house, like the appliances or frosted windows and offer the property at a reduced price. They will consider the cost of replacing this feature and decide whether or not it's worth the extra money.

- **The direct close**: A direct close is best for a stalling or slow closing process. If the deal has been taking too long to finalize, start by conditioning the seller to give you their best, most positive responses. Then, you can start asserting yourself. You could say, "I think this deal is right for us. Where would you like me to send the offer?"

Using this technique, you will know how far you have come with the seller, and if the process might drag on for longer. This is because the seller has to make a decision to agree to your proposal or continue negotiations. The direct close also forces the other party to speak up about any objections they might have, because they have to explain why they don't want to make a deal. Otherwise, you are through to concluding the deal.

- **Assumptive close**: This technique revolves around positive thinking. All you need to do is follow the interests, objections, and interactions of a potential buyer during the negotiation process. Then, after the meeting, you inquire if the property meets their expectations, or if they have additional demands.

- **Sharp angle close**: It's normal for potential buyers to ask about extra features in a property, like if they can keep some appliances at a discounted rate or get a discount on the pricing. The real estate agent of the buyer can agree to these conditions to close the deal, but not before seeking the opinion of the seller. This technique promises quick closing at the cost of added demands.

- **The now or never close**: This closing technique involves using special benefits with limited time frames to get the deal done as quickly as possible. Usually, the idea is to close the deal within the day that the offer is made.

What's Next After Closing a Deal?

You'd think that all is done after closing a deal. But the real work has only just begun. Once you have put pen to paper, your next responsibility is to protect your investment. As soon as you complete the deal, get insurance on the property regardless of how you are financing the deal, whether with out-of-pocket cash, angel financing, or crowdfunding. Apart from insurance, you also need to start thinking about security. Have the locks changed and use plywood to board up any broken windows. If there is a basement or garage, you want to get padlocks for those, too. With these measures in place, you will avoid any potential risks that might ruin your investment.

You should already be thinking about property improvement projects when closing the deal. But if you don't have anything in mind already, now is a good time to start thinking. Take some time out to visit the property and check out things that need fixing, maintenance, or brushing up. Get a contractor to accompany you to see the place. Once you have made up your mind on projects, set clear expectations for costs and duration. It's your property, so feel free to check with as many contractors as it takes to get the price that fits your budget. You don't have to settle for the first or most expensive option.

A contractor from your team or one that you regularly work with is your best shot in this case. If you plan on flipping the property, having the right plan and people on the job will make the process smooth and seamless. If everything goes as planned and you flip the property for a profit, you still aren't quite done... sorry. This is proof that real estate is not quick and easy money. It is long and difficult.

To make sure that your next deal closes just as quickly and smoothly as possible, you must keep track of your results. Moving from one deal to the next and changing marketing plans may eventually leave you in a loop without any improvements to show for it. Even if you already have a property in mind and have begun the negotiating process, take some time out to note the processes you took to close this deal. You can use a journal. Take note of important things, like the profits made, how long it took to close, the buying and selling price, things you did well, things you could have handled better, and so on.

Keeping track of your activities will help you identify how you managed your money and help with your business plan in the future. You can also use it as a learning curve for your mentees.

Finally, update your portfolio with details of the property you just closed on. If you didn't already do this, start now. Always update your portfolio to show all the deals you closed. You could track these details using presentations, spreadsheets, or Word documents—as long as it's organized. The idea is to improve your portfolio and ensure that it reflects the details of your activities and progress. In addition, you can use the information in the future with your partners, investors, or others that you work with. Also, it's important to pour in as many details as possible, so that whoever goes through your portfolio can better understand your skills and history.

Chapter 41:

Real Estate Auctions

Real estate auctions are public property sales held by a property owner, a bank, a home builder, or the government. Homeowners could include their properties in an auction to sell quickly without having to go through real estate listings, brokers, agents, or wholesalers. Meanwhile, home builders could offer several properties at an auction to sell them off together, especially when these properties have been listed for a long time with no interest from the public.

On the other hand, the government usually auctions off seized properties from debtors, tax evaders, and other legal violators. But the most common parties found at auctions are banks. The properties sold off by banks are usually foreclosures from people who couldn't pay back their debts.

Auctions come in three different forms, which determines how the processes involved are carried out. These forms are

- **Reserve auction**: In this type of auction, the highest bid is more of an offer than the winning price that the property will be sold at. That means, the seller can either reject or accept the bid within a fixed time, usually 72 hours. The reason the seller still has a chance to decide on making the sale or not is because the property isn't a distress sale. As a result, property owners looking to make quick sales don't attend or host reserve auctions. Instead, this setting is more suited to long-term investors who are looking for good deals to invest in. The downside of the reserve auction is its biggest feature: the seller's right to refuse or accept the winning bid. Potential buyers looking for a quick deal tend to avoid these auctions to avoid time wasting.

- **Minimum bid auction**: In this type of auction, the seller is allowed to choose a minimum price point for bidding on the property. That is, the seller chooses a minimum price and will only accept bids matching or over that amount. So, even if a bid comes in highest, if it doesn't meet the required price of the seller, the property isn't sold. Like with reserve auctions, minimum bid auctions aren't for distress sales. For instance, banks only host minimum bid auctions when they want to get back a certain percentage of the mortgage and are in no hurry to sell for cheap. This makes this auction type more suited to long-term investors.

- **Absolute auction**: This is the regular type of auction, where the property is won by the highest bid despite what the final price might be. Here, there is no minimum requirement or choosy sellers; so, the property can go for any price, as long as it's the highest offer. For instance, if the highest bid is $1000.50 and no one else bids a dollar above that, then the property goes for exactly $1000.50. While it might seem like the auction to be at, keep in mind that the competition is high. Everyone who couldn't make it into reserve or minimum bid auctions will be here. And since they know that it's a distress sale where sellers want to make a quick buck, they are more than willing to buy the property at a lower value than it's actually worth. If you are a short-term investor or have the cash to spend, then this is the auction for you.

How Does the Real Estate Auction Process Work?

Auctions aren't more difficult than traditional property sales. If anything, the only thing different about it is how the process plays out. But the more auctions you attend, the more familiar you become with them. You might even find them easier than the traditional buying and selling of real estate.

That said, auctions are a great source of good real estate deals, and you should consider getting your properties there sometimes. If it sounds like something you might want to try, here are a few things you can learn about what the process is like:

- Auctions are typically held at local courthouses. It's not the only place it could be held, but many prefer to host there. Although, auction companies may sometimes go for other locations that best suit the number of guests they expect for the event. The goal is to get the highest amount possible to cover the seller's needs, so a good setting is necessary to get the right amount of guests. On the other hand, tax lien accounts are often run and managed by the local sheriff, usually because the government is mostly the seller in this case.

- There is a starting bid in every auction. Even absolute auctions don't start at $0. Otherwise, everyone would comfortably bid nothing. Depending on the type of auction (reserve and minimum bid), if the bid doesn't match what the seller is looking for, the property is kept aside to be auctioned at a different event in the future.

  But generally, once the bidders meet the first bid, the rules of the action kick in. The highest bidder who can meet the requirements of the auction, like make payment within a specific time or offer a cashier's check, wins the property and is given the paperwork to begin processing ownership.

- After the bidded amount is paid in full, the investor will receive a certificate of sale. They can also expect the certificate of title in the mail within another 10 days.

The Benefits of Real Estate Auctions

There are a few benefits to visiting auctions for properties, such as the following:

- Some auctioned properties have huge market potential.

- Auctions sometimes contain the most desirable properties.

- You could get a discount on the sale.

- Settlement times are faster than traditional sales.

Also, while you might find auctioned properties with higher price points than their actual value, and some with too much damage to make them profitable after renovation and restoration, you will also find properties with smaller opening bids than they are worth. You may also find undervalued properties with the right price point, which could bring you huge profits when renovated properly.

For real estate investors, lien and foreclosure auctions allow you to invest in one or several properties at reduced prices. With some work, you can set up the properties for rent or sale and get good returns on your investment. Usually, foreclosure auctions give potential buyers a walk-through of the property. This allows investors to conduct due diligence and take note of the ones they find interesting.

Another upside of buying at auctions is that you get enough time to negotiate with the property seller. Auctions are a one-time thing, and the property always goes to the winning bid. The process is quick and straightforward, because the seller or auction company has already set the requirements for the auction. So, the selling price can't change overnight, and you don't have to deal with junk fees or stalling negotiations. And in just a few weeks, the property will be yours, complete with all the necessary documentation. All you have to do is pay for the property if your bid wins through out-of-pocket cash, crowdfunding, or angel investing.

The Risks of Real Estate Auctions

There are two types of properties you will find in every auction, namely:

- **Normal properties**: These properties are regular with little to no issues that can be fixed without a hassle. Usually, the seller chooses to auction the property due to the convenience of the method. So, the buyer has nothing to worry about.

- **Problem properties**: These properties come with baggage. Usually, the seller has to get rid of the property, but can't sell it on the open market because of several problems. Properties that fall within this category will test you in every way, and may leave you wondering why you even bothered.

  But, sometimes these properties also turn out to be gold mines. Just because they are trouble doesn't mean they should always be avoided. As long as you can get them at a good price and have the time and resources to invest into fixing any problems it might have, you could turn a decent profit.

Making a success out of problem properties boils down to two things: having the finances and time to get rid of all the things that make the property a bad purchase on the open market.

It all begins with knowing the problems involved. Otherwise, you might bid too high or not have enough money left to fund the property and get it back to market standard. If this is the case, the property will end up as a disaster. Not only would you have paid too much for a bad property, but you may not even be able to fix the problems. At that point, the property becomes a money pit that just takes your money and produces no results.

This is most likely the biggest risk with buying properties at an auction. In fact, a lot can be wrong with these properties at once. Here are some of the most common problems you can find:

- wood rot or dry rot

- Japanese knotweed

- fire damage

- neighboring property problems

- structural problems

- problematic tenants

- derelict properties or homes that need to be entirely renovated

- short leases

- roof problems

- substandard construction

- flood damage, and so on...

Stiff Competition

A lot of people from different parts of the real estate industry attend auctions, from developers to builders, contractors to investors, and realtors to brokers. If you will be actively participating in an auction for the first time, then you must be aware that competition is stiff. This is an important detail, because the stiff competition may lead you to pay way over the price of the property or your budget. And that's the start of bad business.

Legal Risks

It would be great news if the problems with auctioned properties were only with bad purchases, but that's hardly the case. Some properties come with legal baggage, which can take forever to get rid of and rack up a huge bill.

In a normal property sale, when you buy a property from a real estate broker or agent, you only start to deal with the property directly after you have settled on a price. Like most huge assets, properties come with complicated legal structures that affect how they are bought and sold.

Here are some common legal issues that real estate attorneys check for when closing deals:

- **Title checks**: This ensures that you get full legal ownership of the property you are paying for.

- **Covenants**: Positive covenants means that you are obligated to perform a task, such as contributing to the maintenance of a wall or road network. Negative covenants, on the other hand, limit how and what you can do on the property.

- **Easements**: This is the confirmation that no one else has a right over the property, except for the buyer.

- **Local area**: This confirms whether or not there are plans for major developments or roads bearing property.

- **Enforcement notices**: These obligate you to do certain things after purchasing the property.

- **Encroachments**: This is done to ensure that your neighbor's land doesn't overlap into the property.

- **Tenancy checks**: Doing this will check if there are tenants on the property and if they live without disputes and pay rent on time.

Most of these checks require the expertise of a lawyer to figure out and highlight any issues. Also, it might be challenging to read and understand the legal pack on your own.

Preference for Cash Buyers

There is a common myth about buying auction properties: that it only works with cash. This isn't the case, though, because you can finance with other options, including loans, crowdfunding, etc. However, the approval time for anything but cash is very slow, which makes buyers with cash more likely to edge you out. So, if you don't have ready cash to pay, you might find yourself losing out on bids, no matter how much you want them. This preference makes auctions unpopular for non-cash buyers.

Risks With the Auction Process

So, you have checked out the property, done due diligence, and got the legals simplified by an attorney. Your cash is also ready for the purchase. Sounds like nothing else could go on, right? Wrong. The auction process itself is a risk that you might not know about.

- **Sunk costs**: As we mentioned before in other chapters and even here, it's important that you do due diligence on a property before bidding for it. But due diligence isn't free. It costs money, and could be as expensive as $300 or more. You could also pay well over $500 for the attorney's legal pack. If you foot these charges, then attend the auction and lose the bid, you aren't getting your money back. That $800 is now sunk costs.

  There is no way to avoid this. The only other alternative is to go in without legal advice, which is not recommended. But having to pay for things that don't pan out is a huge risk, especially if you regularly attend auctions.

- **Auction terms**: When going through the traditional method of buying and selling properties, the fees involved are usually out there. Even if you don't know all of it, you can expect the other parties will bring it up. Usually, the seller covers them, with about 1% to 2% plus value added tax (VAT).

  With auctions, the fees aren't so straightforward.

  For one, you can expect to pay higher, like 3% to 4% (+VAT), depending on the property. Also, it's not a given that the seller will cover the fees. Sometimes, they fall to the buyer and you can expect some extra fees.

  This is why it's important to read and understand all the auction terms before bidding on a property. You want to be sure who is covering all the additional fees and how much they cost. It won't be the first time someone gets the winning bid only to meet a huge, undisclosed bill. Imagine making the winning bid of $250,000 on an auctioned property, only to be slapped with a 4% (+VAT) fee. That's over $10,000 in unplanned expenses.

- **Overpaying**: The processes involved in auctioning properties didn't start recently. They have been around for many years, and have been developed to get the seller the best possible prices, even in distress sales. So, a huge part of the process is getting you to pay more than the actual worth of the property through competitive bidding.

  The only way to get around this risk is to set a budget before going into the auction. But this is not new advice. Many people have gone into auctions with a fixed price in mind, only to end up going over budget and paying way too much for a property.

- **Little to no property inspection**: The auctioned properties are sold as they are. Meaning, you aren't allowed to inspect the properties before buying them, like you would in a traditional setting. This is because the properties are usually sealed up and don't allow for internal walk-throughs. So, you can't properly inspect it. As a result, all the problems are hidden and a surprise after you have won the bid. By then, it just might be too late to back out of the deal.

How to Bid at Auctions

There are different rules for auctions in each state. However, the basics are still the same. To join an auction and bid on properties, you must register for the event before the due date. Registration is fairly straightforward. All you have to do is look for auctions or auction companies near you and inquire about the process. Once you have successfully registered, you will be given a bidding package.

Once that is out of the way, you need to start preparing for the event. Start your research. A property is a good or bad deal depending on factors like: its auctioning value, your bid amount, how much renovation and resources it needs, and its eventual value as a rental or resell. You need to be sure of these factors before even attempting to bid on a property. Never bid blindly.

Here are some other steps to keep in mind leading up to the time of auction:

- Read up on all the documents and transactions from your due diligence before attending the auction.

- Find out the market value of the property after working on it.

- Drive by the property you are interested in and inspect the external view.

- Prepare your financials if you are sure of the property. In most states, you will be required to make the payment once your bid is accepted. So, prepare a money order, cash, or a cashier's check.

- Check again to be sure that the auction is still on. You'd be surprised how many are canceled or rescheduled.

- Make payment for the pre-auction deposit. It's usually 5% of the complete debt on the property.

- At the auction, raise your bidder card at the right time and for the right property. As long as you have done your financials and due diligence, you should already know how much you'd be willing to part with for the property.

How to Get the Right Properties at Auctions

When going to auctions to buy property, due diligence is just as important in this case as in traditional real estate purchases, maybe even more so. This is especially important for first-time property buyers, who may not be familiar with the processes involved. Usually, auctions are hubs for experienced real estate investors and agents, so it would do you a world of good to know your stuff. You can get some practice by attending a couple of auctions before settling on one to buy a property. Don't worry about standing out. Not everyone at an auction buys something. You can even approach someone with a winning bid for insights.

Remember, even though auctions and traditional processes are different, it's still pretty much the same idea: to get good property deals. So, whether you are buying one or more properties, you need to go through the details and be sure that the property won't sink your time, finances, and resources without results.

That said, the most important thing to keep your eye on is the property in question. You need to be even more careful in this type of property sales, because auctioned properties are usually not kept in the same conditions as traditional real estate sales. For instance, sellers in a traditional setting might still be living in the property up until the deal is completed. Auctioned properties, on the other hand, are usually vacant and sealed. This makes them magnets for vandalism, neglect, insect attacks, pests and rodents, and mold.

So, during your walk-through, take some time to check if the home will require a lot of work and still be profitable in the end. This might mean checking for mold or if copper pipes are in place.

Chapter 42:

Mobile Home Investing

The invention of mobile homes caused a bit of a head-scratcher back in the day. No one could tell if they were classified as properties or vehicles. And who could blame them? It makes sense to wonder about the place of mobile homes, because it combines two assets that are treated and regulated differently.

Let's go over this in more detail.

Mobile homes are personal properties registered under the Division of Motor Vehicles (DMV). So, it's considered a vehicle. Even the title registration and ownership rights are transferable in the same way as any other automobile's. It makes sense, because mobile homes are vehicles, and remain so until connected to a real property. Also, if you own the piece of land housing your mobile home, you have two separate rights and property interests. You get one for the personal property (the mobile home) and another for the real property (the land).

So, if you decide to sell the land, you will still retain ownership and the rights over the mobile home. That is, the land and the mobile home are independent of each other. The only other way you will be giving off both at once is when the mobile home has been converted into a landed property.

The History of Mobile Homes

We have covered what mobile homes are and how they differ from landed properties. But how exactly did they come about?

'Trailer' was used as a collective term for describing mobile homes way before 1953. At that time, the properties started to evolve and catch on, so it was important that travel trailers be differentiated from factory-built homes. And so, "mobile home" was born.

Even after we began using the new term, there were no federal policies on how mobile homes should be built. But all of that changed in 1974, when congress assigned the United States Department of Housing and Urban Development (HUD) to set building standards. So, the HUD created some regulations to ensure that only quality mobile homes were produced. The new federal guidelines concerned several parts of the production process, including:

- overall quality

- fire resistance

- construction and design

- transportability

- energy efficiency

- durability and strength

But that's not all; The HUD also made these regulations compulsory for documentation of mobile homes. But in the document, they were called "manufactured homes." So, technically, mobile homes were the unregulated properties built before the HUD got involved with codes and standards. And what we have now are manufactured homes, built and inspected under HUD guidelines.

Modular homes are another property that are often mistaken for mobile or manufactured homes. But they couldn't be any more different. That's because modular homes aren't built according to HUD standards, but by the same regulations as site-built properties.

For the remainder of this chapter, we will use manufactured homes and mobile homes interchangeably. But we mean the same thing.

Types of Mobile Homes

The Single-Wide Mobile Home

This mobile home has a narrower and longer style than most houses. The floor plan differs based on preference, but this style is often used by new couples or young families still starting out. It contains all the necessary amenities and manages to stay affordable.

Single-wide mobile homes also work well for people who move around more, because it's cheaper and easier to move than the other types. On the other hand, it makes for a good temporary residence for people waiting to complete their regular homes. It's more comfortable and affords users their own space, at a much lesser cost than rentals and relative fees.

Newly built single-wide mobile homes go for about $63,600 on average.

The Double-Wide Mobile Home

Double-wide mobile homes are between 2,000 to 2,500 square feet. They are also more or less 90 feet long and 20 feet wide. Most designs come with two bathrooms and two to three bedrooms, a dining room, and several entryways. Double-wide mobile homes in the United States are the exact size as a regular home.

The design of most double-wide mobile homes is on par with the average ranch style home. During production, the home is made as two different parts, which are then combined into one upon arrival at the chosen location. Some buyers fear that using two pieces instead of one might make the property unstable and leaky. But that's hardly the case. As long as you purchase mobile homes from certified and reliable dealers and have it assembled by expert hands, you will get good value for your money.

The double-wide mobile homes work well for average-sized families of two to four people, who might be too cramped in a single-wide. Anything above this number of people will make the house feel smaller, so you might want to go for something bigger.

Getting a new double-wide mobile home can set you back around $109,100. You also have to consider lot rents if you don't have land of your own—prices for these differ across states. For instance, in Delaware a lot's rent is about $800, while it's only $140 in Indiana.

The Triple-Wide Mobile Home

Although double-wide mobile homes are also known as multi-section homes, this term is mostly used when talking about triple-wide mobile homes and other bigger designs. This form of mobile homes is very spacious, and can come with as many as three bathrooms and five bedrooms.

Triple-wides are usually between 3,000 to 4,500 square feet on average. And even though they appear shorter than double-wides, they are bigger and have more of a square shape. Triple-wides often look like traditionally built homes, but they are sometimes larger than some regular homes.

They work best for larger families of five or more people who might struggle with three bedrooms and two bathrooms. The price range is usually over $100,000.

Should You Invest in Mobile Homes?

From an investor's point of view, a mobile home is not the best investment. From a financial perspective, it's like throwing lots of money on a big car to sleep in. And like every other car, value is lost over time.

The main argument for fans of mobile homes is that it beats leasing or renting a property or an apartment. But is that really the case? For example, if you pay a rent of $1,500 a month, that's the only amount that goes into the property besides utility bills and other petty charges. But with a mobile home, not only do you chuck in a higher amount than basic rent, but you also have to cover other petty charges, too. And since the property is yours, the reducing value is on you. So, even though mobile homes are great on your tax burden, their resale value isn't worth the trouble.

In the end, it's a gamble to invest in a mobile home. A mobile home park is perhaps a better investment. But for just the home alone, the odds are more against you than for you. And you don't want to involve your loved ones in a bad deal.

The Upsides of Mobile Homes

- **Mobility**: Mobile homes can be moved—it's basically the selling point. And even though the process isn't easy and requires professional help, it still allows for owners to move conveniently without having to change properties.

- **Low costs**: The most talked about upside to getting a mobile home is that they often cost less than building a regular home. With the current cost of building materials, you could get a decent-sized mobile home for way less and have some leftover finances for furnishings. This is because the cost per square foot for a regular home is more than that of a mobile home. As a result, it's much easier to become a homeowner of a mobile home, and you get more space for the same amount.

- **Flexibility**: Another upside of a mobile home is the flexibility it brings. The mobile part of this property means you can up and leave at any time. Imagine moving to a new place and taking your house along with you. That it's both semi-permanent and affordable makes it one of the most flexible assets you will ever own.

  But the removal and movement isn't nearly as easy as hitching your car to a recreational vehicle (RV) and just driving into the sunset. You need experts because of delicate systems like plumbing and power. All in all, the flexibility allows you to live in different places at different points in your life, without being limited like with regular houses.

Other upsides of owning mobile homes include:

- They have high-quality construction and design.

- Mobile homes are in high demand; so they have come to stay.

- The property attracts lower taxes, which means you can improve your rental portfolio without breaking the bank.

- Mobile homes are easier to manage due to lower costs of repairs and renovation.

The Downsides of Mobile Homes

- **Depreciation**: Regular properties grow in value depending on how they are managed and the location they are in. But that's not the same for mobile homes. The moment you buy one, the value starts to fall. It doesn't matter if the property sits on prime real estate. The value almost never goes up. It works just like a vehicle. Also, since the land it sits on isn't connected to the property, there is no hedge to protect against depreciation. Instead, the value of the land might rise, but your property won't.

- **You're a property owner but pay rent**: If you don't own land, you might have to set up your mobile home in a mobile home park. And even though you are the owner of the property, you still have to pay rent to the owner of the park and adhere to certain rules and regulations. The park owner can also evict you at any time, which will make you move your property or sell it and move elsewhere. Basically, mobile homes make you a property owner without the convenience and rights of a regular homeowner.

- **Poor resale value**: Besides losing value over time, it's not the easiest thing to sell a mobile home, especially if the property is located in a park. This is because mobile homes usually become somewhat permanent until they need to be moved. And unless the buyer wants to live in the same location, that would be extra costs that they might not want to make. So, finding a buyer that wants to live in the park or foot relocation fees is hard.

- **Susceptibility to damage**: Unlike regular properties that are erected on permanent foundations buried in the ground, mobile homes sit on temporary structures. So, should a natural disaster happen—like a storm, earthquake, or a hurricane— mobile homes aren't secure enough to survive the situation.

- **Stigma**: Over the years, the media has contributed to the stereotype around people living in mobile homes. So, there is somewhat of a stigma around the property. And despite how much better mobile homes are currently than when they were first invented, the stigma remains, and could be a huge turnoff for some property buyers or investors.

Profiting From Mobile Home Investing

Here are a few methods to make decent profits from investing in mobile homes, especially single-wide designs, as well as the pros and cons of each method.

Before we dive in, keep in mind that the system of return on investment (ROI) is the same across all the methods discussed in this section.

That is:

Cash Flow = Rent - Lot Rent

- Own the property, but not the land: This method of investing involves buying an already existing property in a mobile home park, or moving one into a park.

    o **Pros**: If you invest in the property alone, not the land, you only have to pay rent for occupying the space. Other bills—like utilities, for instance—fall to the park owner. This means less financial strain and more cash flow.

    o **Cons**: Even if you save on petty living charges, the cost of moving a mobile home is astronomical. What's more, there are regulations and fees that you must review and pay before the property can be transported to a different location.

- **Own both the park and the mobile homes in it**: This has to be the best investment strategy for mobile homes. Owning the park and the properties in it gives you optimum cash flow. When choosing a location for the park, go for lands that are connected to the water supply and sewage network of the area.

    o **Pros**: In this case, you get to live rent-free and charge rent—meaning higher cash flow.

    o **Cons**: Investing in both a park and mobile homes isn't nearly as inexpensive as buying a single property and paying rent monthly. Additionally, as the park owner, you are responsible for repairs, maintenance, and utilities for the properties.

- **Own the park but not the properties**: You can invest in mobile homes part-time or full-time, depending on your commitments and needs. Investing in a park but not mobile homes is a great way to reduce your responsibilities and costs, while still getting returns.

    o **Pros**: For this investment method, the upside is that you can manage your investment passively. Also, you only have to worry about fewer things, like the park and utilities. The repair and maintenance of mobile homes fall to their owners. And just like with traditional properties, you can increase rent and improve your cash flow.

- ○ **Cons**: Since you can only charge a lot rent, cash flow is lower than if you owned the mobile homes.

- **Own the park, but seller finance the properties**: Seller financing mobile homes in a park you own is another investment strategy to consider. However, this time, it's important that you carry out inspections periodically over the course of the lease, so that you can keep an eye on your properties. It's best to use a property manager or agency to keep a tab on things.

  - ○ **Pros**: The upside of this technique is that you still own the park and sell the properties on a note, while still earning income through rent.

  - ○ **Cons**: The downside is that this method can lead to a lot of tenants leaving. When a new management takes over the park, they might update the regulations, which could force people to leave—leading to vacant lots, which is bad for business.

Investing Through Semi-development Deals

Think of this strategy as flipping mobile homes. You start by purchasing land with a disused mobile home. Then, you take out the old property and put a new one in its place. Now, you can sell together as a land and home deal.

Of course, the deal will come with utilities and amenities.

Investing Through Land Property Deals

This strategy is similar to seller financing. It also involves lenders. First, the buyer collects a loan and begins making payments to the seller or park owner until the agreed price is met.

Processes Involved in Buying a Mobile Home

The process of buying a regular apartment or property differs widely from a mobile home. So, before you get into a mobile home dealership, check with the DMV near you to learn the basics. On the other hand, if you will be settling for a used mobile home, here are some items to check for: Form 400, bill of sale, and title (including HUD plate, VIN, brand, and year).

Title

When purchasing mobile homes, especially used ones, you could experience title problems. Here are a few issues that might come with it and how best to solve them:

Lost Titles

It might surprise you to know that sellers sometimes put up mobile homes for sale without a title. Usually, they might say the title is lost. Here are some questions to find out what happened:

- Is the title faded or lost?

- Is it a legal property?

- Is the title really lost?

- What's going on with the title loss?

Solution: There is a walk-around for legal mobile homes with faded or lost titles. All you have to do is visit the DMV and get a duplicate.

Incorrect Owner and No Title

Sometimes, it could be that the owner of the title doesn't match the seller's name, and they don't have the title to prove themselves. This may happen if there was a previous seller who sold the property but didn't change the title.

Solution: The only way around this is to find the first owner of the mobile home. But this isn't an easy task because a lot could have happened. For instance, they may have passed, leaving you to search for the estate executor.

But you can skip all the searching by looking for the bill of sale. It's usually the first document signed by the original owner. The bill of sale is recognized as proof of ownership and transaction.

Moving Mobile Homes

After buying a mobile home and updating the title, you might want to relocate it to another place of your choosing. If the new location is less than 100 miles away, movers can do the job for cheaper, like $5,000.

Before calling the movers, make sure to check for the guidelines for moving properties in your area.

Understanding the Guidelines for Installation

- Find out about the fees involved.

- Learn about the inspections needed.

- Find the time allowed for moving mobile homes.

Rehabbing Mobile Homes

If you are investing in mobile homes for rehabbing, there are two crucial questions you must answer:

- Are you planning to sell or rent?

- How much time and resources are needed to make it work?

Here are a few factors to help you make up your mind when choosing properties for rehab:

- Consider the long-term.

- Inspect thoroughly for any faults, especially leaks.

- Don't add a carpet just yet.

- Go with used appliances.

- Imagine the income bracket of your target audience.

- Get a contractor that has expertise on repairing and maintaining mobile homes.

- Check out your neighbors.

Red Flags to Watch Out for When Investing in Mobile Homes

Just because mobile homes don't appreciate doesn't mean you can't invest in them and get good returns. Instead, you should be focused on avoiding things that might make your investment go bad. One way to do this is to ensure that you are pouring your money into the right property and not buying a red flag.

For instance, water damage is huge for mobile homes. It's expensive and time-consuming, and can affect both used and new properties. So, before purchasing a mobile home, ensure to inspect it thoroughly. Check the roof for exposed underlining and low points, which may hold and let water in. If the cover for the air conditioning unit is broken, that could also be a sign that the property has problems.

Another thing you want to look for is tire treads and the date of production. You will find four-digit numbers that stand for the week and year or manufacture. For instance, 2519 means the tire was produced on the 25th day of 2019.

If you find anything during your inspection that sets off red flags, don't try to make it work. Look at other options instead. But if you are fixated on the property, consider asking the seller to reduce the asking price.

Here are a few things to watch out for, which are huge red flags:

- Damages on the floors is bad business.

- Faulty or poor coverage by the AC cover means leakages.

- Problems with the roof can lead to water damages.

- Older tires with worn-out treads make the property unsafe for roads.

Chapter 43:

Property Management

Buying or building a property is only half of the work involved. There is still a business side of it that needs to be taken care of, whether the owner intends to sell or rent. This aspect of ownership can sometimes be too much for the property owner, and they might need to outsource the processes to someone else.

This is how property management is born. The idea is for a third-party to handle the upkeep of the property, but the owner still maintains ownership. A professional real estate representative who takes on this management role is known as a property manager.

Property management isn't limited to residential real estate alone. It also works for industrial and commercial real estate. From a general point of view, property management oversees the day-to-day upkeep, maintenance, security, and repair needs of a property. Property management usually goes hand in hand with investment properties like industrial parks, private home communities, condominium complexes, apartment complexes, and shopping centers.

Think of property management as the next step after closing a deal, designed to deal with routine tasks that maintain and improve property value and bring in income. Also, property management can be seen as a niche in real estate. It's not unusual to see real estate agents and brokers working in this field. For instance, a residential real estate agent may offer property management services during negotiations or to sellers' and buyers' agents.

Property Managers: Who Are They and What Do They Do?

As we have discussed so far, property managers perform a lot of tasks on the properties under their care and management. They could manage one or multiple properties at the same time. The ones who manage investment properties are tasked with protecting and ensuring the success of the investment.

With a property manager in the picture, property owners can decide how much they want to be involved in the running of the property. The ones who want to stay in the loop regularly keep in touch with their property managers to make decisions. On the other hand, property owners too busy with other commitments can leave rest assured knowing that their property is in safe hands. Even without regular communication, property managers will ensure that things are run as agreed.

Property Management Agencies

Property managers don't always fly solo. Sometimes, they work for property management agencies. So, to get management oversight, property owners get in touch with these companies. In turn, the agency delegates property managers to deal with the property. If you are considering getting a property manager for your property, check for agencies near you or ask your real estate agent or broker.

Licensing

Property managers don't just start managing properties without any form of vetting. They usually need a real estate broker's license or a property management license to work in this field. Not only does the license certify them to work in the industry, but it also gives them the legal backing to make business decisions when managing properties.

Getting a license is important, not just for freedom to operate, but also for your career and image.

The requirements for licensing differ from state to state. To get licensed, you need to be 18 years old, at least, with a high school diploma. While this degree is fine for the regulatory bodies issuing the license, most property management agencies require their managers to have a bachelor's degree at the minimum in fields like real estate or business.

Who Needs a Property Manager?

Property owners hire property managers for different reasons. Some require oversight for the multiple properties on their portfolios, which might be too much work for one individual. Others may not have the skill or time to run a property and deal with tenants directly. Also, some just want to own properties and get returns on their investments without any involvement in the running process.

Another set of individuals who require the services of property managers are absentee property owners. Individuals in this category often own single and seasonal properties, such as vacation homes and condos.

We also have property owners from affordable housing schemes. These sets hire property managers due to the nature of their investments. The properties built or bought under these schemes are heavily regulated by federal guidelines. Hence, the property owners need expert guidance to navigate their investment.

Responsibilities of Property Managers

The responsibilities of a property manager depends on the agreement reached with the property owner. So, there can be as few or as many as both parties agree. For instance, while some property owners might want property managers to verify tenants and collect rent alone, others might want them to manage every aspect of the property.

That said, here are some of the responsibilities a property manager deals with:

- **Rent management**: One of the primary responsibilities of a property manager is managing rent. Sometimes, this might involve deciding the amount tenants pay as rent. To do this, the property manager first checks out the property, the current state of the real estate market, and the location.

  When tenants move into the property, the property manager decides on a date, medium, and cycle for collecting rent. For instance, they could collect rent on the first day of each month via bank transfer or check. Property managers also get to decide when to increase rent, as long as they do so within the legal boundaries of the laws in the city or state.

- **Marketing**: Another major reason why property owners use property managers is for marketing. Property owners may not always have the time or expertise to market to tenants. Property managers, on the other hand, take photographs of the property and list it correctly on the right mediums.

  Property managers with a huge presence or brand in the real estate space will usually draw more interest for properties that they manage. And when they get enough offers, they can begin to interview the potential tenants and choose the right ones.

- **Tax management**: Sometimes, property owners need help with taxes, and require property managers to file them correctly and on time. In some cases, the process is outsourced to property managers to handle on their own.

- **Tenant management**: When dealing with rental properties, property managers are required to oversee tenancy. So, they deal with marketing the property to tenants, screening and choosing potential tenants, and running credit checks to ensure that the accepted tenants can pay for occupying the property.

Property managers could also be tasked with managing tenant leases. But it doesn't end there. They also have to deal with evictions, moving out, and emergencies. Before a tenant moves out of the property, property managers have to carry out inspections to ensure that there are no damages. If there are no damages, the tenant is refunded their deposit. Otherwise, the property manager figures out the cost of repairing the damage and deducts it from the tenant's deposit.

Once the move-out is complete and damages have been inspected and seen to, the property manager starts preparing the unit to be rented out again. In the case of evictions, property managers kick-start the process when they find a tenant violating the agreements of the lease.

- **Understanding the rules and guidelines of the landlord-tenant relationship**: Property managers can only succeed at their jobs if they understand the federal and state laws governing landlords and tenants. This deals with knowing how to stop a lease, start an eviction, and screen potential tenants, among other duties. Property managers who understand these policies are better suited to running a property, while ensuring that tenants are treated fairly and the owner receives reports duly.

- **Budget management**: Property managers could also deal with budgets for properties and other key financial details. Managing a property budget typically deals with handling the costs of repairs and maintenance, complaints, tenant leases, and more.

- **Managing repairs and maintenance requests**: The general idea of property management is to ensure that the property is running smoothly and good enough for the renters (in the case of residential properties). So, property managers are tasked with making sure that tenants' requests for repairs and maintenance are seen to quickly. This might involve issues like trash disposal, pest and rodent extermination, water leaks, etc.

Property managers can handle these requests themselves if they have the skills. Otherwise, they can just get third-party services, like a pest control service, plumber, trash collector, and electrician. Property managers that stay on top of these minor situations keep tenants happy, prevent huge turnovers, maintain property value, and make the property more appealing to future renters.

- **Employee supervision**: Sometimes, property owners may employ other hands to help with the running of the property, such as a security guard. These staff fall under the supervision of property managers. The latter may also be in charge of discussing the salary and employment of the other staff, including termination.

Tips for Success as a Property Manager

- **Availability and reliability**: To succeed in the role, a property manager must be dependable and available to work. These qualities make you trustworthy to the property owners you work with. You also need to maintain regular and prompt communication via calls, texts, and emails. You need to be available for when your clients, tenants, and potential clients and tenants need to reach you. If you are bad at managing your time, you won't be taken seriously or trusted with anything of importance.

That is, good quality service is all you need to get your career on the upswing as a property manager. The better you do, the more referrals you get, and the bigger the portfolios you will be given to manage. By now, you should already have an idea of the responsibilities that fall within your jurisdiction. So, sharpen up your skills to meet current standards.

- **Understand the property under your management**: This tip goes for whether you only deal with sales and promotion of properties. You need to know your properties inside out. For example, would you buy a product—say, a donut—from a vendor that can't tell you in detail how the snack is made? If they can't, then that's your cue to move on to another vendor.

You ought to know your properties, not only because it's the job, but because you also have to speak to clients and renters or buyers and convince them of the property in your care. Having no idea of the property makes that difficult, if not impossible.

People pay attention and trust the words of figures of authority in a field. Property managers are authority figures in managing properties, and however you project a house goes with your audience. But how can you tell them about the good features of a property or its shortcomings if you don't even know about these?

And even when you do know about the property, don't limit your knowledge to it alone. Learn about the amenities in the neighborhood, like social facilities, banks, shopping centers, etc.

- **Improve your experience**: Property managers take on multiple roles for the job, depending on who they are relating to: a client, renter, or buyer. So, it's crucial that you are learned and up-to-date with the required experience. If you want to take on the role full-time, it's best that you enroll for formal courses in fields like business, management, real estate, and other related areas. Mentorship can also help you learn on the go and absorb good strategies from another expert with a more successful career.

On another hand, you can sign up for the property managers association in your state. These groups usually get together for regular meetings, where members are allowed to air specific job-related issues, find answers to key questions, and bond and share ideas for improving and staying relevant in changing times. Another great idea is to sign up for webinars and workshops. Just be careful not to fall prey to faux real estate gurus, while you're at it. Search online for workshops near you and read books from successful people in real estate.

Steps Needed to Become a Property Manager

- **Identify the requirements for the role**: Every state has their own rules and licensing requirements for becoming a property manager, especially for residential properties. Also, the rules and requirements differ depending on the type of property you manage. For instance, property managers that handle public housing schemes subsidized by the government are often required to get special licenses. So, it's up to you to decide the type of laws that apply depending on the type of properties you want to manage.

  To begin your research on the requirements for becoming a property manager in your locale, check with the National Association of Realtors chapter in your state. Once you get all the details that you need, it's time to begin the journey to qualifying for the license.

  If you didn't already know, most states do not allow individuals to become property managers without proper licensing. Meaning, you might not be able to start the job before you get the license. The reason for this limitation is because your duties as a property manager are similar to those of a real estate agent.

  Even if you decide to settle for a real estate license, there are different requirements across the states. The easiest way to learn about these is to look them up online. That way, you can tailor your search to fit your state of residence. Alternatively, you can find out more about the recommended coursework from the Internet. More often than not, real estate project managers don't just depend on the requirements of their state. They may also take other classes, like a real estate exam, prep courses, and other things necessary for passing the real estate exam.

- **Take courses in real estate**: Although a high school diploma is the basic degree that you need to provide to a property management agency, most companies prefer knowledgeable agents educated up to tertiary level in fields like finance, business administration, accounting, real estate, and public administration. A bachelor's degree will go a long way.

However, if you can't imagine yourself going back to school, try vocational real estate training or get licensed by your state. There are usually courseworks tailored for other audiences, such as property management, urban planning, real estate development, affordable housing administration, housing for the elderly, real estate management, and real estate finance.

If none of these options work for you, consider investing in online courses to improve your skill set and boost your knowledge of real estate. You can also learn more on the job. Don't be afraid to start from an entry-level position and gradually work your way up the ranks as you get better at the job.

- **Get specialized certifications**: Even if your state doesn't make licenses compulsory for managing properties, getting specialized certifications is a good way to keep your stock high. Not only will potential clients and companies recognize your professionalism, but it will also speak to your commitment.

  You can get licenses like the real estate salesperson's license or a real estate broker's license. These licenses open you up to many opportunities within and outside property management. For more specialized certifications, consider the Certified Apartment Manager (CAM), Certified Manager of Community Associations, Certified Property Manager, or Residential Management Professional (RMP). To get most of these certifications and licenses, you have to apply, meet certain educational requirements, and take a series of tests or exams. Of course, it takes some time and effort to get these certifications, but it's all worth it in the end.

- **Work toward your first gig**: After figuring out the requirements, taking courses, and obtaining a license or specialized certification, the time is right to begin working toward your first gig as a property manager. Even though this might be easier said than done, here are a few ways to ease into the job search process:

- ○ **Start with your network**: Inform your family, friends, and professional contacts about your search for a job in property management. It could be someone who you know that gives you your first run at the role. Do this before getting the word out and marketing yourself to the rest of the market.

- ○ **Get in touch with real estate agents**: The agents in your neighborhood are more likely to know about openings for a property manager before anyone else. So, take the initiative to meet with them to pitch your services and credentials. You can even get tips from them on how best to get into the business. That way, they can keep an eye out for openings or hire you themselves when they want the help.

- ○ **Go online**: You can start your property management career by going through online career resources and job boards. Don't just limit your search to offline job listings, conduct searches online as well and see what turns up. If you find an opening, you can do some digging around to find the hiring manager and use their details in your cover letter.

- **Stay up-to-date on the best practices**: When you successfully land your first gig, don't see it as finished work. There is still much growing left to do, so you shouldn't just sit back and stop improving yourself. You want to be better at the job every day, so that your stock is valuable when you decide to move. So, get out there and connect with other property managers near you and keep abreast of changing practices in the market. You can study property management blogs to stay updated on needs in the industry. Here are a few that might interest you:

- ○ **Multifamilyexecutive.com**: This blog is your one stop destination for all the current news about the factors affecting the real estate market.

- **30Lines.com**: This blog deals with the different ways of using technology to improve the happiness levels of your residents and appeal to new clients.

- **AppFolio.com**: This blog delivers property management news that is easy to read.

Chapter 44:

Different Real Estate Formulas for

Success

Whether you are just starting out in real estate or have been in the industry for several years now, it's no news to you that there are formulas that make real estate work. Things won't always be smooth sailing, because you have to deal with many things at the same time— like assessing property calculations to find the ones that work, or dealing with many different figures at the same time.

In this section, we will be going through some formulas in real estate that guarantee success:

Return on Investment

When you invest in real estate, it only makes sense that your investment brings in a profit after a certain amount of time. As someone in real estate, you would have heard of the term known as "return on investment" (ROI). It is the value or profit that you get from investing in something, in this case real estate properties.

But how do you find your ROI? The answer to that isn't as straightforward.

The concept of ROI, from a general point of view, is that you earn per investment you make. However, when dealing with real estate, there are several metrics you can use during investing. They include:

- **Operating expenses**: There are several expenses you have to make when you own property, such as financing costs, the cost of identifying and closing the property, and maintenance costs, among others. These expenses are known as the operating expenses, or cost of running the property.

  Whether you settle these payments one time or they are recurring, they must all feature in your calculations to determine the ROI of your property. That said, here are some common costs that are classified under operating expenses:

  - **One-off costs**: agent fees, renovation costs, down payment, and closing fees

  - **Recurring costs**: taxes, HOA Fees, maintenance costs, insurance, utilities, depreciation, and loan payments

  Of course, the list is much longer than this. So, try to check your costs and include as many expenses as you make in the calculations. Because, they all play a role in the eventual value of your property and the ROI you get out of it.

- **Gross operating income**: A property's income is the regular inflow of cash that it generates weekly, monthly, or yearly. The amount depends on the type of property you own and how it is run. When dealing with rental properties, income typically comes from rent. However, it's not unusual for property owners to find new ways to increase income from their properties.

  For instance, a property owner may offer the sidewalk of their property for rent to be used as a parking space—especially when they don't park there or have tenants who park there, either. Alternatively, they could also offer the garage for rent as a storage space.

  Regardless of how the property owner chooses to generate money from their property, all the sources of income combine to form the gross operating income. So, how is gross operating income calculated when dealing with rental properties?

The formula is pretty straightforward:

Gross Operating Income = (Annual Income from Rent × Rate of Vacancy) + Sum of Other Income

The rate of vacancy refers to the amount of time in a year when tenants do not occupy the property, and therefore the property does not generate income. It can also be called turnover rate.

It helps to keep in mind the appreciation rate of your property. More often than not, many property owners fail to include this factor in their calculations. You shouldn't ignore the appreciation of your property, because it's one of the things that makes real estate a great investment in the first place.

So when you are calculating long-term math for your property next, don't forget to add the appreciation rate. You'd be surprised at the great opportunities that could pass you by otherwise.

The 30/30/3 Rule

There are three main rules to follow when investing with the 30/30/3 method. The concept is about following all three rules. But if that seems like too much work, stick to one at the very least. The rules are:

- **Do not spend over 30% of your gross income on monthly mortgage payments**: A traditional rule of thumb is to ensure that you aren't spending 30% of your gross income to a lender to offset your mortgage. However, mortgage rates haven't been the same throughout the years, so more people are starting to exceed this rule to ensure they don't default on their loans.

  If you manage to get a low mortgage deal, you will be able to invest in another property if only a fixed percentage of your gross income goes into your expenses. The only time that's a bad idea is when mortgage rates are high, or the cost of investing in another property is even higher. Investors in the low and middle income brackets are more likely to break this rule.

For example, if your gross income per month is $70,000, and you spend 43% on your mortgage payment, you will be left with $39,900. However, if that same rate applies for when your property only brings in $6,000 in gross income, you won't have much of a financial cushion at the end of the day.

The amount left after you have offset your monthly payments should be enough to take care of your needs. So, it's better to spend less of your gross income per month on a mortgage, especially when you are strapped for cash.

- **At least 30% of your property value should be in semi-liquid assets or cash savings**: Before starting the process of buying a property, it's best to have up to 30% of the value of the property as cash savings. You only need 20% to cover down payment, get good mortgage rates, and avoid PMI insurance. The remaining 10% will provide a financial cushion for when you run into financial issues.

Granted, some programs allow for even smaller down payments less than 20%. But there's no telling what might happen, so you'd be better off with a bigger financial cushion. During the last recession, the property owners who were hit worst by the situation were those who made smaller down payments. Why? Well, they had minimal equity, and it was more tempting to leave the mortgage behind. There were several thousand property owners who took this high road from 2008 to 2012, and they ended up missing out on one of the most dramatic recoveries in the real estate industry.

So, if you have any plans to invest in a property any time soon, ensure that you have at least 20% in down payment saved up. Don't try to play it smart by investing your down payment into the stock market to increase it before you are ready. That's a risk you shouldn't be taking, especially if you are on a short time line. If you had, say, a five-year wait period before buying a property; then it makes sense to invest in a stable stock and watch your down payment appreciate before the due date.

- **The cost of your target property should not exceed three times your yearly gross income**: Your ability to afford a property based on income level determines the price you should be willing to pay on a property. So, if you can stick to the first two rules of the 30/30/3 method, this final rule is all that ties them together.

This rule allows you to check for properties within a price range you can afford. It also takes factors like percentage of down payment into consideration, and stops you from stretching your finances thin—even with high down payment rates.

The goal is to buy properties within your affordability range, which is your yearly income times three. For example, if you earn $150,000 per annum, then a $400,000 property isn't so far off your affordability range. In another instance, if you earn around $500,000 yearly, you can comfortably spend $1,500,000 on a property. And as mortgage rates have started to reduce, houses are getting even more affordable. If you buy with cash, though, this wouldn't affect you either way—except for making properties even more affordable.

It's not advisable to stretch this rule by going for properties five times above your yearly earnings. That would mean a huge debt profile for you, higher maintenance costs, more expensive property tax, etc. Do the math before settling on a property.

Break-Even Ratio

The break-even ratio is mostly applied to rental properties. The formula allows you to figure out the rate of occupancy needed for your property to break even and begin paying for its running costs.

The formula is as follows:

Break-Even Ratio = Total Expenses / Gross Operating Income

Let's consider an example: If your property racks up $45,000 in operational expenses, but only brings in $52,000 in gross operating income, the break-even ratio is:

45,000 / 52,000 = 86%

Where 86% is the rate of occupancy you need to maintain for your property to bring in enough income to break even. Anything below this percentage will lead to losses, which you will have to cover yourself.

The math also shows that properties with higher break-even ratios will struggle to cover their running costs.

Capitalization Rate

Capitalization rate is another popular real estate formula that most real estate investors use. It helps to figure out the investment potentials of a property using its market value. Cap rate is different from most other formulas, because it doesn't care about how you financed the property—whether it's a loan, cash, crowdfunding, or the one-off costs involved in closing the deal.

Instead, the formula is all about finding out how the property performs in the market from an investment perspective. This makes it easier to compare performance with other similar properties on the market. The cap rate formula works best when you want to choose a property from a list of several similar structures. Checking out the cap rate will help you narrow down the list, allowing you to invest in properties that have potential values for success.

To find the cap rate of a property, we use the formula:

Capitalization Rate = Net Operating Income / Market Value of the Property

Price per Square Foot

The price per square foot formula is similar to the cap rate formula, in that it is also used to compare the value of investment properties. However, the difference is that investors typically use this formula to figure out whether a property (especially rentals) is more than the market value before purchasing it.

The formula for calculating price per square foot is:

Market Value of Property / Property Square Footage = Price per Square Foot

- **Net operating income**: Although the gross operating income of a property is the total income generated by a property, the net operating income (or cash flow) is the percentage of the gross operating income that is left after every expense has been covered, including running costs.

  That is, net operating income is the difference between the operating expenses and the gross operating income. In formula is:

  Gross Operating Income - Operating Expenses = Net Operating Income

  The NOI of cash flow of a property can be both negative and positive. When negative, it means that the revenue the property generates is lower than the cost of keeping it running. As a result, the property is a bad investment that takes more money to manage than it brings in. It goes without saying, then, that a positive cash flow is good business. Without it, you will be out of business.

Gross Scheduled Income

The gross scheduled income is a formula used to determine the income flow from a rental property when all the units are fully occupied without defaults in payment of rent. The formula works for investors who want to make comparisons with income flow:

$$Rental\ Income + Lost\ Rental\ Income\ from\ Vacant\ Units = Gross\ Scheduled\ Income$$

Cash Flow after Financing

Although there are multiple ways investors finance properties—like crowdfunding, angel investing, cash, and so on—taking a loan out remains one of the most popular methods. The formula for cash flow after financing allows investors to figure out the cash flow performance of their property.

The formula is as follows:

$$Cash\ Flow\ from\ Operations - Financing\ Costs = Cash\ Flow\ after\ Financing$$

Equity Buildup Rate

Instant cash flow isn't always a sign that an investment was the right choice. Investors prefer some properties for their abilities to build and maintain equity over time. Thus, becoming more valuable as time passes. The equity buildup rate formula is used to measure these gains. The process is fairly simple: divide the amount of the loan or mortgage in the first year by the total cash invested in the property within the same year.

That is:

$$Mortgage\ Principal\ Paid\ (First\ Year)\ /\ Initial\ Cash\ Invested\ (First\ Year) = Equity\ Buildup\ Rate$$

Debt Service Coverage Ratio

The debt service coverage ratio is a formula used to determine the inflow of income currently available to offset the debt used in financing the property. The formula is:

Net Operating Income - Annual Debt Service = Debt Service Coverage Ratio

Cash on Cash Return

It's crucial for investors to know the cash on cash return in their properties. As a result, this formula is one of the most used ones, allowing investors to accurately make comparisons between investments and identify profitable properties based on the method of financing.

To determine the cash on cash return on a property, the net operating income is divided by the total cash investment. Usually, the total cash investment involved is made up of renovation expenses, closing costs, down payments, and other fees paid up-front when purchasing property.

Here is the breakdown of the formula:

Net Operating Income / Total Cash Investment = Cash on Cash Return

Price to Rent Ratio

The price to rent ratio is a measure of how much rent a property generates with respect to its cost price at the time of purchase. The value obtained from this formula helps investors to compare the profitability of their different investment properties.

The formula is:

Gross Rent Multiplier

Investors use the gross rent multiplier to find out the value of a rental property in a particular market. This formula is usually best for investors that list rental properties for sale. Using the gross rent multiplier, they can easily find out and set the perfect price for the property during listing.

Investors who want to purchase investment properties can also use the gross rent multiplier formula to find out whether the investment is worth their time and resources.

That said, the formula is:

Market Value + Gross Scheduled Income = Gross Rent Multiplier

Occupancy Rate

This formula is used to show the amount of times a property was occupied by tenants over a given time line. It goes without saying that occupancy rate is a good indicator of how a property performs. Low occupancy rate, for instance, is a sign that a property needs some work to preserve the investment.

The formula for occupancy rate is:

Number of Days Occupied / Total Number of Days in One Year = Occupancy Rate

Cash Flow From Operations

How to spot a successful property: it brings in more money than it takes. A property's cash flow from operations is obtained by subtracting the capital expenses (that is, the one-time huge expenses that you made) from the net operating income.

That is:

Net Operating Income - Capital Expenditures = Cash Flow From Operations

Prorated Taxes

Most buyers pay a certain amount as prorated tax during the closing process. To prorate tax on your property, you must find out how much property tax you have to pay for the rest of the calendar year. To do this, count the number of days left in the year and divide by 365 days.

That is:

Prorated Taxes (%) = Number of Days Left in a Year / 365 days

The resulting percentage is the tax bill you have to pay. Next, find the product of the percentage and the tax bill left to pay. This will produce the tax left on the property during closing.

Down Payments

Whether you are buying a property to live in or as an investment, you have to make a down payment. But how do you know how much to pay?

Here's the formula to calculate down payment:

Down Payment Amount = Sales Price x Percentage Down

So, for instance, if the cost price of a property is $300,000, and the buyer used the traditional down payment rate of 20%, you have to pay:

$$\$300,000 \times 20\% = \$60,000$$

Homeowners Insurance

You need insurance for your property to safeguard your investment and earnings. When calculating how much you could spend on homeowners insurance, several factors come into play, including: past claims, age of home, location of property, deductible amount, roof condition, property value, coverage level, proneness to natural disasters, and insurance policy type (see Chapter 30).

The average homeowner in the United States may pay up to $1,000 per annum for homeowners insurance. To get an accurate breakdown of how much you will pay for your property, see an insurance company for a quote. If you play your cards right by adding safety features to your property—like storm shutters, smoke detectors, and a new roof—you will get a better deal on insurance costs. However, the cost will likely be influenced by any of the factors mentioned above.

Loan-To-Value Ratio

This is one of the most common formulas investors use in real estate. As an agent, realtor, or broker, you will also use the formula:

Loan-To-Value Ratio = Loan Amount / Assessed Value of the Property

Let's take an example. Say a property is valued at $250,000, with a mortgage of $100,000. The loan-to-value ratio of the property then is 40%, or 0.4.

Property Taxes

When you aren't dealing with prorated taxes during closing, you have to deal with property taxes properly. Now, although the government automatically collects the charges, it still helps to know why you are charged a certain amount and how much it totals to at the end of the year.

The tax on your property is determined by two factors: property value and the tax rate of your location.

As we have covered in previous chapters, property value isn't determined by the selling price alone. You will need a tax assessor to give you a breakdown of your property value. An appraiser could also work. They will look into the appropriate records and give you a number.

After you get the assessed value, it's time to start calculating. Multiply the number by the tax rate to get your property tax costs for the year. Then, divide the yearly costs by 12 to get the monthly costs to add to your mortgage payment.

Bear in mind that you may also be charged a transfer tax when selling a property in some areas. This tax is handled by the seller. But you should be aware, so it doesn't get added to your junk fees.

28/36 Rule (Qualification Ratios)

When dealing with investors who want to purchase properties, it's important to know the qualification ratio—the amount they could potentially get on a mortgage. In the 28/36 rule, the 28 aspect states that buyers can get up to 28% of the gross monthly pre-tax income produced by their property before taxes.

For instance, if a buyer makes $32,000 per month, they qualify for the 28% rule, meaning they get to pay a mortgage of $8,960.

For the 36 aspects of the rule, we take debt payments into account, such as student loans, credit card fees, car loans, etc. The formula is still to multiply their earnings by 36%. So, we get $11,520 instead.

What these figures mean is that the buyers have to keep their monthly debt payments below $8,960 and $11,520.

Mortgage Payments

Principal and Interest

A mortgage principal refers to the amount collected from a lender or the loan amount. It's the total of the debt you currently owe your source of financing. For instance, if a buyer has $60,000 as a 20% down payment on a property valued at $300,000, they still need $240,000 to complete the payment. When a lender steps in, $240,000 becomes the loan amount.

To find out the interest rate per month on a property, you need to find out the yearly mortgage interests rate around the area. Visit your local mortgage lender to learn more about the rates.

Once you get the number, divide it by 12 to find the monthly rate. So, say, there is a 5% yearly interest rate, your monthly interest rate would be 0.42%.

Monthly Mortgage Payment

To find out how much mortgage payment you have to make per month, excluding taxes and insurance, use the formula:

$$M = P\,[\,i(1 + i)\char`\^n\,] \,/\, [\,(1 + i)\char`\^n - 1]$$

Where,

- M is the mortgage payment per month

- P is the loan amount

- i is the interest rate per month

- n is the number of payments (this is usually capped at 30 years)

For instance, if a property has a 3% annual interest rate, we can calculate the monthly mortgage payment as follows:

$M = \$450,000 \ (0.00416 \ (1 + 0.00416) \ \verb|^|360) \div ((1 + 0.00416) \ \verb|^|360 - 1)$

Therefore, M = $2,416

If you need to calculate monthly mortgage payments anywhere outside a real estate exam—like with a client, for instance—it's easier to use an online mortgage payment calculator.

Rent to Cost Ratio

This formula comes in handy for making comparisons of properties (especially smaller apartment buildings and family units) with other similar properties. For this formula, the monthly rent is divided using the cost of the property.

For example, if tenants pay $800 in rent per month for a property sold for $300,000, the rent/cost ratio is:

$$\$800 \ / \ \$300,000 = 0.00267$$

This formula works best when there are no tenant vacancies, so you can work out the rent rate until the lease term runs out. Otherwise, use a value similar to what other similar properties are outputting.

Private Mortgage Insurance

Investors only need private mortgage insurance (PMI) when they make a down payment that is less than 20% of a property's selling price. The PMI is then added to their monthly mortgage fees.

Unlike other expenses, the cost of private mortgage insurance is determined by the lender and the loan estimate. But, there is usually a range: between 0.2% to 2% of the loaned amount. The PMI on a property is considered paid in full when the investors reach 20% equity on the property.

The cost of PMI can also be influenced by other factors, such as:

- **Credit score**: The higher an investor's credit score, the better the deal they get on PMI costs.

- **Loan-to-value ratio**: PMI isn't included in mortgage payments with 20% or more down payment.

- **Loan term length**: Loans with shorter terms mean higher monthly payments, but it helps build equity much faster.

Private mortgage insurance comes in four different forms, including:

- lender-paid mortgage insurance

- single-premium mortgage insurance

- borrower-paid mortgage insurance

- split-premium mortgage insurance

Chapter 45:

Property Tax

Property tax refers to the levy charged on properties owned by individuals and other legal entities, like businesses. This tax is usually not fixed and depends on the value of the property in question, as well as the land it's located on. As such, it's a regressive tax. The local government is responsible for calculating the property tax to be paid by the owner of a property. While buildings might be considered as the only property in this case, other assets like boats and cars are also taxed in some areas, even though they are considered as personal property.

After collecting taxes, the local government directs the funds toward making the area better by financing education, libraries, fire protection, sewer and water improvements, road and highway construction, law enforcement, and other things and services that improve quality of life.

The types of properties taxed and the property tax rate in an area differ from one place to another. So, before investing in an area, make sure you are familiar with the tax laws that apply there. In most countries under the Organization for Economic Co-operation and Development, property tax contributes to a small portion of the national revenue when compared to value-added taxes and income taxes. But things are different in the United States, where tax rates are significantly more than most European nations.

How Does Property Tax Work?

The amount property owners are charged as tax depends on the value of the land and the tax rate in the area. That is, the property tax rate multiplied by the land's market value. Many taxing agencies typically calculate the tax rate again every year. As mentioned earlier, property taxes are almost exclusively charged on real property—which is legally categorized and defined by the state. The most common examples of real property are structures, land, and fixed buildings in general.

So, how does the local government determine the tax rate? Usually, a municipality obtains the services of a tax assessor to assess properties in an area. In turn, the assessor assigns tax rates to property owners using the fair market value of their properties at the time. As such, the tax rate is the assessed value of a property.

Furthermore, property tax is paid differently across each state and locality. Also, local property tax codes come with built-in mechanisms that allow property owners to reach out to the assessor about their tax rates. This allows them to formally debate the rate. If owners go a long time without paying property taxes, then the local government slaps a lien against the property. This is why it's important for buyers to review any outstanding liens against a property before agreeing to buy.

How Property Tax Is Assessed

Tax assessments differ based on property types and the land and structures involved. For instance, the tax rate on a piece of land will be significantly lower than a comparable property due to lower assessment values. Because of this, the property tax paid on the land will be much lower. However, if the land is closer to public services—like gas, water, and sewer—it could receive a higher assessment. Additionally, if the assessor thinks that the land could potentially be developed, the assessment will also increase—meaning higher taxes for the landowner.

Property taxes contribute to a significant chunk of the income of the governments in a city or county. The legislatures, councils, and boards come together to decide on the best rates for properties in the area. They hold budget meetings to figure out the right amount to allocate toward financing projects in the local community.

If property tax is determined by property value and tax rate alone, does it mean that there are no limits to how much one can pay as tax? Not really. The Tax Cuts and Jobs Act made $10,000 the highest tax rate per annum since the 2018 tax year, based on federal deductions on state and local taxes. The amount also takes care of other taxes on a property, including sales tax, income tax, and real estate tax.

How to Pay Property Taxes

It's not enough to know how to calculate your property tax—you also want to know how to pay it. That's how you don't get on the bad side of the law and attract liens.

There are two methods of paying the tax, namely:

- setting up a monthly escrow payment each time you pay your mortgage

- paying online or writing a check on a cycle of once per six months or once per annum when you receive the tax bill from your municipality

Over the course of this book, we have mentioned adding your property tax to your mortgage a few times. While that's all well and good, you must remember that a mortgage isn't the same as property tax. One is the money you owe a lender, and the other is the money you owe the government. Also, your escrow company you own an account with isn't the government. Instead, what you are doing is putting some money away, so you can conveniently pay your tax when the bill comes in. And escrow companies use the money saved up in your account to cover the tax bills on your behalf.

If you prefer to use the online method, then look up the website of the tax assessor in your area. You can also check for other details, like your tax records and the tax rate in your neighborhood.

Can You Lower Your Property Tax Bill?

Sometimes, the tax assessor can be wrong about your assessed tax and charge you higher than you believe your property is worth. If this is the case, you are within your rights to contest the assessed valuation of your property. But you need to convince the municipality that your property has a lesser value than they were led to believe. If you succeed with your appeal, then your tax bill will be lowered.

To begin, start by looking up your tax records. Ensure that the assessment data corresponds with all your property details. Next, you want to get your hands on other comparable property listings. Reach out to a real estate agent for a record of sales of comparable properties in the area. You can even go online to locate the tax records of other similar properties.

When you are done gathering these details, reach out to your assessor and find out about the dispute process. Then, follow the directions and convince them that the properties within the same tax bracket as yours are better. You can begin telling them about your findings in person or via phone. And if you still aren't satisfied with how they handled the situation, consider pursuing the case with an independent tax appeals board.

Real Estate Taxes

Real estate taxes are the levies placed on immovable land by the government, such as residential property, land plots, and buildings. They are payable per year. Immovable land is considered as a real property, because it's a land or structure that you can't move whenever you'd like to. So, definitely not mobile homes.

These taxes are collected by the state or local government of an area and used to finance community projects, schools, infrastructure, and other things. Like property tax, real estate taxes are payable via direct payments to your local tax assessor or indirectly via an escrow account, while dealing with mortgage payments.

It's not uncommon for people to use property taxes and real estate taxes interchangeably. And while they might mean the same thing in some cases, they mean different things sometimes.

How Do Real Estate Taxes Work?

Real estate taxes are calculated in the same way as property taxes: by finding the product of the local tax rate and the property's assessed value. So, real estate tax is also an ad valorem tax (these are taxes that are charged based on financial value).

There are no fixed real estate tax rates—not across school districts, cities, counties, or states. For example, in 2020, the median real estate tax rate by state in New Jersey was 1.89%, while Louisiana only paid 0.18%. For perspective: if you own a property in Louisiana that has an assessed value of $300,000, your real estate tax is:

$$0.18\% \times \$300,000 = \$540 \ per \ Annum$$

In contrast, a property in New Jersey of the same assessed value would pay:

$$1.89\% \times \$300,000 = \$5,670 \ per \ Annum$$

As long as you own a piece of real estate, you have to pay these taxes promptly and in full. The repercussions are the same with property taxes if you fail to pay: a lien will be issued against your real estate property from the municipality, and foreclosure procedures will be carried out.

Similarities Between Property Taxes and Real Estate Taxes

Both taxes are collected by government bodies either at a local or state level. They both aid the development, economic growth, and quality of life in an area by funding developmental projects.

They are both determined by a tax assessor and under governmental control and supervision.

Differences Between Property Taxes and Real Estate Taxes

Although these terms are used interchangeably and have some similarities, they are still different from one another. The biggest distinction is that while all real estate taxes are property taxes, all property taxes aren't real estate taxes.

In many areas, property taxes are charged on everything from real estate to tangible personal property. The Tax Foundation revealed in a 2019 report that tangible personal property is taxed in about 43 states. Both real estate tax and property tax are deductible if a Schedule A is filed with income taxes. However, since passing the Tax Cuts and Jobs Act, taxpayers could now deduct up to $10,000 per annum for either single or married couples taxpayers. Before the Act, there were no limits to the deductible amount of state and local taxes on federal income. Also, married couples filing separately were capped at $5,000.

That said, the real difference between real estate tax and property tax is: property tax levies both tangible personal property and real property, while real estate tax is used on real property alone.

Chapter 46:

Tenant Screening

Tenant screening is the process of selecting the best tenants for a rental property. The process aims to find tenants that pass your screening checklist and are interested in occupying your property. Once you have successfully screened every potential renter, the next step is to sieve out the unqualified ones until you are left with only the best.

You'd be surprised how many property owners and managers don't perform a tenant screening exercise.

Why many might be opposed to the process of interviewing people for showing interest in your property, tenant screening is more than just getting instant gratification. Think of it as vehicle maintenance. If you regularly schedule oil changes and servicing, your vehicle will run smoothly and for longer. Not only that, but you'll also stay abreast of any problems before they break down the vehicle.

Tenant screening is important and should be done correctly, so that you have fewer things to worry about and can rest assured that your tenants aren't devaluing your property.

Tenant Screening Companies

Like property managers, tenant screening companies exist to aid property owners in securing the right renters. These agencies collect data about potential tenants and forward them to property owners and managers as proof that the applicant is willing and capable of affording the rent, paying promptly, and isn't involved in disruptive or illegal activities that could implicate the property owner. Disruptive tenants are more likely to damage a property, be noisy, and pose a risk to others within the property and neighborhood.

Sometimes, local renting license regulations demand property owners to run criminal background checks or employ tenant screening companies to ensure that the neighborhood remains crime-free. Failing to keep to these demands makes property owners responsible for the actions and behaviors of their renters.

Tenant screening companies went mainstream during the 1970s as technology—especially the use of databases and the Internet—allowed for data to be stored and shared easily, securely, and cheaply. The screening technology has continued to fall in price as it has aged, making it even more affordable now. Hence, why tenant screening is a requirement in some areas.

How Tenant Screening Companies Work

Tenant screening companies retrieve the data of potential renters from different sources, like utility companies, court records of evictions, credit reports, state courts, police blotters, and bad check reports. Most will also check and verify previous landlords, social security numbers, and employment and work history. Some could go the extra mile and check the Terrorist Database and the National Sex Offender Registry for more insights.

Typically, though, screening companies compile information on potential tenants from public sources into different package levels. For example, CreditLink offers basic background checks, including bad checks, employment verification, credit report, public records, address, and social security number for $13.95. For a higher fee of $34.95, they will provide a more extensive report, including a terrorist and criminal background check. Not to worry, though, the screening fee is usually covered by the potential renter using their application fee.

Tenant screening companies go as far as providing a risk prediction score—a number, much like a credit score, that is determined based on the data the agency has collected on a potential renter. The risk score helps property owners and managers to decide on prospective renters without having to study the paperwork. However, the risk score isn't a definite phenomenon, like a credit score; because every agency has a different algorithm and style of calculating it. As a result, it's not unusual for a potential renter to rank differently in the risk analysis of different screening companies. The only time risk score works is when all applicants are screened using the same agency.

The Importance of Tenant Screening

- **Finding the right tenants**: The entire point of the screening process is to find the right tenants. You want renters that will adhere to the rules of their leases, care for your property like it was theirs, and relate well with others. And although tenant screening isn't the perfect judge of character, it helps you narrow down on tenants with good property etiquette and a history of conducting themselves properly.

  The screening process is designed to check for possible red flags in behavior and lifestyle; hence, the use of criminal history, credit score, employment history, etc. Not only do these factors help you get the right renters, but it's also useful for adhering to the mandates of the location of your property.

  By doing so, you will be keeping away problematic and disruptive renters from your property and neighborhood. This is good for both your income and the property value in your neighborhood—because people are less likely to want to move in next to disruptive neighbors, which could impact your finances greatly.

- **Lower liability risks**: As a property owner, you are liable for everything that occurs on your property, whether it's an injury or damage to personal effects. So, having the wrong tenants just increases your liability risk. But by screening tenants, you will be doing yourself a solid.

Imagine having a lawsuit filed against you because a disruptive tenant got in a fight and injured someone else or stole their personal data.

And besides just protecting yourself, you also want to look out for your other tenants. A disruptive tenant can lead to high vacancy and turnover rates—which won't keep you in business for long.

- **Reducing the risk of rent defaulting**: Screening tenants helps you to know the financial aspect of a potential tenant. This way you can determine who is more likely to pay their rent regularly and on time. From their employment history and current position at their jobs, you will be able to narrow down the interested parties to ones who can easily afford the rent.

When screening tenants, a big part of the requirement is that they have a verifiable proof of income. If a tenant is unable to provide a standard source of income, then you can request their bank statement as proof that they receive income and can pay.

This aspect of the screening safeguards you from running your property without income. Bear in mind, though, that tenants won't always have flourishing finances. Sometimes, they could experience a bit of a dry spell and ask for an extension. But that is less likely to happen with tenants with jobs than ones without any standard employment, source of income, or ability to afford the rent.

- **Lower rate of vandalism and crime**: Again, while tenant screening isn't the absolute judge of character, it helps you to weed out red flags before they happen. And one potential red flag it prevents are destructive and disruptive tenants, who engage in vandalism and crime. Not only will it save you from property damage, but you will also be keeping other tenants and the neighborhood safe.

Property vandalism and crime are very expensive for landlords. And if you aren't facing repair and renovation costs, you could be dealing with lawsuits. Screening helps you reduce the risks of such grim outcomes.

- **Lowering eviction rates**: Evictions aren't fun, not for the evicted tenant or the landlord—especially as things could get complicated and affect all parties involved. But it remains that evictions can be avoided.

There are many reasons why a property owner has to evict a tenant, but it's mostly due to disobedience of the rules of the lease or defaulting in payment. For property owners, you can't guarantee that tenants will adhere to the rules of the lease 100%. But you can reduce the risk of having to begin the eviction process by screening tenants before they move in.

Start by looking through their rental history and getting in touch with their former landlords or landladies. If they have a history of evictions, that's your cue to look for someone else. Of course, their history doesn't define their behaviors or mean they are prone to breaking the rules of engagement. But it's a red flag you can't ignore during the screening process.

Tenant Screening Checklist

As a property owner or manager, you want to choose tenants that will be prompt with their rent payments and care for your property. But that can sometimes be wishful thinking. The tenant screening process is complicated, and you are well aware of the consequences of wrong choices, which makes it all the more difficult. But you can ease the pressure by creating a well-defined screening process that takes into account all the vital information you need. This is where a tenant screening checklist comes in, making it easier to compare and judge potential tenants fairly using the same factors.

Bear in mind that each step of the screening process is crucial to getting the right tenant, whether you are doing background checks or looking into more private details like income and employment verification, credit checks, and eviction checks. Of course, the process is tedious, but it will save you the trouble in the future.

That said, here is a step-by-step guide on how to begin the checklist screening process:

- **Identify the screening criteria**: Before deciding on the criteria for screening applicants, check out the tenant policies in your area. Not only do you want to be fair in your judgements, but you also want to be aware of the criteria required of tenants in the area. For instance, some areas don't allow property owners to conduct criminal background checks or choose tenants based on criminal history. However, some areas want to be crime-free and would rather renters didn't have criminal backgrounds.

  While you are free to have your own requirements, here are a few standard ones to include in your checklist:

  - lifestyle requirements (like smoking or pets)

  - steady employment (alternatively, you could ask for a co-signing)

  - attitude and problem-solving style

  - income to rent ratio

  - rental history

- **Prescreening the applicants**: Instead of having to screen every interested renter individually, you could set up a rental listing that shows all you expect from applicants. This will be like a prescreening process that contains important requirements for potential renters. This way, the ones who don't qualify (those who default on rent, damage property, or don't adhere to rules) will self-select out. For instance, your listing could show that interested parties must turn in a rental application, authorize a credit check, and agree to have their rent history sent to a credit bureau (e.g., Equifax and Landlord Credit Bureau).

Alternatively, you can ask interested parties to schedule a phone call. This way, you can double down with crucial questions, such as:

- How much do you earn monthly?

- Will you be able to turn in a rental application?

- What is your living situation presently?

- Will you be able to provide a reference from your former employer or landlord?

- Do you own any pets?

- Why do you want to leave your current place?

- Do you smoke?

- Will you agree to report your rent to a credit bureau?

- When do you plan to move?

- Will you agree to a credit check?

- **The application form**: If you are satisfied with the response from the phone call, you could send the potential renter an application form ahead of your meeting. It's imperative that the form contains a section for the tenant to give you the go-ahead to check their tenant history and credit report. Other important questions you should include in the form are:

  - **Personal Information**: full legal name, residential address, date of birth, phone numbers, and email address (don't forget to request a copy of their ID as well)

  - **Residential history**: previous home address and owner's contact details

  - **FrontLobby lease record**: proof of payment for previous rentals

- o **Employment and proof of income**: employment status, position, supervisor or head personnel information

- o **Financials**: outstanding debts and authorization to check for a credit report, and emergency contact information

- **Outline your expectations in the listing**: When making a rental listing, ensure to clearly highlight your expectations for the tenants. That way, you won't have to give every interested person a tour of the property. Also, potential renters who don't meet your requirements will self-select out, leaving only the ones that qualify.

It's important that you are deliberate with each aspect of the screening process, whether you are doing background checks, verifying employment or credit checks, or eviction history. Sure, the process seems like a lot of work. But it would save you the headache of problematic tenants.

Reviewing the Application

Ensure that the renter completes and turns in the application form before starting the next stage of the screening process: credit check and reference verification. Here are a few extra questions for your checklist when going through the applications:

- Has the renter ever declared bankruptcy?

- Does the renter have a history of eviction?

- Does the renter smoke?

Once you have received the application and screened all the details to your satisfaction, you can now begin choosing the right tenant.

The Screening Process

- **Landlord reference**: The behavioral habits of a tenant at their previous rental will give you a profile of what they are prone to and if they are right for your property. So, get in touch with the other landlords or landladies and find out what to expect. If you can, get in touch with their current landlords or landladies to see if the behaviors match up. This will give you better insight into how the potential renter has evolved over the years.

  When reaching out to the past or current landlords or landladies, you can ask the following questions:

    o How did the tenant leave the property?

    o Would you rent to them again?

    o How quick did they pay their rent?

    o Did other tenants or neighbors complain about them?

    o Did they manage the property to a reasonable extent, or was there vandalism?

  And don't just take the property owner's word for it. Confirm that the reference they provided is not a false lead to cover up bad rental history. You can log into the Landlord Credit Bureau to look up and verify landlord contact information.

- **Tenant credit check**: The credit check is necessary to ascertain the financials of a prospective renter. You can go through a screening company for a credit check or ask the tenant to turn in details like: current and prior addresses, credit balances, inquiries, credit score, financial history, credit history, bankruptcies, aliases, employment details, and a verified tenant record from the Landlord Credit Bureau.

- **Employer reference**: It helps to verify that your tenant is employed at the place and position they filled out in their application. This is crucial for the screening process; you want to ensure that they are earning legally to avoid drawing criminal risks to you and your property. Also, it can help you assess their financial ability to afford rent. When reaching out to their employers, ask questions to confirm specific details, like the position they occupy, how long they have worked there, and their standing with their colleagues.

Why You Need a Tenant Screening Checklist

A standard tenant screening checklist gives you a standard list of criteria for judging tenant applications. That ensures that you get good tenants and are fair in your judgements. It also helps you keep track of the really important factors instead of getting carried away with unimportant details. Finally, a screening checklist is better organized than asking questions at random, helps to streamline communication, and regulates applicants with prescreening.

Chapter 47:

FAQs About Rental Real Estate

Do I Need Rental Property Insurance?

Although landlord insurance isn't compulsory in some areas, it's important that you sign up for it, because it gives you better insurance coverage than standard homeowners insurance. Think about damages to your property by third-parties, natural disasters (storms, earthquakes, etc.), fires, and liability protection (loss or damage of tenant properties or injuries to tenants). The goal is to ensure that your property is well protected, even from factors that you may not imagine.

How Much Should I Charge as Rent?

The amount you charge tenants as rent is determined by the state of the real estate market. Check out properties similar to yours in size and feature around your area and find out how much they charge for rent. You can then price your property competitively.

How Do I Get Good Tenants?

Tenant screening is the key to getting good tenants. Provided you cover all the bases—like source of income, rental history, employment history, and credit checks—you will find tenants that meet your criteria. As a rule of thumb, also try to meet in person with interested parties before they move in. That way, you will better understand them, instead of just relying on all the data from their application.

Do I Need a Real Estate Attorney When Renting Out My Property?

While you don't need an attorney to put up your property on a rental listing, you might need their services for staying within the confines of the law regarding rental properties in your area. If you decide against hiring an attorney, ensure to check out the Landlord and Tenant Act in your state before drafting and sending out lease agreements to potential tenants.

Here are some common laws to keep in mind:

- abandoned tenant property rules

- security deposit rules

- Human Relations Act (places like Pennsylvania)

- tenants' rights to refuse paying rent should essential services be denied or unprovided

- lead disclosure requirements

- right to refuse renters based on references and bad credit

- notice to terminate tenancy

- prohibition of landlord retaliation

Ensure that your lease agreement is in accordance with the law; and that you, your property, and tenants, will be free from legal risks and their consequences.

What Are Comparables In Real Estate?

Properties that have been listed and sold recently that share similarities in features, size, and location to another listed property are known as comparables. This term is usually used by realtors or appraisers when determining a property's market value.

Should I Hire a Property Manager for My Rental Property?

Rental properties can be a lot to deal with. For instance, someone has to see to the day-to-day running of the business, conduct regular inspections, run ads, manage finances, prepare tax returns, review insurance policies, prepare lease and renewals, and handle tenant emergencies.

These responsibilities might be too much for a property owner, so you could use the help if you want it. If you don't want to be a full-time landlord or don't want to be directly involved with your property, then a property manager is ideal for the job. Otherwise, you don't really need the extra hand. Not only will it save you on costs, but you will also grow on the job. After all, no one knows your property any better than you.

What Are Contingencies in Real Estate?

Contingencies refer to the possibilities or what-ifs that might present in a sale or purchase contract. They are put there by sellers or buyers to make a contract unusable if their requirements aren't met. Some common examples of contingencies in real estate are loan approvals, inspections, appraisals, and house sales.

Do I Get Tax Breaks for Owning Residential Real Estate?

Rental properties that are only used for investment purposes can get several tax benefits. The IRS website states that, "If you receive rental income for the use of a dwelling unit, such as a house or an apartment, you may deduct certain expenses. These expenses, which may include mortgage interest, real estate taxes, casualty losses, maintenance, utilities, insurance, and depreciation, will reduce the amount of rental income that's subject to tax" (U.S. Internal Revenue Service, 2022).

However, the IRS also went on to differentiate between properties used personally and rented out occasionally (like a condo or vacation home) and ones that are only used as rentals year-round. So, how you use your property determines if you will get tax benefits and how much of it. Check out the IRS website to find out more about tax breaks you can get as a property owner and what to avoid.

What Is Earning Money in Real Estate?

Earnest money, also known as consideration sometimes, is an amount that a buyer presents as a binding agreement during closing processes. If the buyer fails to follow through on the deal, they could lose a certain percentage of the money. Think of it as money paid up-front to convince the seller of how serious the buyer is about buying a property.

Earnest monies are often paid into escrow accounts, and goes toward the down payment for the property.

How Can I Build Equity on My Property?

There are three ways of building equity into your property.

- The first and simplest method is market appreciation.

- The second method is to pay a little higher than your mortgage costs each month—the extra amount will go toward offsetting the loan, instead of interest. But before trying this, ensure that the lender is informed, so they can direct the money toward the loan instead of the next payment.

  The extra amount on your mortgage payments doesn't have to be huge. It could be as little as $50. As long as you are consistent, you will build equity over time and reduce your loan period.

- The final method is to make home improvements. There are multiple ways of remodeling and making changes around your property. For instance, you could change the decor. Another example is to add more square footage or living space to your property.

What's the Difference Between a Real Estate Realtor, Broker, and Agent?

While these terms are often used interchangeably, they mean different things. A realtor is a real estate professional. It's more than just being a salesperson or real estate agent. That's because not all real estate agents are realtors. A person in real estate can only be called a realtor if they continue to learn about real estate, adhere to the code of ethics, oppose housing discriminations, and support private property rights.

On the other hand, a real estate broker is an agent who has the license to own and manage an agency. By law, every real estate agent has to have, at least, one main broker. Meanwhile, real estate agents usually come in two forms: sellers' and buyers' agents.

A seller's agent is one who is contacted by a seller to help in listing, negotiating, and selling off property. As such, they are discrete, loyal, and hold the seller in good faith. Despite owing duties to the seller, a seller's agent must also disclose potential bad aspects of a property to prospective buyers. Of course, the state of the property is well-known by the broker.

On the other hand, a buyer's agent is one who is hired by a buyer to help with finding and closing a property. The agent works for the buyer and owes them duties, much like the seller's agent, including fidelity, loyalty, and good faith.

Why Is My Property's Market Value Different From Its Assessed Value?

Differences in assessed and market values sometimes confuses property owners. But before you start a dispute on your property assessment, be sure that you understand the difference and why.

The market value of a property is determined by buyers and sellers, while assessed value comes from the calculations of a tax assessor. During sellers' markets, the market value of your property could rise beyond its assessed value. That's usually due to buyers' willingness to pay more than the worth of the property due to high demand and low supply. However, when the tables are flipped to a buyers' market, competition is higher because supply is more than the demand. Thus, buyers will not be willing to part with more than a property's assessed value.

Conclusion

The aim of this book was to turn newbies in the real estate market into savvy investors and landlords. My hope is that *Rental Property Investing* has achieved this with the simplicity, thoroughness, and comprehensiveness that it promised. Each chapter was designed to gently introduce the reader to greater depths in real estate and rentals, in particular.

Each chapter was a knowledge-packed piece that completed the puzzle that is this book. The style of writing in this book was neither too simple that it was condescending, nor too complicated that it spoke over the heads of you, the readers. Fortunately, this book straddles the sweet and coveted spot between easily understandable and sophisticated.

In Chapter 1, we analyzed the mind of investors to understand the mechanism under the hood—what makes them different from the average entrepreneur. You now know that one distinguishing quality is that investors typically have more patience than most businesspeople. Some, in fact, are willing to let decades pass before reaping the full rewards of their investments. Patience and long-term planning are uncompromising characteristics shared by successful investors all over the world.

But we also found that risk-taking is another defining quality that's found in successful investors. However, this doesn't refer to careless and imprudent risks, for which many people have become bankrupt and disillusioned. In fact, winners in the game of investment spend a lot of time learning so that they can take *educated* risks. Investors are also far less emotionally attached to their investments than entrepreneurs are to their ventures. This prevents them from being in too much of a hurry or making errors for sentimental reasons.

The succeeding chapter described the various ways by which anyone can raise money to invest in rental real estate. You may have observed that Chapter 2 steered clear of mortgages and, in general, loans. This is because the weight of such commitments can be so heavy that the potential investor is made bankrupt. But not to worry, because interest-based financing isn't the only way to raise capital. In fact, there are better methods of financing—some of which aren't talked about nearly enough in the industry.

So Chapter 2 revealed the relative ease and efficacy of crowdfunding, angel investing, partnerships, savings (personal cash), and wholesaling. In comparison to loans for which you may be hounded and lose much of your ROI, these alternatives are safer and quite profitable.

As we saw in the first chapter, some investments take a while to mature. And investors are often willing to wait as long as they need to get a safe and bountiful win. This also implies that investors are often the best at planning long-term goals, because it's necessitated by the nature of their trade. As such, investors need to know how to be patient and plan long-term goals.

It is this issue of long-term goals that the third chapter of this book tackled. It showed exactly what characterizes long-term goals and how anyone can utilize them. In this chapter, you also learned how to identify short-term goals and how they can be set.

Afterward, Chapter 4 discussed the all-important subject of correctly identifying profitable rental real estate properties. Every aspect of your investment in real estate is made futile if you choose the wrong property. Now, there's no guarantee that you'll ever pick a problem-free building. It's par for the course that whichever property you invest in, there'll be room for improvement.

However, you can reduce your risk of picking an unsalvageable building or one with issues that exceed your know-how and financial capabilities. To help you with this, Chapter 4 described the shared characteristics of profitable rental real estate.

Chapter 5 continued from where the preceding chapters stopped by providing more foundational knowledge. In this chapter, we saw why networking is indispensable for serious investors. We learned that those who try to be players in the real estate market all by their lonesome—

without the moral, financial, and experiential support of a strong network—are quite likely to fail.

We also saw that while the benefits of networking for the investor might be obvious and plentiful, they mustn't forget to give more than they take. By doing so, you would effectively gain the respect and trust of your contacts, and they'll be even more willing to come to your aid.

Having prepped you with the prerequisite skills and knowledge to make the best use of in-depth real estate information, this book journeyed toward more complex and salient topics. Issues like property flipping, analysis paralysis, finding a mentor, promoting your real estate business, money management, and market segmentation (among many others) were laid bare and dissected. Very little is left unexplained, as this book strived to be more comprehensive than many others in the same niche. All 47 chapters of this book bear the same discernable mark of meticulousness that is required of a subject as important as real estate investment.

At this point, you know how to write a purchase offer and how to understand the nuances of foreclosures and REOs. However, you should know that real estate is never fully grasped, as the market continues to adapt to various political, social, and economic factors. As such, you must never stop learning and growing as an investor.

Glossary

Appraisal: An appraisal is needed to calculate the estimated value of a real estate property. When there is a home sale, an appraiser is needed to assess the value of the property and provide a professional view. Usually mortgage lenders require this to determine if a property is worth the amount of loan a potential buyer wants to get. Property buyers also use it to determine if the property is worth the amount they are bidding for it.

Appraisal Contingency: An appraisal contingency is a clause that permits a buyer to break a purchase agreement after finding out that a property's sale price is far greater than the appraised value.

As-is: When the condition of a property is indicated as "as-is," it means that the seller cannot do the major (or all) repairs on the property. This could also mean the property price is "as-is" because it is below the market price.

As-is indicates the condition of the property during the writing of the offer; and if the property happens to be altered from the time of creation of the offer to the closing time, then the property has ceased to be as-is. Since the state has changed, it has to be returned to the original as-is condition at the time of offer, at the expense of the seller. Alternatively, the buyer is no longer obligated to buy and should be released from the contract with the seller refunding all monies spent by the buyer, like earnest money.

Backup Offer: If a buyer shows interest in buying a property that another person has a contract for, the buyer can provide a "backup offer," which will take effect if the original transaction does not work out. A backup offer is still subject to negotiations, and necessary payments have to be made—like earnest money—to secure its place as the next available offer. Legally, a property can only have one backup offer.

Blind Offer: If a buyer makes an offer before seeing a property even when they could have chosen to see it, it is regarded as a "blind offer." This is a common occurrence in highly competitive areas, and is done so that a buyer could win the property before the others.

Broker: A broker is a real estate agent that has had further education than the typical real estate agent and has passed the broker license exam. The broker understands real estate law, construction, and property management. The brokers usually supervise the work of real estate agents.

Buyer's Agent and Listing Agent: A buyer's agent (also called a selling agent) is a licensed real estate expert whose duties involve finding a property for a buyer, negotiating price, and property deals to serve the buyer's best interest. The agent functions as the buyer's fiduciary.

The listing agent (also called a seller's agent) is a licensed real estate expert who markets the seller's property, negotiating the best price and selling scenario on behalf of the seller to get deals that serve the best interest of the seller. The listing agent serves as the seller's fiduciary. Usually, the buyer and listing agent charge 2%-3% of the contract price for every sale.

Call Option: A call option is a contract that confers the right to buy and sell a certain property at a later date and price to different parties.

Cash Reserves: This refers to money put away by a business or an individual for emergency purposes.

Capitalization Rate: Capitalization rate (or cap rate) is a real estate metric that evaluates the potential return on an investment property.

Closing: When every process of a property sale is finalized, the deal is considered closed. This usually involves all parties' signatures appearing on the necessary documents, all payments made, and a lender's approval where relevant. Some real estate markets regard recording the deed with the county clerk's office as the last step of closing a deal. When all the relevant details are finalized, the buyer is given access to a property and is then regarded as the new homeowner.

Closing Costs: Closing costs refer to the multitude of fees including those paid to: the title company, attorneys, taxing authorities, insurance companies, real estate agents, a lender, homeowners associations, and other companies involved in the closing. The closing costs are usually paid when the real estate deal is ending.

Commercial Leases: Commercial leases are leasing agreements that refer particularly to commercial real estate. A real estate agent should know the seven different kinds of commercial leases.

Commission: Commission in real estate is typically around 5%-6 % of the home's sale price. The seller pays the commission when the deal is closing, and the buyer's and seller's agents split the amount.

Common Area Assessment: Part of the fee which the Homeowners Association (HOA) charges often goes to a common area assessment to manage an area accessible to everyone in the community.

Community Property: Community property is a property which a married couple buys and has equal ownership of.

Comparative Market Analysis: Comparative market analysis is a report that compares the values of similar properties in the area to determine an accurate value for a defined property.

Comparable Sales: An appraiser uses comparable sales to determine the worth of a home compared to the sale price of other similar homes in recent times. Comparable sales only refers to homes that have legally closed, and many lenders and insurance providers demand that appraisers use a minimum of three closed sales.

Contract: A written agreement indicating transaction details that binds a seller and buyer legally to a real estate deal.

Curb Appeal: Curb appeal refers to the exterior appearance and appeal of a property.

Covenants, Conditions, and Restrictions: Covenants, Conditions, and Restrictions CC&Rs are the rules and regulations which bind a real property. These rules are made by a homeowners association, neighborhood group, developer, or builder and outlines the requirements and boundaries of what homeowners can do with their property. Oftentimes, it includes monthly (or annual) fees or special assessments.

Conventional Sale: A conventional sale occurs when the owner completely owns the property (no mortgage left to be paid on it), or the amount which the owner owes on the mortgage is less than what the market determines they sell the property for. The sales process of a conventional sale is much easier than nonconventional sales like foreclosures, probate related sales, and short sales.

Days on Market: Days on market (DOM) is the number of days from when the property appears on the sales list on the local real estate broker's multiple listing service to when the seller signs a contract to sell the property to a buyer.

The DOM is used to indicate a metric for the homes sold in the market during a certain period of time. If the DOM average is low, the market is strong and favors sellers. If the DOM average is high, the market is weak and favors buyers. One major factor that affects DOM is the season.

Homes leave the market faster in spring than winter, because more people want to buy and sell when the weather is pleasant rather than when it is uncomfortable.

Deed: A housing deed refers to the legal document that transfers title from a property seller to a buyer. The document must be in writing, and is often called the vehicle of the property interest transfer.

Due Diligence: A purchase agreement can allow a due diligence period, whereby the buyer is allowed to completely examine the property. Within a specified time frame, the buyer hires professionals to inspect the property and carry out tests that inform their buying decision.

The buyer may get the chance to renegotiate the contract following the result of their due diligence, or end the contract in a specified time period so they do not default on a contract. Carrying out due diligence on a property helps the buyer completely understand it before they seal the deal.

Dual Agency: Dual agency refers to when a single agent is a representative of both parties, instead of having a separate buyer's agent and listing agent.

Earnest Money Deposit: The earnest money deposit (EMD) is also known as "a good faith deposit." It refers to the earliest payment that a buyer makes to the seller when the buyer's offer is accepted, and indicates that the buyer is completely serious about buying the property. The buyer can pay around 1%-5% of the sales price as EMD. Usually, an escrow company—or any other company which the purchase and sales agreement indicates—is responsible for receiving the EMD.

Easement: An easement legally permits another individual to use a person's land or property as long as the title remains in the owner's name.

Eminent Domain: The right of eminent domain allows the government to repurpose private property for public use. This only applies when and if the government fairly compensates the property owner.

Encroachment: Encroachment refers to a scenario where a property owner transgresses upon the rights of a neighbor by erecting a structure that outstretches to a neighbor's land or property line.

Encumbrance: In real estate, encumbrance refers to a claim against a property that obstructs usage or transfer, like an easement or property tax lien.

Escrow Holder: An escrow holder is an agent or unbiased third party whose duty is to hold money, written instruments, personal property, documents, or other valuable items pending when certain events or conditions which have been indicated by the relevant parties happen. Basically, they are in charge of relevant contract details until the need arises.

Equity: This is the investment a homeowner's home has accumulated. The equity value of a property is the current market value after any mortgages and liens have been subtracted. For instance, if you pay $240,000 for a home worth $250,000, you get instant equity because the difference between the cost and the value is $10,000. If you sell a property you bought for $250,000 at $260,000, the equity on the home is yours to keep after the deal is completed and all expenses have been paid.

Homeowners need to build equity, because they can leverage it to receive loans for other financial needs.

Foreclosure: This is a legal process following the failure of a property owner to keep to their mortgage agreement and make necessary payments. The mortgage lender reclaims the property and sells it to recover the losses.

Homeowners Association: A homeowners association (HOA) is a private association in charge of a planned community or condominium. Buying an HOA managed property implies that you are ready to operate by the HOA's rules and pay any monthly or annual HOA dues. Failure to pay or comply will lead the HOA to issue a lien against your property with the possibility of a foreclosure.

Home Sale Contingency: A buyer uses a home sale contingency to signify to a seller that a portion of their condition to buy the seller's property depends on if the buyer can close a sale on their current property. This negotiation is done with a clause in a contract or an addendum to a contract. A likely scenario where a contingency will be used is if a buyer wants to sell their property to raise the down payment needed to buy the new property. A contingency may affect the negotiations between a buyer and seller.

Home Warranty: A home warranty provides protection from future problems that could arise due to issues in the property that are expensive to fix, like plumbing and heating.

iBuyer: An iBuyer is a company that makes offers on homes instantly. iBuyers relieve you of the responsibility of owning, marketing, and reselling your home. The iBuyer offers different services and guarantees that you'll get an all-cash offer.

Inspection: An inspection is carried out on a property when a buyer pays a licensed professional inspector to assess a property, and report its condition and any required repairs. The inspection is usually done during a due diligence period, so that the buyers can determine if they want to buy the property in its current state or demand that the seller completes or pays for certain repairs.

Inspection Contingency: The inspection contingency is also referred to as "due diligence contingency," and is a clause written into a purchase agreement that allows the buyer to have a window period during escrow to carry out any needed inspections.

Liens: This is the legal right given to creditors to seize assets used as collateral until the owner satisfies their debt.

Land Lease: Ideally, buying a property makes you the owner of the property and the land the property is built on. But in some cases, a land lease becomes necessary for making you the owner of the property, wherein you still pay rent to the landowner for using their land.

Multiple Listing Service: A multiple listing service (MLS) is a database where real estate agents and broker members access and add details about properties on sale in an area.

After a seller lists a home for sale, a listing agent registers it on the local MLS. To know what houses are available, buyer's agents view the MLS; it also helps them determine the sale price of similar homes.

Natural Hazards Disclosure Report: The Natural Hazards Disclosure (NHD) Report is needed in many states to disclose if a property is sited in a location with greater risk of natural hazards. The seller pays for the report and hands it over to the buyer during escrow. An NHD report covers these natural hazard zones:

- earthquake fault zone

- area of potential flooding

- seismic hazard zone

- special flood hazard area

- very high fire hazard severity zone

- wildland area that could contain substantial forest fire risk and hazards

Net Operating Income: This value determines the amount of profit that a commercial real estate property can provide.

Offer and Counteroffer: When a buyer sees a home they like, they make a formal offer. The offer contains either the full price list or a price which the buyer and their agent considers a fair market value.

The buyer's agent puts the offer in writing for the buyer to sign before submitting it to the seller's agent. If the seller accepts it instantly, it becomes the parties' purchase contract. If the seller doesn't accept it, they might make a counteroffer. The offers are simply the art of negotiation recorded in paperwork.

Open Listing: An open listing occurs when a property owner decides to sell their home on their own. Because there is no exclusive agreement, the property owner can list the property with multiple agents.

Open House: A real estate open house is an event which opens a property to potential buyers without appointment for a stipulated duration. Potential buyers visit the property to determine if they are interested.

Option Period (Texas Only): The option period (or termination option period) is a type of due diligence period that is exclusively available to a buyer who buys this right for a certain amount of money and a certain period of time.

After a buyer has acquired the right to terminate, it is in their best interests to complete all other inspections and due diligence during this option time frame. If the buyer decides to end the contract during the option period, they get back their earnest money.

Pocket Listing: A pocket listing is when a property is up for sale, but is not publicly accessible to buyers or agents.

Pre-approval: A pre-approval means homebuyers have to complete an application that authorizes a lender to find out their financial situation, debt-to-income ratio, ability to repay, and creditworthiness. When this has begun, the lender issues a letter to the buyer that states they have been pre-approved for a certain loan amount.

The pre-approval letter indicates the buyer's estimated down payment and the interest rate. Sellers usually prefer it when an offer comes with a pre-approval letter.

Preliminary Report: A preliminary report indicates every problem with a title that should be resolved by the seller before a clear title is delivered. It indicates information like ownership history, liens, and easements. The title company compiles this report by looking through the available property records at the county recorder's office.

A preliminary report is one of the requirements for a title insurance company before issuing a title insurance policy. Usually lenders mandate borrowers to get title insurance coverage to safeguard their interest in a property. In many regions it is the custom for a seller to pay for this policy, even though it's negotiable.

Prequalification: A prequalification is the amount a lender estimates that a property buyer can get when they seek a loan. It involves the lender assessing the buyer's financial situation based entirely on what the buyer tells the lender and not proof or verifications.

Principal: A principal balance refers to money owed to a lender which does not include interest. For instance, if you borrow $300,000, that's the principal of the loan. Usually buyers pay a total of the principal and interest every month. They make payments first toward the interest, and then toward the principal. The bank's motivation for agreeing to the loan is the interest, anyway.

Probate Sale: When a property owner dies without making a will or assigning their property to someone, a probate sale occurs. Usually, the probate court authorizes an estate attorney or other representatives to find a real estate agent who will sell the home. The probate sale has a rather complicated process, and takes a longer time to complete than a conventional sale.

Proof of Funds: After making an offer, sellers demand that you submit proof of funds. The proof of fund indicates that a buyer has enough cash for a down payment and closing costs if buying with a mortgage. If you decide to pay cash, the proof of funds indicates that you have all the money.

These are the documents usually accepted as proof of funds:

- an open equity line of credit

- original or online bank statements showing bank letterhead

- a copy of a money market account balance showing the bank's logo or letterhead

- verified financial statements like an income or cash flow statement that are signed off by an accountant

Purchase and Sale Agreement: A purchase and sale agreement (PSA) is the written contract between the buyer and the seller which points out the terms binding the parties who intend to buy and sell real property. If a property goes "under contract," it means that the buyer and seller now have a formal commitment to sell and buy the property.

Real Estate Owned: Real estate owned (REO) is a title assigned to properties owned by a lender as a result of a failed foreclosure sale at auction. REO properties usually give the buyer a chance to buy a property below market value, as many banks would rather reinvest the proceeds than keep the property on the market for a long period of time.

Again, REO properties are usually listed "as-is," indicating that the lenders do not have any plans of repairing any part of the property— and this complicates the finances.

Realtor: Although the term 'realtor' is used to mean an actively licensed real estate agent, not every real estate agent is a realtor. A realtor is an agent that belongs to the National Association of Realtors.

A realtor is bound by the Code Of Ethics of the association to hold members accountable in their service to the public, clients, customers and one another, to a high standard of practice and care.

Rent-back: A rent-back is also known as a leaseback, and describes an arrangement where a buyer who has become the new homeowner decides to let the seller, the current tenant, live in the house after the close of escrow. The agreement terms are discussed beforehand and usually involve a lease deposit, a daily rental rate, and an allowable length of time. The rental rate is often determined by considering the payments which the new homeowner makes for mortgage and the possible inconvenience that the agreement may cause by delaying their move.

Seller Concession: Sometimes, sellers provide concessions on a property to make the deal more interesting and give buyers more reason to buy the property. A concession is referred to as the seller's contribution to the buyer's closing costs, including some limitations and approvals which the buyer's lender makes. Ultimately, the buyer has more money left at the end of the deal.

Seller Disclosure: A seller's disclosure is when the seller shares every detail they have about the property, which could influence the buyer's decision to buy the property.

A seller has to include items that are not particularly related to the property, but can impact the buyer's enjoyment of the property like pest problems, odd odors from a nearby factory, property line disputes, information regarding nearby major construction projects, legal problems, noises linked to military bases, or even recent deaths on property, as the law permits.

Short Sale: When a short sale occurs, the debt secured on the property is more than the amount it is sold for. A short sale is only done following the approval of the seller's lender(s), as the funds received from the sale will be lower than the debt owed. The process of approving a short sale is usually extended and complicated, thus these sales need a longer time to close than the average sale.

Subject to Inspection: Subject to inspection, otherwise known as "submit offers subject to inspection," refers to a sale situation where the seller does not allow viewing of the property without having an accepted offer. Sellers often do this to protect the privacy of the occupants, or due to tenants who refuse to cooperate.

The average buyer might be skeptical about buying a property without seeing it; but on the upside, the clause pushes the overall interest lower than usual. Besides, with a standard purchase contract, the buyer is allowed an inspection period in which they can terminate the sale without paying a fine.

Tenancy in Common: Tenancy in common (TIC) is a form of joint ownership of a property, be it a commercial building or a single-family property. The tenants in common have varying ratios of ownership to the property, but are all owners.

The property type determines how easy or difficult it will be to get financing. When one of the partners dies, the tenants in common are not allowed the right to survivorship (the surviving owners cannot share the deceased partner's property interest), rather the ownership interest or percentage returns to their own estate according to their will or the governing law.

Termite Report: Termites are insects that consume wood and are very destructive. The Wood Destroying Insect Report (WDI) is also called the Termite Report, and it shows a diagram of the property and the location in which WDI infestation is occurring or has occurred.

Title Search: A title search checks the public records for the history of the home, including sales, purchases, tax, and liens, where applicable.

A title examiner uses title plants and the county records to search for the record owner of the property. After getting information on the property owner, any liens or encumbrances discovered on the property will be indicated in the preliminary report for the interested parties to review before closing escrow.

Trust Sale: A trust sale refers to a property being sold by a trustee of a living trust. Usually, this occurs because the original homeowner is now deceased and has assigned their assets over to a living trust.

If the trustee is not as emotionally attached to the property as the original owner, they most often will accept poorly attractive offers just to off-load the property from their care.

References

Boss, J. (2015, March 20). *How to overcome the 'analysis paralysis' of decision-making.* Forbes. https://www.forbes.com/sites/jeffboss/2015/03/20/how-to-overcome-the-analysis-paralysis-of-decision-making/?sh=7626193b1be5

Depersio, G. (2021, August 17). *What are the main segments of the real estate sector?.* Investopedia. https://www.investopedia.com/ask/answers/052715/what-are-main-segments-real-estate-sector.asp

Kejriwal, S. (2021). *Gaming the commercial real estate talent conundrum.* Deloitte. https://www2.deloitte.com/ce/en/pages/real-estate/articles/commercial-real-estate-talent-conundrum-predictions.html

Toussaint, K. (2020, February 11). *Even business-to-business companies benefit from having a purpose.* Fast Company. https://www.fastcompany.com/90462281/even-business-to-business-companies-benefit-from-having-a-purpose

U.S. Internal Revenue Service. (2022). *Internal Revenue Service.* Irs.gov. https://www.irs.gov

Image References

Angelo_Giordano. (2015, February 9). [*Magnifying glass sheet*]. [Image]. Pixabay. https://pixabay.com/photos/magnifying-glass-sheet-writing-desk-626174

DTS Videos. (2017, July 20). *Gray steel fence on green grass field*. [Image]. Pexels. https://www.pexels.com/photo/gray-steel-fence-on-green-grass-field-532006

Geralt. (2014, October 23). [*Dollars currency money*]. [Image]. Pixabay. https://pixabay.com/photos/dollars-currency-money-us-dollars-499481

LoboStudioHamburg. (2018, January 28). [*Internet WhatsApp*]. [Image]. Pixabay. https://pixabay.com/photos/internet-whatsapp-smartphone-3113279

Mellish, B. (2015, October 29). *Blue and gray concrete house with attic during twilight*. [Image]. Pexels. https://www.pexels.com/photo/blue-and-gray-concrete-house-with-attic-during-twilight-186077

Nattanan23. (2017, September 7). [*Money home coin*]. [Image]. Pixabay. https://pixabay.com/photos/money-home-coin-investment-2724248

Pixabay. (2016, February 16). *1 US bank note*. [Image]. Pexels. https://www.pexels.com/photo/1-us-bank-note-47344

Succo. (2015, January 26). [*Hammer money euro*]. [Image]. Pixabay. https://pixabay.com/photos/hammer-money-euro-currency-611582

Vaitkevich, N. (2020, December 7). *White round wall clock at 10 10*. [Image]. Pexels. https://www.pexels.com/photo/marketing-dawn-blue-wall-6120249